The Secret Wars

Volume III

International Terrorism, 1968–1980

The Secret Wars: A Guide to Sources in English

Volume I: Intelligence, Propaganda and Psychological Warfare, Resistance Movements, and Secret Operations, 1939–1945

Volume II: Intelligence, Propaganda and Psychological Warfare, Covert Operations, 1945–1980

Volume III: International Terrorism, 1968–1980

"The Secret Wars: A Guide to Sources in English"

Volume III

International Terrorism, 1968–1980

MYRON J. SMITH, JR.

With a Foreword and Selected Chronology by

LLOYD W. GARRISON

ABC-Clio

Santa Barbara, California

Oxford, England

Library of Congress Cataloging in Publication Data

Smith, Myron J
  The secret wars, a guide to sources in English.

  (War/peace bibliography series; no. 12–14)
  Includes indexes.
  CONTENTS: v. 1. Intelligence, propaganda, and psychological warfare, resistance movements, and secret operations, 1939–1945.—
[etc.]—v. 3. International terrorism, 1968–1980.
  1. Military intelligence—Bibliography. 2. Espionage—Bibliography.
3. Psychological warfare—Bibliography. 4. World War, 1939–
1945–Underground movements—Bibliography. 5. World War,
1939–1945—Secret service—Bibliography. 6. Commando troops—
Bibliography. 7. Guerrilla warfare—Bibliography. 8. Terrorism—
Bibliography. I. Title.
Z6724.I7S63 [UB250] 016.3553'43 79-25784
ISBN 0-87436-271-7 (v. 1)
ISBN 0-87436-304-7 (v. 3)

ABC-Clio, Inc.
Riviera Campus
2040 Alameda Padre Serra, Box 4397
Santa Barbara, California 93103

Clio Press, Ltd.
Woodside House, Hinksey Hill
Oxford OX1 5BE, England

Manufactured in the United States of America

The War/Peace Bibliography Series

RICHARD DEAN BURNS, EDITOR

This Series has been developed in cooperation with the Center for the Study of Armament and Disarmament, California State University, Los Angeles.

About the War/Peace Bibliography Series

With this bibliographical series, the Center for the Study of Armament and Disarmament, California State University, Los Angeles, seeks to promote a wider understanding of martial violence and the alternatives to its employment. The Center, which was formed by concerned faculty and students in 1962–63, has as its primary objective the stimulation of intelligent discussion of war/peace issues. More precisely, the Center has undertaken two essential functions: (1) to collect and catalogue materials bearing on war/peace issues; and (2) to aid faculty, students, and the public in their individual and collective probing of the historical, political, economic, philosophical, technical, and psychological facts.

This bibliographical series is, obviously, one tool with which we may more effectively approach our task. Each issue in this series is intended to provide a comprehensive "working," rather than definitive, bibliography on a relatively narrow theme within the spectrum of war/peace studies. While we hope this series will prove to be a useful tool, we also solicit your comments regarding its format, contents, and topics.

RICHARD DEAN BURNS
SERIES EDITOR

Other Bibliographies by Myron J. Smith, Jr.

Navies in the American Revolution. Vol. I of the American Naval Bibliography Series.

The American Navy, 1789–1860. Vol. II of the American Naval Bibliography Series.

American Civil War Navies. Vol. III of the American Naval Bibliography Series.

The American Navy, 1865–1918. Vol. IV of the American Naval Bibliography Series.

The American Navy, 1918–1941. Vol. V of the American Naval Bibliography Series.

The European Theater. Vol. I of *World War II at Sea: A Bibliography of Sources in English.*

The Pacific Theater. Vol. II of *World War II at Sea: A Bibliography of Sources in English.*

General Works, Naval Hardware, Home Fronts, Special Studies, and the "All Hands" Chronology (1941–1945). Vol. III of *World War II at Sea: A Bibliography of Sources in English.*

General Works, European and Mediterranean Theaters of Operations. Vol. I of *Air War Bibliography, 1939–1945: English-language Sources.*

The Pacific Theater; Airpower, Strategy and Tactics; Escape, Evasion, Partisans, and POW Experiences. Vol. II of *Air War Bibliography, 1939–1945: English-language Sources.*

Multi-theater Studies and The Air Forces. Vol. III of *Air War Bibliography, 1939–1945: English-language Sources.*

The Aircraft. Vol. IV of *Air War Bibliography, 1939–1945: English-language Sources.*

World War I in the Air: A Bibliography and Chronology.

Cloak-and-Dagger Bibliography: An Annotated Guide to Spy Fiction, 1937–1975.

Air War Southeast Asia, 1961–1973: An Annotated Bibliography and 16mm Film Guide.

Men-at-Arms: A Fiction Guide.

The War Stories Guide: An Annotated Bibliography of Military Fiction.

Sea Fiction Guide. With Robert C. Weller.

for Russ, Carol, and Jeff

Virtue lies in shedding blood
—Adolf Hitler

Contents

Foreword

Terror.

That simple noun has been used historically to describe the lack of civility displayed by such worthies as Torquemada, Robespierre, Hitler, and Arafat. Terror, the power to hurt, was monopolized, until recently, by sovereigns —kings, princes, popes, and a few generals. Every civilization —Egyptian, Sumerian, Hindu, Babylonian, Greek, Roman, Christian, Muslim, and Jewish, as well as those of the modern states of east and west, north and south —has engaged in attempts to legitimize mass violence on the one hand while deploring murder by individuals on the other. The record of our frequently undistinguished past is filled with baleful tales of terror —conflict, violence, killing, and coercion —always condoned under the broader rubric, war. The best minds of the aforementioned civilizations[1] occupied themselves, extensively, with considering and codifying the "laws of war." Their codes, in every instance, legitimized terror when it was employed in defense of empire, to protect the property and person of sovereigns, or to extend the natural rights of a righteous authority. The codes invariably described various restraints to be exercised by "civilized" states in employing the tools of terror in wartime. Torture was forbidden, armies could not use poison, soldiers were permitted to kill male prisoners and encouraged to spare women and children, guilt on the part of the participants could be absolved through penance. Despite those restraints and the best efforts of theologians, jurists, philosophers, teachers, and politicians the human penchant for intimidation has rarely been inhibited. We apparently have a masochistic affinity for terrorism —provided our cause is righteous and our conduct is condoned by the laws of war. Telford Taylor affirms that:

> War consists largely of acts that would be criminal if performed in time of peace —killing, wounding, kidnapping, destroying or carrying off other people's property. Such conduct is not regarded as criminal if it takes place in the course of war, because the state of war lays a blanket of immunity over the warriors.[2]

The general acceptance of the concept of a *justum bellum* (just war) renders all of us vulnerable to terrorism since anyone with a powerful sense of godly cause creates, for himself at least, a kind of *justum terrorem*. Governments legitimately kill thousands to preserve the state and its interests; so terrorists assume that fear and murder are justified to ensure that their rights are inviolate.

The notion that "extremism in defense of liberty is no vice . . . and moderation in the pursuit of justice is no virtue"[3] failed to sway the American electorate in 1964, but it may have appealed to the Symbionese Liberation Army in 1974. By that time, the activities of terrorist groups had introduced a new term into the lexicon of international relations —*transnational terrorism.*

Professor Smith notes that terrorism rarely appeared in the New York Times *Index* until the late 1960s. The term was never indexed in the standard textbooks used in teaching international politics prior to 1970 (although it may have appeared in text). European histories used *terror* to describe the activities of Robespierre and Torquemada, but neither the word nor the practice achieved particular significance until the 1970s. Now, of course, international terrorism is a subject worthy of detailed scholarly attention. The proliferation of literature cataloged in this bibliography is positive proof of the need for definition, understanding, and eventual control of criminal intimidation. It is also, sadly, an indictment of human behavior.

Transnational terrorism reflects the deepening social conflicts resulting from the unprecedented technological advances we have experienced in this century. Modern communications and transportation systems advertise —and exacerbate —the radical cultural, economic, political, and social differences of previously unknown and miniscule minorities that entertain real and imagined grievances against the existing social order. Those systems are also convenient targets for terrorist activity. Newly developed weapons simultaneously altered military strategy and the conduct of war while providing small groups of determined terrorists the means of bringing entire nations to heel. The modernized western nations may well be so preoccupied with the grand vistas of history —the October Revolution, World Wars I and II, the Long March, Korea, Vietnam, great battles, and political disasters —that their people have failed to note that the future is threatened by demented factions.

Several nineteenth-century political writers left modern dissidents a heritage of anarchy, revolution, and terror which culminated in the awful events at Lod, Munich, and Entebbe. The early anarchists — William Godwin, Pierre Proudhon, Max Stirner (Kaspar Schmidt), Friedrich Nietzsche, Mikhail Bakunin, Enrico Malatesta, Pëtr Kropotkin, and others —advocated opposition to government through the use of force and violence. They were no strangers to terror. Similarly, the revolutionists —notably Marx, Lenin, Trotsky, and Stalin —encouraged violent insurrection and fear as a means of developing a socialist society. Lenin, the architect of the Soviet revolution, believed that "not a single problem of the class struggle has ever been solved . . . except by violence."[4] Lenin rarely departed from the doctrines of Karl Marx, yet he believed that terror was compatible with Marxist socialism —when it served the psychological purposes of the communist elite. Lenin combined every legal and illegal form of struggle to achieve his revolutionary goals. Modern terrorists obviously follow his example, like him they believe they are "justified in using violence on a massive scale against ordinary individuals."[5] Transnational terrorism is a revolutionary tool.

According to some theorists terrorism does not include guerrilla warfare and political assassination. They theorize that factions are too weak to launch general insurrections, too diverse to support guerrilla warfare, and that political assassinations are more likely to occur as part of a domestic coup. In that context terrorism is defined as a "weapon of the weak." That theory, however, is not consistent with the views of one of the foremost exponents of anarchistic terrorism —Johann Most (1846–1906). Most advocated "mass slaughter in public places." More significantly, he advised that "especially obnoxious public officials should be singled out and assassinated as a means of *striking terror* into the hearts of all members of the governing classes."[6] But, no matter how terrorism is defined, there is no doubt fear will continue to be employed to achieve the political objectives of determined minorities. Terrorists will exploit vulnerable public targets in the future; they will attack aircraft and airports, embassies and consulates, diplomats and businessmen. Whole cities will not be immune when weapons of mass destruction become available to terrorist organizations.

So far international efforts to control terrorism (for example, the Tokyo Convention, 1963; the Hague Convention, 1970; the Montreal Convention, 1971) have had little success. There is little agreement between governments about the measures that can be applied, and, as Professor Smith reports, even the effort to define terrorism in the United Nations evokes controversy and discord. Certainly, the sanctions that could be applied by international organizations are restricted in the interests of differing interpretations of international law, and conflicting interpretations of national sovereignty. Unless those issues can be resolved quickly the future is bleak. Ideological conflicts — between capitalists and communisits, radicals and conservatives, Muslims, Christians, atheists, and Jews —will inevitably incite revolution, conflict, violence, and terror. The noted Russian emigré Alexandr Solzhenitsyn warns that communism:

cannot survive as an ideology without using terror . . . consequently to coexist with communism on the same planet is impossible.[7]

The struggle against international terrorism has barely begun and although this bibliography is only a small contribution to the larger battle it is a beginning.

Lloyd W. Garrison
Santa Barbara, California

Notes

1.   The list of important writers who have dealt with the laws of war is extensive. It includes Sennacherib, Euripides, Moses, Plato, Socrates, Hippolytus, Thucydides, Livy, Cicero, Virgil, St. Basil, St. Augustine, Thomas Aquinas, Francisco de Vitoria, Francisco Suarez, Alberico Gentili, Hugo Grotius, Francis Lieber, and all the participants at The Hague, in Geneva, and at Versailles.

2.   Telford Taylor, *Nuremberg and Vietnam: An American Tragedy* (Chicago: Quadrangle Books, 1970), p. 19.

3.   Statement by Barry M. Goldwater made in his acceptance speech before the Republican National Convention in San Francisco, 1964.

4.   N. Lenin (Vladimir Ilyich Ulynov), *Report to the Third All-Russian Congress of Soviets* (1918).

5.   Thomas T. Hammond, ed., *The Anatomy of Communist Takeovers* (New Haven: Yale University Press, 1975), p. 59.

6.   Edward McNall Burns, *Ideas in Conflict: The Political Theories of the Contemporary World* (New York: W. W. Norton, 1960), p. 43.

7.   Alexandr Solzhenitsyn, "Misconceptions about Russia are a Threat to America," *Foreign Affairs*, LVIII, no. 4 (Spring 1980), p. 797.

Chronology 1975–1979

The following chronology lists major terrorist activities and govern-ment actions reported in the press from January 1975 through Decem-ber 1979. The list is selective and no attempt was made to define terrorist activities in accordance with any particular point of view. For a chronology of terrorist activities prior to 1975 consult B. M. Jenkins and Janera Johnson, *International Terrorism: A Chronology, 1969–1974* (Santa Monica, California: Rand Corporation, 1975).

1975

January		FALN bombs New York City tavern. Four killed, fifty-three injured.
February	11	Malagasy Republic President Richard Ratsiman-drava assassinated.
	26	U.S. Consul John P. Egan kidnapped and mur-dered by the Montenaros in Cordoba, Argentina.
	27	Chairman of the West Berlin Christian Democratic Union (CDU), Peter Lorenz, kidnapped by ter-rorists (released on 5 March).
March	5	Eight Al Fatah guerrillas attack Tel Aviv.
April	24	*Rote Armee Fraktion* terrorists blow up West Ger-man embassy in Stockholm. Military attaché killed, twelve hostages taken, in reprisal for West German government's refusal to release twenty-six impris-oned anarchists.

May   6   Judge Giuseppe de Gennaro kidnapped in Rome
                 by NAP group.
          21   Ulrike Meinhof, Andreas Baader, Gudrun Ensslin
                 and Jan-Karl Raspe (members of the *Rote Armee
                 Fraktion*) on trial in Stuttgart.

July   4   Terrorists bomb Zion Square in Jerusalem. Forty-
                 three Israelis killed, eighty injured.
          30   Francisco de Sola, industrialist, kidnapped by PRA
                 group in El Salvador. Rafael Aguiñada Carranza,
                 leftist labor leader, shot to death.

August   4   Five members of the *Rengo Sekigun* (Japanese Red
                 Army) attack the U.S. and Swedish embassies in
                 Kuala Lumpur, Malaysia, and take fifty-three hos-
                 tages.
           6   Red Army terrorists and four hostages flown to
                 Libya. Japanese granted sanctuary by Libyan gov-
                 ernment.
          22   Anti-terrorist law imposing mandatory death sen-
                 tences for terrorist activity approved by Spanish
                 cabinet.

September   Five Basque terrorists, convicted of killing Spanish
                 policemen, are executed on order of General
                 Franco.

October   IRA terrorists bomb home of MP Hugh Fraser in
                 London. One killed.

November   Ross McWhirter, British sportswriter, murdered
                 by IRA members in reprisal for his attempt to
                 establish a reward fund for information leading to
                 the arrest of terrorists.

December   2   South Moluccan terrorists seize train near Beilin,
                 the Netherlands. Two killed, fifty hostages taken.
           4   South Moluccan terrorists seize the Indonesian
                 consulate in Amsterdam. Twenty-five hostages
                 taken.
          14   South Moluccan train terrorists surrender to
                 police.

19	Seven South Moluccan terrorists release twenty-five hostages taken at the Indonesian embassy on 4 December.
21	Pro-Palestinian terrorists take sixty hostages at a meeting of OPEC ministers in Vienna. Two killed.
22	Algerian government grants asylum to pro-Palestine terrorists flown from Vienna to Algiers. Ten hostages freed.
23	U.S. CIA station chief Richard S. Welch murdered by terrorists in Athens.
29	Bombing at La Guardia airport, New York City, kills eleven, injures seventy-five.

1976

January	4	Outbreak of violence in Belfast. Five Catholics killed.
	5	Ten Protestant workmen shot and killed in Belfast. British order troop reinforcements to Ireland.
February		FCLS terrorists hijack school bus near Djibouti. French and Somali troops engage in firefight. Six terrorists, one child killed, several children wounded.
	13	General Murtala Ramat Mohammed, Nigeria's head of state, shot and killed by revolutionaries.
March	11	Former defense minister and twenty-nine others executed in Nigeria for complicity in attempted coup and murder of General Mohammed on 13 February.
June	16	U.S. Ambassador Francis E. Meloy, his advisor Robert O. Waring, and their chauffeur shot and killed in Beirut. Palestinian hijackers seize French airliner carrying Israeli passengers from Paris to Tel Aviv and divert it to Entebbe, Uganda.
July	3–4	Israeli commandoes rescue Israeli hostages in Entebbe. Seven hijackers, twenty Ugandan soldiers, one Israeli soldier killed. Ninety-one passengers and twelve aircrew members returned to Israel.

15	Ulster Freedom Fighters bomb the Special Criminal Court in Dublin.
21	British Ambassador Christopher T. E. Ewart-Briggs and his secretary killed by a land mine at his residence in Dublin.

September

Air India airliner hijacked and diverted to Lahore, Pakistan. Crew and passengers released 11 September.

10–12 New York to Chicago jetliner hijacked by Croatian terrorists and diverted to Paris. Propaganda leaflets dropped over several U.S. cities.

26 Palestinian guerrillas seize hotel in Damascus and hold ninety hostages. Syrian troops kill one terrorist and four hostages. Three guerrillas hanged 27 September.

November

Maire Drumm, officer of the Provisional IRA, shot and killed by Protestant gunmen in a Belfast hospital.

1977

January 11 Abn Doud, member of the Palestinian Revolutionary Council, suspected leader of the terrorists who murdered Israeli athletes during the 1972 Olympic Games in Munich, released by French authorities.

February 6 Black Rhodesian guerrillas kill seven Catholic missionaries near Salisbury.

March 4 Four *Totenokai* terrorists occupy the Tokyo office of the Federation of Economic Organizations.

11 Twelve Hanafi Muslim gunmen surrender in Washington, D.C. after seizing three buildings and holding 134 hostages since 9 March.

18 Marien Ngouabi, Congolese head of state, murdered in abortive coup.

April

Siegried Buback, Chief Federal Prosecutor, West Germany, ambushed, shot, and killed. Andreas Baader, Jan-Karl Raspe, and Gudrun Ensslin sentenced to life imprisonment for murdering four American soldiers in 1972.

May	1	Leftist extremists fire into a crowd of one hundred thousand in Istanbul. Thirty killed, two hundred wounded.
	23	Two groups of South Moluccan terrorists seize 165 hostages in a school near Groningen and board a hijacked train. Terrorists demand release of twenty-one South Moluccans imprisoned by the Netherlands.
June	11	Royal Dutch Marines assault terrorists. Six terrorists and two hostages killed in the attack on the train. One hundred children held by terrorists at the school had been released on 27 May.
July	23	Three Hanafi Muslims convicted of kidnapping, conspiracy, and second-degree murder for crimes committed on 9–11 March. Nine codefendants convicted of conspiracy and kidnapping.
September	5	Hanns-Martin Schleyer, President of the West German federation of industry, kidnapped by terrorists in Cologne.
	6	Muslims, convicted on 23 July, sentenced to life imprisonment.
	28	Japan Air Lines jetliner hijacked by Red Army terrorists in India. Japanese government pays $6 million ransom and releases six terrorists from jail. Terrorists flown to asylum in Dacca. One hundred fifteen of 151 hostages released in Bangladesh, ten in Damascus, seven in Kuwait, nineteen in Algiers.
October	10	Moros kill a Philippine army general and thirty-three others on Jolo Island.
	11	Colonel Ibrahim al-Hamdi, President of Yemen, and his brother, Abdullah Mohammed al-Hamdi, assassinated in San'a'.
	18	Eighty-six hostages, held on a Lufthansa jetliner hijacked in Majorca, freed by a West German commando unit in Mogadishu, Somalia. Pilot killed in Yemen. Plane flown to Italy, Cyprus, Bahrain, Dubai, and Yemen before landing in Somalia. Three of four hijackers killed.
		Jan-Karl Raspe, Gudrun Ensslin, and Andreas

Baader, principles in the Baader-Meinhof gang, commit suicide in Stammheim Prison near Stuttgart. Leftists claim they were murdered by prison officials.

19   Hanns-Martin Schleyer found murdered in Eastern France.

November 17   France extradites Klaus Croissant, defense attorney of the Baader-Meinhof gang, suspected of establishing covert communications for the members in prison, to West Germany.

1978

January   10   Pedro Joaquin Chamarro Cardenal, editor of *La Prensa,* assassinated in Nicaragua. Thousands riot in protest against President Somoza's regime.

February   18   Palestinian terrorists assassinate Yusuf as-Sibai, editor of Cairo's daily *al-Ahram*, and seize thirty hostages at the Hilton Hotel in Nicosia. Cypriot officials allow the terrorists to fly off in a jet aircraft in exchange for nineteen hostages.

19   Hijacked aircraft returns to Larnaca Airport after being refused landing rights in Kuwait, Somalia, Ethiopia, Greece, Yemen, Libya, and Algeria. Egyptian commandoes attack the terrorists and claim that the Cypriot National Guard and a PLO unit opened fire on them. Fifteen of seventy-four Egyptians killed. Hostages freed by the terrorists. Anwar Sadat severs diplomatic relations with Cyprus.

March   11   PLO guerrillas kill thirty Israeli civilians on a bus between Haifa and Tel Aviv.

14   Israel conducts land, sea, and air attacks against PLO bases in Southern Lebanon in reprisal.

16   Aldo Moro, former Italian premier, kidnapped in Rome by Red Brigade terrorists. Five bodyguards killed. Terrorists demand release of fifteen Red Brigade members on trial in Turin.

April   4   President Sardar Mohammed Daud Khan, Afghanistan, killed during military coup. Revolutionary council led by Nur Mohammed Taraki assumes control.

May	9	Aldo Moro murdered in Rome following Italian government's refusal to release fifteen Red Brigades from prison.
	11	Congo National Liberation Front (FNLC) guerrillas invade Shaba province, Zaire. President Mobutu Sese Seko accuses the USSR, Algeria, and Libya of backing the FNLC. Forty-four Europeans murdered in Kolwezi, an estimated one hundred fifty whites and three hundred blacks killed in the fighting.
	19	French and Belgian paratroops, airlifted in U.S. and British aircraft, rescue two thousand five hundred Europeans and Americans in Kolwezi.
June	23	Twenty-nine Red Brigade terrorists sentenced to prison in Turin. Renato Curcio and Pietro Bassi sentenced to fifteen years in prison for arson, kidnapping, and robbery. Sixteen acquitted.
	26	Radicals bomb the Palace of Versailles. French officials blame the Breton Liberation Front.
July	17	West Germany, Canada, France, Great Britain, Italy, Japan, and the U.S. agree to cancel flights to any country that refuses to extradite or prosecute air hijackers —and to deny landing rights to that country's aircraft.
	28	Iraqi officials attacked in London in reprisal for Iraq's refusal to negotiate peace with Israel.
	31	Iraqi terrorist seizes eight hostages at the Iraqi embassy in London.
August	2	Iraqi officials attacked in Pakistan and Lebanon.
	13	PLF headquarters in Beirut bombed. One hundred fifty members of various guerrilla factions killed.
	19	Four hundred thirty killed in a crowded theater in Abadan, Iran, burned by Muslim arsonists.
	22	Twenty-five Sandinist National Liberation Front guerrillas seize Nicaraguan National Palace in Managua. Six killed, twelve wounded, one thousand held captive.

24   Sandinista guerrillas fly to Panama with fifty-nine released prisoners and $500 thousand ransom.

September 20   Corrado Alunni, Red Brigade leader, suspected in murder of Aldo Moro, sentenced to twelve years in prison for illegal possession of firearms.

November   Early in November the Spanish government approved stringent security measures in the Basque provinces. More than forty killings claimed by the ETA during the year.

1979

January   29   Emilio Alessandri, Public Prosecutor, assassinated by BR terrorists in Milan.

February   14   U.S. Ambassador to Afghanistan, Adolph Dubs, kidnapped, shot, and killed in Kabul by Muslim extremists.

24   Italian court sentences right wing terrorists Franco Fredo, Giovanni Ventura, and Guido Gianettini to life imprisonment for bombing Milan bank in 1969.

March   1   Egyptian President Anwar Sadat warns Muslim Brotherhood that religion cannot be involved in Egyptian politics.

22   Provisional IRA terrorists shoot Sir Richard Sykes, British Ambassador to the Netherlands.

23   One hundred members of the Independent Fighting Brigades for Popular Autonomy riot during labor demonstrations in Paris.

30   MP Airey Neave killed by IRA bomb in the House of Commons garage, London.

April   20   Palace of the Senators, Rome, bombed by members of the Armed Revolutionary Cells (or the Italian Popular Movement, both groups claimed responsibility).

May   1   Several night explosions occur in Paris and a number of terrorist organizations claim responsibility. Similar bombings occurred frequently throughout France during late April.

3	Ten to fifteen Red Brigade terriorists bomb the Christian Democrat headquarters in Rome. One killed, two injured.
6	Third anniversary of the Corsican National Liberation Front. Twenty-seven bombings occur in Corsica.
8	BPR terrorists occupy the cathedral and seize the French and Costa Rican embassies in San Salvador. Both ambassadors taken hostage. Terrorists demand release of imprisoned BPR members. Twenty-three shot and killed by the police.
11	BPR members take over the Venezuelan embassy. West German police shoot Elisabeth van Dyck, suspect in the kidnapping and murder of Hanns-Martin Schleyer.
21	El Salvador officials cut off food, water, and electricity in the Venezuelan embassy held by BPR terrorists.
22	Fourteen pro-BPR supporters killed by police while trying to supply the Venezuelan embassy in San Salvador. Guerrillas assassinate the minister of education in reprisal.
25	BPR guerrillas peacefully vacate the Venezuelan embassy.
June 25	Red Brigades attempt, and fail, to murder General Alexander Haig, NATO commander, in Belgium.
28	Syrian government executes fifteen members of the Muslim Brotherhood convicted of murder and subversion. Three sentenced to life imprisonment.
July 13	Colonel Antonio Varisco, Security Chief, Rome Central Courts, murdered by terrorists. Palestinian terrorists seize the staff of the Egyptian embassy in Ankara, Turkey. Two Turkish policemen and one Egyptian killed. PLO representatives mediate end to the siege.
August 27	IRA terrorists murder Lord Mountbatten in his fishing boat off the coast of Ireland. Two boys and Lady Brabourne also killed. IRA terrorists ambush and kill eighteen British soldiers and one civilian in northern Ireland.

30   Irish police arrest two IRA members for the murder of Lord Mountbatten.

September 21   Carlo Ghiglieno, Fiat executive, murdered by the Red Brigades in Turin.

26   Cesare Terranova, Sicilian judge, murdered by terrorists in Palermo.

October   10   Police arrest twenty-four students in Manila for opposing martial law in the Philippines.

November   4   Iranian militants seize the U.S. embassy in Tehran and take ninety hostages, including sixty Americans.

11   Bassam Shaka, mayor of Nablus on the West Bank, Israel, arrested by Israeli military officials for allegedly supporting terrorists (Shaka freed on 5 December on the recommendation of the Israeli cabinet).

20   Muslim extremists attack and invade the Grand Mosque in Mecca. Two weeks of bloody fighting follow before the extremists are driven out. One hundred fifty killed.

23   Thomas McMahon convicted of Lord Mountbatten's murder in Dublin and sentenced to life imprisonment.

December   3   Puerto Rican terrorists kill two American sailors near San Juan. Ten others injured.

4   UN Security Council unanimously passes resolution demanding release of U.S. hostages in Iran.

11   Front Line (Red Brigade) terrorists "kneecap" ten students/faculty at the University of Turin.

15   International Court of Justice rules 15–0 that Iran must release U.S. hostages in Iran.

Preface

Background

Until the latter part of the 1960s, "terror" and "terrorism" were words most often associated with historical events in, say, eighteenth-century France or nineteenth-century Russia, or atrocities committed as part of guerrilla warfare. Entries for these terms could seldom be found in the *New York Times Index*. If one thought in terms of what we now call "terrorism," be it domestic or international, one usually meant revolutionary activity or irregular combat.

Then followed a series of bombings, abductions, assassinations, and aircraft hijackings by individuals or small groups who, if not criminal or mentally ill, represented a variety of often little-known and less-understood causes and who sought to effect political changes violently and with a maximum of publicity. According to a report prepared for the 1976 Department of State Conference, "International Terrorism in Retrospect and Prospect," cases of political violence, which now may be labeled terroristic, rose from an average of under 50 per year to over 100 per year in the late 1968–1970 period. After dipping back to some 75 in 1971, incidents in succeeding years exploded to 175–200 per annum until late in the decade.[1] Clearly there has occurred such an upshot in politically motivated—if somewhat mysteriously reasoned—violence that, by whatever definition is applied, the world since 1968 has a significant new problem.

Unfortunately for those who like their topics nailed down between concrete perimeters, no precise definition of either domestic or international "terrorism" is yet universally accepted. What definitions there are vary greatly, among governments, individuals committing terrorist acts and those charged with combatting them, and throughout that growing segment of the academic community now examining what J. Bowyer Bell calls a "trendy" subject.[2] There is much to be said for the phrase "one man's terrorist is another man's freedom fighter."

Perhaps nowhere is the effort to define "terrorism" so controversial as at the United Nations. Despite a number of sessions devoted to grappling with the problem, delegates refer not to "terrorism" but to "Item 92." Formally, "Item 92" has the rather lengthy subtitle:

> Measures to Prevent International Terrorism Which Endangers or Takes Innocent Human Lives or Jeopardizes Fundamental Freedoms, and Study of the Underlying Causes of Those Forms of Terrorism and Acts of Violence Which Lie in Misery, Frustration, Grievance, and Despair, and Which Cause Some People to Sacrifice Human Lives, Including Their Own, in an Attempt to Effect Radical Changes.

That all-encompassing sort of terminology, which nods toward both the terrorist and the victims of "terrorism," leaves a lot of room to maneuver. Other people and agencies have attempted to be more precise. Let's look at the products of a few of these.

The American Intelligence Community defines international terrorist actions in two slightly different ways. First, according to the Intelligence Community Staff, international terrorism is defined as:

> The calculated use of violence, or the threat of violence, to attain political goals through fear, intimidation, or coercion; usually involves a criminal act, often symbolic in nature, and is intended to influence an audience beyond the immediate victims. International terrorism transcends national boundaries in the carrying out of the act, the purpose of the act, the nationalities of the victims, or the resolution of the incident; such an act is usually designed to attract wide publicity in order to focus attention on the existence, cause, or demands of the perpetrators.[3]

Second, as viewed in Executive Order No. 12086, "U.S. Intelligence Activities," dated January 26, 1978, international terroristic activities means:

> Any activity or activities which: (a) involves killing, causing serious bodily harm, kidnapping, or violent destruction of property, or an attempt or credible threat to commit such acts; and (b) appears intended to endanger a protectee of the Secret Service or the Department of State or to further political, social, or economic goals by intimidating or coercing a civilian population or any segment thereof, influencing the policy of a government or international organization by intimidation or coercion, or by obtaining widespread publicity for a group or its cause; and (c) transcends national boundaries in terms of the means by which it is accomplished, the civilian population, government, or international organization it appears intended to coerce or intimidate, or the locale in which its perpetrators operate or seek asylum.[4]

The learned British authority Brian Crozier, in testimony before the U.S. Congress, sought to differentiate terrorism from both vandalism and nonpolitical crime when he stated simply that it constituted "motivated violence for political ends."[5] Later, his Yugoslav colleague, Milivoje Karanović, noting that "there are two types of terrorism, domestic and international," provided another definition in the April-June 1978 issue of *Jugoslovenska Revija za Krimologiju i Krivicno Pravo:*

> Terrorism may be defined as systematic and organized violence against nonresisting persons to create fear in them for the purpose of retaining or

gaining governmental authority, or for the purpose of using that authority for exploitation or oppression or to extract political concessions.[6]

Another British author, Paul Johnson, former editor of the *New Statesman* is more blunt in his assessment: "Terrorism is the deliberate and
cold-blooded exaltation of violence over all forms of political activity."[7]

Almost every student of terrorism has at one time or another offered
a definition of his topic in an effort to set guidelines by which he may
discuss it. The examples above constitute only a few of the many. For
purposes of this guide, we concur with Edward Mickolus of the CIA's
International Issues Division, Office of Regional and Political Analysis,
in that our effort is concerned with

> The use, or threat of use, of anxiety-inducing extranormal violence for
> political purposes by any individual or group, whether acting for, or in
> opposition to, established governmental authority, when such action is
> intended to influence the attitudes and behavior of a target group wider
> than the immediate victims and when, through the nationality of foreign
> ties of its perpetrators, its location, the nature of its institutional or human
> victims, or the mechanics of its resolution its ramifications transcend
> national boundaries.[8]

In addition to international terrorism, this guide also addresses the
topic of domestic terrorism, the exact parallel of the transnational
variety, which Mickolus goes on to define as "behavior that has the
aforementioned characteristics of extranormal violence but does not
involve nationals of more than one state."[9]

Objectives

In the years since 1968 and especially of late, a vast amount of terrorism
literature has appeared in many languages, seemingly to keep pace
with events. The variety of this literature is very uneven. Institute
papers, whole journals, documents, anthologies, and many books have
appeared on the Palestinian and Irish problems. On the other hand,
only a handful of journal or newsmagazine references are available
concerning terrorism in, say, Turkey or Malaysia.

Some effort has been made to control this growing literature with
bibliographies, "one of the sure and certain signs of a novel and popular topic in academic eyes," writes J. Bowyer Bell.[10] In preparing this
work, I found only a few bibliographies in English devoted to our topic,
although several have been issued bearing on certain activities like
violence or revolution which are related to it. At least two (Mickolus and
Norton-Greenberg) are extremely well annotated. Most, however, contain far fewer than one thousand citations, are unpublished, or are
extremely difficult for the layman to obtain.

This guide is intended to serve as a working bibliography for
English-language sources about domestic and international political

terrorism written during the years 1968 through mid-1979. Due to the many clandestine features of terrorism, the topic seemed a natural for the third volume of our Secret Wars series. While aimed primarily at scholars and especially graduate and undergraduate students, it should also prove useful to librarians, general readers, journalists, and law enforcement officials.

This guide is not definitive, but it attempts comprehensiveness in that virtually all facets of domestic and international terrorism are covered. As a reference tool, it will permit the user to quickly determine what kinds of materials are available and help him to establish a basis for further research. In general and with the exception perhaps of certain conference papers, items are cited which the user might reasonably expect to find in large university, public, or government libraries. In practice, students should be able to find many of the more recent newsmagazine and book titles in small or medium-sized college or public library collections. Should you be unable to turn up a given reference locally, keep in mind that many items cited are available through interlibrary loan, details of which service may be obtained at your nearest library.

The criteria for selection in this guide are the same as those for the first and second volumes in this series. The following types of unpublished or circulated material are represented: books and monographs, scholarly papers, periodical and journal articles, government documents, doctoral dissertations and masters' theses. Although much has been included, it was necessary to draw a line somewhere and omit certain kinds of information. Excluded materials include fiction, obvious childrens' works, newspaper articles (unless reprinted in other works), book reviews, and poetry.

Arrangement

The eight main sections of the table of contents, with their subsections, form a classified subject index to this guide and the key to the manner in which the book is laid out. Within the text, each main section receives a brief introduction outlining its task. Every subsection is arranged alphabetically, and from sections 2 through 8, each is further subdivided as to type of material: book, article (including those in anthologies), or documents, papers, and reports. All main sections contain a note on "further references" designed to guide the user to other sections and subsections containing related materials. The references themselves are not repeated from one section to another.

Each citation receives an entry number. These entry numbers run consecutively throughout the book. An author index keyed to entry numbers is provided. Unnumbered cross-references to joint authors and editors and to aliases are provided within the body of the text where appropriate.

Acknowledgments

For their advice, assistance, or encouragement in the formulation, research, and completion of this endeavor, the following persons and libraries are gratefully acknowledged.

Mr. Robert B. Lane, Director, Air University Library

Hon. Edward P. Boland, U.S. House of Representatives Permanent Select Committee on Intelligence

Mr. Charles E. Wilson, Chief, Plans and Policy Branch, U.S. Central Intelligence Agency

Ms. Joyce Eakin, Library Director, U.S. Army Military History Institute

Mr. V. L. Krohn, Chief, Operations Liaison Staff, Office of Civil Aviation Security, Federal Aviation Administration

Mr. Jung Ra, *Terrorism* journal

Ms. Iris J. Gilbert, Office for Combatting Terrorism, U.S. Department of State

West Virginia University Libraries

West Virginia Library Commission

Harrison County (W.V.) Public Library

Interlibrary Loan Division, Central Intelligence Agency Library

National Criminal Justice Reference Service, Law Enforcement Assistance Administration, U.S. Department of Justice

Special appreciation is reserved for my colleagues at Salem College, without whose backing and aid this project would not have been completed. President James C. Stam and Dean Ronald O. Champagne provided continuous support and encouragement to proceed. The Political Science Department, including Dr. Robert Chalouhi and former chairman Dr. Jesse Kelly, gave stimulation, insight, and resources. Mrs. Sara J. Graham, Margaret Allen, Jacqueline Isaacs, and Sara A. Casey of the Benedum Learning Resources Center staff gave bibliographic and interlibrary loan assistance.

To series editor Richard Burns, editor Shelly Lowenkopf, and production editor Paulette Wamego go my appreciation for their support and guidance, to say nothing of their endurance.

Finally, hearty thanks is due to Lloyd W. Garrison for his excellent foreword and stimulating chronology.

Notes

1. Chalmers Johnson, "Perspectives on Terrorism," in Walter Laqueur, ed., *The Terrorism Reader: An Historical Anthology* (Philadelphia: Temple University Press, 1978), p. 270.

2. "Trends on Terror: The Analysis of Political Violence," *World Politics,* XXIX (April 1977), p. 476.

3. U.S. Central Intelligence Agency, "Glossary of Intelligence Terms and Definitions Published by the Intelligence Community Staff for the Director of Central Intelligence, with the Advice of the National Foreign Intelligence Board, June 15, 1978," in U.S. Congress, House, Permanent Select Committee on Intelligence, *Annual Report* (95th Cong., 2nd sess.; Washington, D.C.: U.S. Government Printing Office, 1978), p. 43.

4. *Ibid,* pp. 65–66.

5. U.S. Congress, Senate, Committee on the Judiciary, Subcommittee to Investigate the Administration of the Internal Security Act and Other Internal Security Laws, *Terroristic Activity, Part 4: International Terrorism—Hearings* (94th Cong., 1st sess.; Washington, D.C.: U.S. Government Printing Office, 1975), p. 180.

6. Cited in Marjorie Kravitz, ed., *International Summaries: A Collection of Selected Translations in Law Enforcement and Criminal Justice, v. 3* (Rockville, Md.: National Criminal Justice Reference Service, Law Enforcement Assistance Administration, Department of Justice, 1979) pp. 83, 88.

7. "The Seven Deadly Sins of Terrorism," *The New Republic,* CLXXXI (September 15, 1979), p. 20.

8. "Transnational Terrorism" in Michael Stohl, ed., *The Politics of Terrorism* (New York: Marcel Dekker, 1979), p. 148.

9. *Ibid.*

10. J. Bowyer Bell, *A Time of Terror: How Democratic Societies Respond to Revolutionary Violence* (New York: Basic Books, 1978), p. 280.

I/Reference Works

Introduction

The purpose of this section is to provide information in one place on research tools. These citations should prove useful to those seeking treatments such as encyclopedia articles, statistical data, bibliographic sources, or further "terrorism" definitions. Additionally, by watching current sources, the reader may readily update this guide well into the early 1980's.

Encyclopedia articles will often give the student a quick, general overview and background to his topic, while biographical materials such as *Current Biography* can provide leads to specific personalities. Current and retrospective English-language sources relative to all aspects of terrorism may be located among the citations in various bibliographies, abstracts, and indexes. Terms useful in interpreting language or concepts in some of the works cited in this guide may be found in dictionaries, while additional meanings for the word "terrorism" can be found in our subsection on definitions. Handbooks and manuals not only provide information on police-military procedures but act as guides to nations and international organizations. Yearbooks and almanacs provide a variety of ready data on terrorists and their deeds; chronologies on terrorism approach the topic year by year.

Users of this bibliography should also be certain to check the footnotes and bibliographies (where provided) in all of the books, scholarly journal articles, papers, documents, and dissertations cited in this guide.

A. Encyclopedias

1. *Collier's Encyclopedia: With Bibliography and Index.* 24 vols. New York: Collier-Macmillan, 1978.

2. DeConde, Alexander, ed. *Encyclopedia of American Foreign Policy: Studies of the Principal Movements and Ideas.* 3 vols. New York: Scribners, 1978.

3. *The Encyclopedia Americana.* International Edition. 30 vols. Danbury, Conn.: Americana Corp., 1979.

4. Dupuy, R. Ernest, and Trevor N. *The Encyclopedia of Military History.* Rev. ed. New York: Harper & Row, 1976. 1,488p.

5. *Encyclopedia International.* 20 vols. New York: Grolier, 1978.

6. *The Encyclopedia of Psychology.* 3 vols. London: Herder & Herder, 1972.

7. Kurian, George T. *The Encyclopedia of the Third World.* 2 vols. New York: Facts on File, 1979.

8. *The New Encyclopedia Britannica.* 30 vols. Chicago: Encyclopedia Britannica, 1979.

9. Patai, Raphael. *Encyclopedia of Zionism and Israel.* 2 vols. New York: Herzl Press and McGraw-Hill, 1971.

10. Reich, Warren T., ed. *Encyclopedia of Bioethics.* 4 vols. New York: Free Press, 1978.

B. Biographical Materials

11. *Biography Index.* New York: H. W. Wilson, 1968–. v. 22–.

12. *Current Biography.* New York: H. W. Wilson, 1968–. v. 28–.

13. *Dictionary of International Biography.* London, 1968–. v. 4–.

14. *Facts on File,* Editors of. *Obituaries on File* [1940–1978]. 2 vols. New York, 1979.

15. *The International Who's Who.* London: Europa Publications, 1968–. v. 32–.

16. United States. Central Intelligence Agency. Office of Political Research. *Chiefs-of-State and Cabinet Members of Foreign Governments.* A Reference Aid. Washington, D.C.: Document Expediting Project, Exchange and Gift Division, Library of Congress, 1972–. v. 1–.

17. *Who's Who.* New York: St. Martin's Press, 1968–. v. 120–.

18. *Who's Who in America.* Chicago: Marquis, 1968–. v. 30–.

19. *Who's Who in Germany.* 7th ed. 2 vols. New York: Facts on File, 1979.

20. *Who's Who in Italy.* 3rd ed. New York: Facts on File, 1980.

21. *Who's Who in the Arab World.* New York: International Publications Service, 1968–. v. 1–.

C. Bibliographies, Abstracts, and Indexes

1. Bibliographies

22. *ABS Guide to Recent Publications in the Social and Behavioral Sciences: Supplements.* Beverly Hills, Calif.: Sage, 1968–. v. 2–.

23. *Alternative Press Index: An Index to Alternative and Underground Publications.* College Park, Md.: Alternative Press Centre, 1969–. v. 1–.

24. *American Book Publishing Record.* New York: R. R. Bowker, 1968–. v. 8–.

25. *Bibliography of Asian Studies.* Ann Arbor, Mich.: Association for Asian Studies, 1968–. v. 1–.

26. Blackey, Robert. *Modern Revolution and Revolutionists: A Bibliography.* War/Peace Series. Santa Barbara, Calif.: ABC-Clio, 1976. 257p.

27. *Books on Demand Subject Guide.* Ann Arbor, Mich.: University Microfilms International, 1977. 786p.

28. Boston, Guy D. et al. *Terrorism: A Selected Bibliography.* Washington, D.C.: National Criminal Justice Reference Service, National Institute of Law Enforcement and Criminal Justice, Law Enforcement Assistance Administration, U.S. Department of Justice, 1976. 45p.

29. _____ . _____ . 2nd ed. Washington, D.C.: National Criminal Justice Reference Service, National Institute of Law Enforcement and Criminal Justice, Law Enforcement Assistance Administration, U.S. Department of Justice, 1977. 62p.

30. Boyer, Anne. *Soviet Foreign Propaganda: An Annotated Bibliography.* Washington, D.C.: U.S. Information Agency Library, 1971. 45p.

31. *British Books in Print: The Reference Catalogue of Current Literature.* New York: R. R. Bowker, 1968–. v. 2–.

32.   Chilcote, Ronald H. *Revolution and Structural Change in Latin America: A Bibliography of Ideology, Development, and the Radical Left.* 2 vols. Stanford, Calif.: Hoover Institution Press, 1970.

33.   Cooling, B. Franklin, III, and Allan Millett. *Doctoral Dissertations in Military Affairs: A Bibliography.* Bibliography Series, no. 10. Manhattan: Kansas State University Library, 1972. 153p.

Updated annually in the April issue of *Military Affairs.*

34.   Coxe, Betsy, comp. *Terrorism.* Special Bibliography Series, no. 57. Colorado Springs, Colo.: U.S. Air Force Academy Library, 1977. 47p.

35.   *The Cumulative Book Index.* New York: H. W. Wilson, 1968–.

36.   Delupis, Ingrid. *Bibliography of International Law.* New York: R. R. Bowker, 1975. 670p.

37.   DeSchutter, Bart, and Christian Eliaerts. *Bibliography on International Criminal Law.* Leyden: Sijthoff, 1972.

38.   Deutsch, Karl W., and Richard L. Merritt. *Nationalism and National Development: An Interdisciplinary Bibliography.* Cambridge, Mass.: MIT Press, 1970. 519p.

39.   Deutsch, Richard L. *Northern Ireland, 1921–1974: A Select Bibliography.* New York: Garland, 1975. 142p.

40.   DeVore, Ronald M. *The Arab-Israeli Conflict.* War/Peace Series. Santa Barbara, Calif.: ABC-Clio, 1976. 273 p.

41.   Dimitrov, Th. D., comp. *Documents of International Organization: A Bibliographic Handbook Covering the United Nations and Other Intergovernmental Organizations.* New York: UNIFO Publishers, 1975. 301p.

Eliaerts, Christian, jt. author. *See* DeSchutter, Bart.

42.   Emanuel, Muriel. *Israel: A Survey and Bibliography.* London: St. James, 1971. 309p.

43.   Fetsenfeld, Lyn, and Brian Jenkins. *International Terrorism: An Annotated Bibliography.* Santa Monica, Calif.: RAND Corp., 1973.

44.   Great Britain. British Museum. Department of Printed Books. *Catalog of Printed Books: Additons.* London: Clowes, 1968–. v. 5–.

Greenberg, Martin H., jt. author. *See* Norton, Augustus R.

45.   Heath, G. Louis, ed. *Vandals in the Bomb Factory: The History and Literature of the Students for a Democratic Society.* Metuchen, N.J.: Scarecrow Press, 1976. 485p.

46.   Heere, Wybo P. *International Bibliography of Air Law, 1900–1971.* Dobbs Ferry, N.Y.: Oceana, 1972. 569p.

47.   Holler, Frederick L., comp. *Information Sources of Political Science,* 3rd ed. Santa Barbara, Calif.: ABC-Clio, 1980.

48.   Hussaini, H. I. *The Palestinian Probelm: An Annotated Bibliography, 1967–1974.* New York: Arab Information Center, 1974. 81p.

49.   *International Bibliography of Political Science.* Chicago: Aldine, 1968–. v. 16–.

50.   *International Bibliography of Sociology.* Chicago: Aldine, 1968–. v. 16–.

Jenkins, Brian, jt. author. *See* Fetsenfeld, Lyn.

51.   Kelly, Michael J., and Thomas H. Mitchell. *Violence, Internal War, and Revolution.* Ottawa: Norman Patterson School of International Affairs, Carleton University, 1976.

52.   Khalidi, Walid, and Jull Khadduri, eds. *Palestine and the Arab-Israeli Conflict: An Annotated Bibliography.* Oxford, Pa.: Institute for Palestine Studies, 1974. 736p.

53.   Kreslins, Janis R. *The Foreign Affairs Bibliography: A Selected and Annotated List of Books on International Relations, 1962–1972.* New York: Published for the Council on Foreign Relations by R. R. Bowker, 1976. 921p.

54.   Kress, Lee B. "Selected Bibliography." In: Marius H. Livingston, ed. *International Terrorism in the Contemporary World.* Westport, Conn.: Greenwood Press, 1978. pp. 469–503.

55.   Lang, Kurt. *Military Institutions and the Sociology of War.* Beverly Hills, Calif.: Sage, 1972. 337p.

56.   Manheim, J. B. *Political Violence in the United States, 1875–1974: A Bibliography.* New York: Garland, 1975. 127p.

Merritt, Richard L., jt. author. *See* Deutsch, Karl W.

57.   Mikolus, Edward F. *Annotated Bibliography on Transnational and International Terrorism.* PR 76-10073U. Washington, D.C.: U.S. Central Intelligence Agency, 1976. 225p.

58.   "The Military Library." In: *Military Affairs.* Washington, D.C.: American Military Institute, 1968–. v. 31–.

Millett, Allan R., jt. author. *See* Cooling, B. Franklin.

Mitchell, Thomas H., jt. author. *See* Kelly, Michael J.

59. Norton, Augustus R., and Martin H. Greenberg. *International Terrorism: An Annotated Bibliography and Research Guide.* Boulder, Colo.: Westview Press, 1979. 200p.

60. O'Brien, Ann, comp. *Hijacking: Selected References, 1961–1969.* Washington, D.C.: Library Services Division, Federal Aviation Administration, 1969. 22p.

61. Overholt, William H. *Revolution: A Bibliography.* Croton-on-Hudson, N.Y.: Hudson Institute, 1975. 43p.

62. "Periodicals and Pamphlets Published by the Palestinian Commando Organizations." *Journal of Palestine Studies,* I (Autumn 1971) 136–151.

63. Piasetski, J. Peter. *Urban Guerrilla Warfare and Terrorism: A Selected Bibliography.* Exchange Bibliography, no. 1098. Monticello, Ill.: Council of Planning Librarians, 1976. 16p.

64. Pollak, Oliver B., and Karen. *Rhodesia/Zimbabwe: An International Bibliography.* Boston: G. K. Hall, 1977. 622p.

65. Price, Arnold H., comp. *The Federal Republic of Germany: A Selected Bibliography of English-Language Publications.* Washington, D.C.: Library of Congress, 1978. 116p.

66. *Publishers' Trade List Annual.* New York: R. R. Bowker, 1968–. v. 95–.

67. Ridgeway, Susan, comp. *N.P.T.: Current Issues in Nuclear Proliferation, a Selected Bibliography.* Political Issues Series, v. 5, no. 1. Los Angeles: Center for the Study of Armament and Disarmament, California State University, 1977. 57p.

68. Rubner, Michael, comp. *Middle East Conflict from October 1973 to July 1976: A Selected Bibliography.* Political Issues Series, v. 4, no. 4. Los Angeles: Center for the Study of Armament and Disarmament, California State University, 1977. 82p.

69. Russell, Charles A., *et al.* "Urban Guerrillas in Argentina: A Select Bibliography." *Latin American Research Review,* IX (Fall 1974), 53–89.

70. _____ . "Urban Guerrillas in Latin America: A Select Bibliography." *Latin American Research Review,* IX (Spring 1974), 37–80.

71. Schulz, Ann. *International and Regional Politics in the Middle East and North Africa: A Guide to Information Sources.* International Relations Information Guide Series, v. 6. Detroit: Gale Research, 1977. 244p.

72. Simon, Reeva S. *The Modern Middle East: A Guide to Research Tools in the Social Sciences.* Modern Middle East Series, v. 10. Boulder, Colo.: Westview Press, 1978. 283p.

73. Smith, Myron J., Jr. *The Secret Wars, Vol. 2: Intelligence, Propaganda and Psychological Warfare, Covert Operations, 1945–1980.* War/Peace Series. Santa Barbara, Calif.: ABC-Clio, 1980.

74. *Sources: A Guide to Print and Nonprint Materials Available from Organizations, Industry, Government Agencies, and Specialized Publishers.* Syracuse, N.Y.: Gaylord Professional Publications, 1977–. v. 1–.

75. Spjut, R. J., and Paul Wilkinson. "A Review of [Ten] Counter-Insurgency [and Terrorism] Theorists." *Political Quarterly*, XLIX (January and May 1978), 54–64, 231–232.

76. *Subject Guide to Books in Print.* New York: R. R. Bowker, 1968–. v. 11–.

77. *Subject Guide to Forthcoming Books.* New York: R. R. Bowker, 1968–. v. 2–.

78. United Nations. Dag Hammerskjold Library. *Current Issues: A Selected Bibliography on Subjects of Concern to the United Nations.* New York, 1968–. v. 3–.

79. _____ . _____ . *International Terrorism: A Select Bibliography.* New York, 1973. 10p.

80. _____ . _____ . *The Palestine Question: A Select Bibliography.* Bibliography Series, no. 22. New York, 1976. 63p.

81. United States. Federal Bureau of Investigation. Academy. *Hostage Situations: A Bibliography.* Quantico, Va., 1973. 8 p.

82. _____ . _____ . _____ . *Terrorist Activities: A Bibliography.* Quantico, Va., 1975. 79p.

83. _____ . Library of Congress. *The Library of Congress Catalog: Books—Subjects.* Washington, D.C.: U.S. Government Printing Office, 1968–. v. 18–.

84. *Vertical File Index.* New York: H. W. Wilson, 1968–. v. 37–.

Wilkinson, Paul, jt. author. *See* Spjut, R. J.

2.   Abstracts

85. *Abstracts of Military Bibliography.* Buenos Aires: Navy Publications Institute, 1968–. v. 1–.

86. *America: History and Life—A Guide to Periodical Literature.* Santa Barbara, Calif.: ABC-Clio, 1968–. v. 4–.

87. Congressional Information Service. *C.I.S. Annual: Abstracts of Congressional Publications and Legislative Histories.* Washington, D.C., 1969–. v. 1–.

88. *Dissertation Abstracts International: "A" Schedule.* Ann Arbor, Mich.: University Microfilms International, 1969–. v. 1–.

89. *Historical Abstracts: Part B, Twentieth Century Abstracts (1914 to the Present).* Santa Barbara, Calif.: ABC-Clio, 1968–. v. 13–.

90. *International Political Science Abstracts.* Oxford, Eng.: Basil Blackwell, 1968–. v. 16–.

91. *Masters Abstracts.* Ann Arbor, Mich.: University Microfilms International, 1968–. v. 6–.

92. *Psychological Abstracts.* Lancaster, Pa.: American Psychological Association, 1968–. v. 41–.

93. RAND Corporation. *Selected RAND Abstracts.* Santa Monica, Calif., 1968–. v. 5–.

94. *Sociological Abstracts.* New York, 1968–. v. 15–.

3. Indexes

a. Newspapers

95. American Association for the Advancement of Slavic Studies. *Index to Pravda.* Columbus, Ohio, 1975–1977.

96. *California News Index.* Claremont, Calif.: Center for California Public Affairs, 1970–. v. 1–.

97. *The Christian Science Monitor Index.* Corvallis, Oreg.: Helen M. Cropsey, 1968–. v. 9–.

98. *Current Digest of the Soviet Press.* Ann Arbor, Mich.: Committee on Slavic Studies, 1968–. v. 19–.

99. *Facts on File,* Editors of. *Editorials on File.* New York, 1970–. v. 1–.

100. *The German Tribune.* Hamburg: Friedrich Verlag, 1968–. v. 10–.

101. *Index to the Times.* London, 1968–. v. 62–.

102. *The National Observer Index.* Flint, Mich.: Newspaper Indexing Center, 1970–. v.1–.

103. *New York Times Index.* New York, 1968–. v. 55–.

104. *Newspaper Index* [to *Chicago Tribune, Washington Post, Los Angeles Times,* and *New Orleans Picayune*]. Wooster, Ohio, 1972–. v. 1–.

105. *The Wall Street Journal Index.* New York: Dow Jones, 1968–. v. 10–.

b. Periodicals

106. *ABC POL SCI.* Santa Barbara, Calif.: ABC-Clio, 1968–. v. 4–.

107. *Access: The Supplementary Index to Periodicals.* Syracuse, N.Y.: Gaylord Professional Publications, 1975–. v. 1–.

108. American Historical Association. *Writings on American History.* Milwood, N.Y.: Kraus Reprint, 1968–.

109. *Book Review Digest.* New York: H. W. Wilson, 1968–. v. 63–.

110. *Book Review Index.* Detroit: Gale Research, 1968–. v. 1–.

111. Botlorff, Robert M., ed. *Popular Periodical Index.* New York, 1973–. v. 1–.

112. Burke, John G., ed. *The Access Index to Little Magazines.* Syracuse, N.Y.: Gaylord Professional Publications, 1977–. v. 1–.

113. *Essay and General Literature Index.* New York: H. W. Wilson, 1968–. v. 7–.

114. *Humanities Index.* New York: H. W. Wilson, 1975–. v. 1–.

115. *Index to Foreign Legal Periodicals and Collections of Essays.* Chicago: William D. Murphy, 1968–. v. 8–.

116. *Index to Legal Periodicals.* New York: H. W. Wilson, 1968–. v. 61–.

117. *Index to the Contemporary Scene.* Detroit: Gale Research, 1973–. v. 1–.

118. *Index to U.S. Government Periodicals.* Chicago: Infordata International, 1975–. v. 1–.

119. *International Relations Digest of Periodical Literature.* Berkeley: Bureau of International Relations, University of California, 1968–. v. 19–.

120. *The New Periodical Index.* Boulder, Colo.: Mediaworks, 1977–. v. 1–.

121. *PAIS Bulletin.* New York: Public Affairs Information Service, 1968–. v. 53–.

122. *Perspective.* Washington, D.C.: Helen Dwight Reid Education Foundation, 1972–. v. 1–.

123. *Reader's Guide to Periodical Literature.* New York: H. W. Wilson, 1968–. v. 68–.

124. *Social Sciences and Humanities Index.* 9 vols. New York: H. W. Wilson, 1965–1974.

125. *Social Sciences Index.* New York: H. W. Wilson, 1975–. v. 1–.

126. United States. Air Force. Air University. Library. *Air University Library Index to Military Periodicals.* Maxwell AFB, Ala., 1968–. v. 19–.

c. Documents

127. Bernan Associates. *Checklist of Congressional Hearings and Reports.* Washington, D.C., 1968–. v. 10–.

128. *Bibliographic Index to Current U.S. Joint Publications Research Service Translations.* New York: C.C.M. Information Corp., 1968–. v. 5–.

129. Canada. Department of Public Printing and Stationery. *Canadian Government Publications.* Ottawa, 1968–. v. 15–.

130. Congressional Quarterly, Inc. *C.Q. Weekly Report.* Washington, D.C., 1968–. v. 23–.

131. Great Britain. *Catalog of Government Publications.* London: H.M. Stationery Office, 1968–. v. 45–.

132. United Nations. Dag Hammerskjold Library. *United Nations Documents Index.* New York, 1968–. v. 18–.

133. United States. Congress. Senate. Committee on the Judiciary. Subcommittee to Investigate the Administration of the Internal Security Act and Other Internal Security Laws. *21 Year Index: Combined Cumulative Index, 1951–1971, to Published Hearings, Studies, and Reports.* 2 vols. Washington, D.C.: U.S. Government Printing Office, 1972.

134. _____. Library of Congress. Legislative Reference Service. *Digest of Public General Bills and Selected Resolutions, with Index.* Washington, D.C.: U.S. Government Printing Office, 1968–. v. 23–.

135. _____. National Technical Information Service. *Government Reports Announcements.* Springfield, Va., 1968–. v. 22–.

136. _____. Superintendent of Documents. *Monthly Catalogue of U.S. Government Publications.* Washington, D.C.: U.S. Government Printing Office, 1968–. v. 73–.

137. *United States Political Science Documents.* Pittsburgh, Pa.: Publications Center, University Center for International Studies, University of Pittsburgh, 1975–. v. 1–.

D.   Dictionaries and Terrorism Definitions

1.   Dictionaries

138.   Gale Research Corporation. *Acronyms and Initialisms Dictionary.* 3rd ed. Detroit, 1970. 484p.

>   Greenberg, Milton, jt. author. *See* Plano, Jack C.

139.   Hyams, Edward. *A Dictionary of Modern Revolution.* New York: Taplinger, 1973. 322p.

>   Levine, Evyater, jt. author. *See* Shimoni, Yaacov.

140.   Lutwak, Edward. *The Dictionary of Modern War.* New York: Harper & Row, 1971. 224p.

>   Olton, Roy, jt. author. *See* Plano, Jack C.

141.   Plano, Jack C., and Milton Greenberg. *The American Political Dictionary.* 5th ed. New York: Holt, Rinehart & Winston, 1979. 488 pp.

142.   _____, and Roy Olton. *The International Relations Dictionary.* New York: Holt, Rinehart & Winston, 1969. 337p.

143.   Quick, John. *Dictionary of Weapons and Military Terms.* New York: McGraw-Hill, 1973. 515p.

144.   Raymond, Walter J. *Dictionary of Politics: Selected American and Foreign Political and Legal Terms.* 6th ed. rev. Lawrenceville, Va.: Brunswick Publishing, 1978. 956p.

145.   Shimoni, Yaacov, and Evyatar Levine, eds. *Political Dictionary of the Middle East in the Twentieth Century.* Jerusalem: Jerusalem Publishing House, 1972. 434p.

146.   United States. Department of Defense. *Dictionary of Military and Associated Terms.* JCS Publications, no. 1. Rev. ed. Washington, D.C.: U.S. Government Printing Office, 1979. 377p.

2.   Terrorism Definitions

147.   Aaron, Harold R. "The Anatomy of Guerrilla Terror." *Infantry,* LVIII (March-April 1967), 14–18.

148.   Arblaster, Anthony. "Terrorism: Myths, Meanings, and Morals." *Political Studies,* XXV (September 1977), 413–424.

149.   Bouthoul, Gaston. "Definitions of Terrorism." In: David Carlton and Carlo Schaerf, eds. *International Terrorism and World Security.* New York: Wiley, 1975. pp. 50–59.

150.   Conrad, Thomas R. "Coercion, Assassination, Conspiracy: Pejorative Political Language." *Polity,* VI (1974), 418–423.

151.   Dugard, John. "International Terrorism: Problems of Definition." *International Affairs,* L (January 1974), 67–81.

152.   _____. "Toward the Definition of International Terrorism." *American Journal of International Law,* LXVII (November 1973), 94–99.

153.   Firestone, Joseph M. *Exploration in Systems Analysis of Domestic Conflict.* Honolulu: Department of Political Science, University of Hawaii, 1969.

154.   Greisman, H. C. "Social Meanings of Terrorism." *Contemporary Crises,* I (July 1977), 303–318.

155.   Gurr, Ted R. "Some Characteristics of Contemporary Political Terrorism." Unpublished paper, Department of State Conference on International Terrorism in Retrospect and Prospect, 1976.

156.   _____. "Some Characteristics of Political Terrorism in the 1960's." In: Michael Stoke, ed. *The Politics of Terrorism.* New York: Marcel Dekker, 1979. pp. 23–50.

157.   Horowitz, Irving L. "Toward a Qualitative Micro-Politics of Terror." Unpublished paper, Department of State Conference on International Terrorism in Retrospect and Prospect, 1976.

158.   Hutchinson, Martha C. "The Concept of Revolutionary Terrorism." *Journal of Conflict Resolution,* XVI (September 1972), 383–396.

159.   Johnson, Chalmers. "Perspectives on Terrorism." In: Walter Laqueur, ed. *The Terrorism Reader: A Historical Anthology.* Philadelphia: Temple University Press, 1978. pp. 267–285.

160.   Johnson, Paul. "The Seven Deadly Sins of Terrorism." *New Republic,* CLXXXI (September 15, 1979), 19–21.

161.   Karanovic, Milivoje. "The Concept of Terrorism." In: Majorie Kravitz, ed. *International Summaries: A Collection of Selected Translations in Law Enforcement and Criminal Justice,* v. 3. Rockville, Md.: National Criminal Justice Reference Service, Law Enforcement Assistance Administration, U.S. Department of Justice, 1979. pp. 81–88.

162.   Kelly, Clarence M. *Statement on Terrorism.* Washington, D.C.: Federal Bureau of Investigation, 1974. 4p.

163.   Laqueur, Walter. "Interpretations of Terrorism: Fact, Fiction, and Political Science." *Journal of Contemporary History,* XII (June 1977), 1–42.

164. Leber, J. R. "International Terrorism: Criminal or Political?" *Towson State Journal of International Affairs,* VII (Spring 1973), 129+.

165. Leiden, Carl. *The Concept of Terror.* FAR Document 16462-3. Washington, D.C.: Department of State, 1972. 5p.

166. Merari, Ariel. "A Classification of Terrorist Groups." *Terrorism,* I (1978), 331–346.

167. Paust, Jordan J. "Definitional Approaches to Terrorism." Unpublished paper, Ralph Bunch Institute on International Terrorism, 1976.

168. _____. "Some Thoughts on 'Preliminary Thoughts' on Terrorism." *American Journal of International Law,* LXVIII (1974), 502+.

169. Schwarzenberger, Georg. "Terrorists, Guerrillas, and Mercenaries." *University of Toledo Law Review,* III (Fall-Winter 1971), 71–81.

170. _____. "Terrorists, Hijackers, Guerrilleros, and Mercenaries." *Current Legal Problems,* XXIV (1971), 257–282.

171. Sloane, Stephen. "Learning about Terrorism: Analysis, Simulation, and Future Directions." *Terrorism,* I (1978), 315–330.

172. Tophoven, Rolf. "International Terrorism: Challenge and Defensive Measures." In: Marjorie Kravitz, ed. *International Summaries: A Collection of Selected Translations in Law Enforcement and Criminal Justice,* v. 3. Rockville, Md.: National Criminal Justice Reference Service, Law Enforcement Assistance Administration, U.S. Department of Justice, 1979. pp. 105–114.

173. United States. Central Intelligence Agency. "Glossary of Intelligence Terms and Definitions Published by the Intelligence Community Staff for the Director of Central Intelligence, with the Advice of the National Foreign Intelligence Board." In: U.S. Congress. House. Permanent Select Committee on Intelligence. *Annual Report.* 95th Cong., 2nd sess. Washington, D.C.: U.S. Government Printing Office, 1978. pp. 24–69.

174. White, C. A. "Terrorism: Idealism or Sickness?" *Canada and the World,* XXXIX (Fall 1974), 14–15.

175. Wilkinson, Paul. "Three Questions on Terrorism." *Government and Opposition,* VIII (March 1973), 290–312.

176. Wolf, John B. "Analytical Framework for the Study and Control of Agitational Terrorism." *Police Journal,* XLIX (July-September 1976), 165–171.

E.   Handbooks and Manuals

177.   Adams, Michael. *The Middle East: A Handbook.* New York: Praeger, 1971.

178.   Ali, Tariq, ed. *The New Revolutionaries: A Handbook of the International Radical Left.* New York: Morrow, 1969. 319p.

Amoia, Alba, jt. author. *See* Stebbins, Richard P.

179.   Banks, Arthur S., ed. *Political Handbook of the World, 19–: Governments, Regional Issues, and Intergovernmental Organizations as of January 1, 19–.* New York: McGraw-Hill, 1968–. v. 40–.

180.   Garling, Margurite. *The Human Rights Handbook.* New York: Facts on File, 1979. 229p.

181.   *Handbook of Latin American Studies.* Gainesville: University of Florida Press, 1968–. v. 33–.

182.   International Association of Chiefs of Police. *Ambush Attacks: A Risk Reduction Manual for Police.* Gaithersburg, Md., 1974. 97p.

183.   Keegan, John. *World Armies.* New York: Facts on File, 1979. 1,016p.

184.   Mallory, Walter H. *Political Handbook and Atlas of the World.* New York: Council on Foreign Relations, 1968–. v. 41–.

185.   Sellers, Robert C., ed. *Armed Forces of the World: A Reference Handbook.* 4th ed. New York: Praeger, 1977. 288p.

186.   Stebbins, Richard P., and Alba Amoia. *The World This Year.* New York: Simon and Schuster, 1971–. v. 1–.

187.   United States. General Services Administration, National Archives and Records Service, Office of the Federal Register. *U.S. Government Manual.* Washington, D.C.: U.S. Government Printing Office, 1968–. v. 33–.

F.   Document Collections

188.   Amnesty International. *Report on Torture.* New York: Farrar, Straus, and Giroux, 1975. 285p.

189.   "Arab Documents on Palestine and the Arab-Israeli Conflict." *Journal of Palestine Studies,* VI (Spring 1977), 178–197.

190. Council on Foreign Relations. *Documents on American Foreign Policy.* New York, 1968–. v. 30–.

191. Djonovich, Dusan J., comp. *United Nations Resolutions.* Dobbs Ferry, N.Y.: Oceana, 1972–. v. 1–.

192. "Documents on Terrorism." *Terrorism,* I (1978), 97–108, 441–449.

193. Great Britain. Parliament. House of Commons. *Journals.* London: H.M. Stationery Office, 1968–.

194. *International Documents on Palestine.* Beirut: Institute for Palestine Studies, 1968–. v. 2–.

195. United Nations. Dag Hammarskjold Library. *United Nations Documents.* New York, 1968–. v. 18–.

196. United States. Congress. *Congressional Record.* Washington, D.C.: U.S. Government Printing Office, 1968–. v. 91–.

G.   *Yearbooks, Almanacs, and Chronologies*

1.   Yearbooks

197. *Africa South of the Sahara.* London: Europa Publications, 1970–. v. 1–.

198. *Africa Yearbook and Who's Who.* New York: R. R. Bowker, 1976–. v. 1–.

199. *Americana Annual.* New York, 1968–. v. 45–.

200. *Annual Review of Psychology.* Palo Alto, Calif., 1968–. v. 18–.

201. *Annual Review of United Nations Affairs.* Dobbs Ferry, N.Y.: Oceana, 1968–. v. 19–.

202. *Arab Report and Record.* London, 1968–. v. 3–.

203. Bialer, Seweryn, ed. *Radicalism in the Contemporary Age.* Boulder, Colo.: Westview Press, 1977–. v. 1–.

204. *Canada Year Book, 19–.* Ottawa: Statistics Canada, 1968–. v. 63–.

205. *Colliers Encyclopedia Yearbook.* New York: Macmillan, 1968–. v. 18–.

206. Crozier, Brian, ed. *Annual of Power and Conflict.* London: Institute for the Study of Conflict, 1973–. v. 1–.

207. *Economic and Social Progress in Latin America.* Washington, D.C.: Inter-American Development Bank, 1970–. v. 1–.

208. Encyclopedia Britannica. *Britannica Book of the Year.* Chicago, 1968–. v. 30–.

209. *The Europa Yearbook: A World Survey and Directory of Countries and International Organizations.* London: Europa Publications, 1968–. v. 19–.

210. *Facts on File,* Editors of. *Facts on File Yearbook: The Indexed Record of World Events.* New York, 1968–. v. 27–.

211. _____. *Latin America.* New York, 1972–. v. 1–.

212. Haverstock, Nathan A. *Dateline Latin America.* Washington, D.C.: Latin American Service, 1971–. v. 1–.

213. Institute of World Affairs. *The Yearbook of World Affairs.* London: Stevens, 1968–. v. 21–.

214. International Association of Chiefs of Police. *Police Yearbook.* Gaithersburg, Md., 1968–. v. 2–.

215. *International Yearbook and Statesman's Who's Who.* London: Burke's Peerage, 1968–. v. 22–.

216. Israel Police Headquarters. *Israel Police Annual Report.* Jerusalem, 1968–.

217. Legum, Colin, ed. *Africa Contemporary Record.* New York: Holmes & Meier, 1969–. v. 1–.

218. _____. *Middle East Contemporary Survey.* New York: Holmes & Meier, 1978–. v. 1–.

219. Metrowich, F. R., ed. *African Freedom Annual, 1978.* Sandton, South Africa: Southern Africa Freedom Foundation, 1978–. v. 1–.

220. *The Middle East and North Africa.* London: Europa Publications, 1968–. v. 15–.

221. Northern Ireland. Information Service. *The Ulster Yearbook.* Belfast, N.I.: H.M. Stationery Office, 1968–.

222. Rake, Alan, ed. *New African Yearbook.* New York: Franklin Watts, 1978–. v. 1–.

223. Saywell, John, ed. *Canadian Annual Review of Politics and Public Affairs.* Toronto: University of Toronto Press, 1968–. v. 8–.

224. Stockholm International Peace Research Institute (SIPRI). *World Armaments and Disarmament: The SIPRI Yearbook.* New York: Humanities Press, 1969–. v. 1–.

225. Union of International Associations. *Yearbook of International Associations.* Brussels, 1968–. v. 20–.

226. United Nations. Department of Social Affairs. *United Nations Yearbook.* New York, 1968–. v. 22–.

227. United States. Federal Bureau of Investigation. *Crime in the United States: Uniform Crime Reports.* Washington, D.C.: U.S. Government Printing Office, 1968–.

228. _____ . National Criminal Justice Information and Statistics Service. *Sourcebook of Criminal Justice Statistics.* Washington, D.C.: U.S. Government Printing Office, 1973–. v. 1–.

2.   Almanacs

229. *The Annual Register of World Events.* London: Longmans, 1968–. v. 210–.

230. *Canadian News Facts.* Toronto, 1968–. v. 2–.

231. Congressional Quarterly, Inc. *Congressional Quarterly Almanac.* Washington, D.C., 1968–. v. 23–.

232. Dupuy, Trevor N., *et al. The Almanac of World Military Power.* 3rd ed. New York: R. R. Bower, 1974. 387p.

233. *Information Please Almanac.* New York: Viking, 1968–. v. 22–.

234. *Keesing's Contemporary Archives.* London, 1968–. v. 37–.

235. *Reader's Digest 19– Almanac and Yearbook.* New York: Norton, 1968–. v. 2–.

236. Whitaker, Joseph. *Almanac.* London, 1968–. v. 99–.

237. *World Almanac and Book of Facts.* Garden City. N.Y.: Doubleday, 1968–. v. 100–.

3.   Chronologies

238. "Arab Terrorism: A Chronology [1968–1973]." *Congressional Record,* CXIX (December 22, 1973), 43427–43428.

239. Buncher, Judith F., ed. *The CIA and the Security Debate, 1975–1976.* New York: Facts on File, 1977. 240p.

240. _____ . *Human Rights and American Diplomacy, 1975–1977.* New York: Facts on File, 1977. 271p.

241. Carroll, Robert, *et al.* "Year of Terror." *Newsweek,* LXXXVII (January 5, 1976), 24–26.

242. Chakeres, Pauline M. *Developments in Northern Ireland, 1968–1976.* Washington, D.C.: Congressional Research Service, Library of Congress, 1976. 40p.

243. *Deadline Data on World Affairs.* Greenwich, Conn.: 1968–. v. 13–.

244. Deutsch, Richard L., and Vivian Magowan. *Northern Ireland, 1968–1974: A Chronology of Events.* 3 vols. London: Blackstaff Press, 1975.

245. "Earlier Acts of [Arab] Terrorism." *Congressional Record,* CXX (May 16, 1974), 15257.

246. *Facts on File,* Editors of. *News Directory.* New York, 1968–. v. 5–.

247. _____ . *Political Prisoners.* New York, 1979. 285p.

248. Griffin, William D., ed. *Ireland: A Chronology and Fact Book.* Dobbs Ferry, N.Y.: Oceana, 1973. 154p.

249. Hill, Brian H. W., comp. *Canada: A Chronology and Fact Book.* Dobbs Ferry, N.Y.: Oceana, 1973. 153p.

250. Jenkins, Brian. "Chronology of Recent Incidents in International Terrorism." In: David Carlton and Carlo Schaerf, eds. *International Terrorism and World Security.* London: Croom Helm, 1975. pp. 35–49.

251. _____ , and J. Johnson. *International Terrorism: A Chronology, 1968–1974.* RAND Report R-1597. Santa Monica, Calif.: RAND Corp., 1975. 58p.

252. _____ . _____: *Supplement.* RAND Report R1909-1. Santa Monica, Calif.: RAND Corp., 1976. 23p.

Johnson, J., jt. author. *See* Jenkins, Brian.

253. *Latin America.* London: Latin American Newsletter, 1968–. v. 3–.

Magowan, Vivian, jt. author. *See* Deutsch, Richard L.

254. Mickolus, Edward F. "Chronology of Terrorist Activity, January 2–March 9, 1976." In: Michael Stohl, ed. *The Politics of Terrorism.* New York: Marcel Dekker, 1979. pp. 182–187.

255. _____ . "Chronology of Transnational Terrorist Attacks upon American Business People, 1968–1976." *Terrorism*, I (1978), 217–236.

256. *The Middle East: U.S. Policy, Israel, Oil, and the Arabs.* Washington, D.C.: Congressional Quarterly, 1974. 100p.

257. Parker, Thomas F., ed. *Violence in the United States.* 2 vols. New York: Facts on File, 1974.

258. "Record of Arab Terrorism, 1967–1975." *Congressional Record,* CXXI (February 25–27, 1975), 4306–4307, 4521–4522, 4753–4754.

259. Seymour, Gerald. "Middle East: September–October 1970." *Contemporary Review,* CCXVII (December 1970), 303–308.

260. Snitch, Thomas H. "Decade of the Terrorist." *Intellect,* CVI (June 1978), 456–459.

261. Sobel, Lester A., ed. *Palestinian Impasse: Arab Guerrillas and International Terrorism.* New York: Facts on File, 1977. 282p.

262. _____ . *Political Terrorism.* 2 vols. New York: Facts on File, 1975–1978.

263. United States. Department of State. Office of the Legal Advisor. *Treaties in Force.* Washington, D.C.: U.S. Government Printing Office, 1977. 391p.

264. _____ . Federal Aviation Administration. Civil Aviation Security Service. *Domestic and Foreign Aircraft Hijackings* [1931–1979]. Washington, D.C., 1979. 77p.

265. _____ . _____ . _____ . *Hijacking Statistics: U.S. Registered Aircraft, 1961*–April *1975.* Washington, D.C., 1975. 18p.

266. _____ . _____ . _____ . *Significant Worldwide Criminal Acts Involving Civil Aviation.* Washington, D.C., 1974–. v. 1–.

267. "Year of the Terrorist." *National Review,* XXVIII (January 23, 1976), 21–22.

II/General Works:
Violence and Terrorism, 1968–1979

Introduction

As terrorism is usually a violent political action undertaken against society, or a segment thereof, much of the research done on violence as a subject has worth for any student of the topic. The titles in subsection A represent the literature written by those engaged in the general study of violence.

Much has been written on terrorism in books, articles, papers, reports, dissertations, and theses. Subsection B provides bibliographic guidance to those works which are too general in nature or too all-encompassing in design or coverage to fit into any of the sections or subsections below.

A. Violence

1. Books

268. Arendt, Hannah. *On Violence.* New York: Harcourt Brace Jovanovich, 1970. 106p.

269. Bell, J. Bowyer. *Assassin: The Theory and Practice of Political Violence.* New York: St. Martin's Press, 1979. 320p.

270. Bingham, Jonathan B., and Alfred M. *Violence and Democracy.* Cleveland, Ohio: World Publishing, 1971. 188p.

271. Buckman, Peter. *The Limits of Protest.* London: Panther, 1970. 286p.

272. Darby, John, and Arthur Williamson, eds. *Violence and the Social Services in Northern Ireland.* London: Heinemann, 1978. 205p.

273. Davies, James C., ed. *When Men Revolt and Why: A Reader in Political Violence and Revolution.* New York: Free Press, 1971. 357p.

274. Fromm, Erich. *The Anatomy of Human Destructiveness.* New York: Holt, Rinehart & Winston, 1973. 521p.

275. Gunn, John C. *Violence.* New York: Praeger, 1973. 200 p.

276. Gurr, Ted Robert. *The Conditions of Civil Violence: First Tests of a Casual Model.* Princeton, N.J.: Center for International Studies, Princeton University, 1970. 111p.

277. Hibbs, Douglas A., Jr. *Mass Political Violence: A Cross-National Causal Analysis.* New York: Wiley, 1973. 268p.

278. Kutash, Irwin L., *et al. Violence: Perspectives on Murder and Aggression.* San Francisco, Calif.: Jossey-Bass, 1978. 574p.

279. Macky, Peter W. *Violence: Right or Wrong.* Waco, Tex.: Word Books, 1973. 210p.

280. Madden, Dennis J., *et al. Rage, Hate, Assault, and Other Forms of Violence.* New York: Halstead Press, 1976. 265p.

281. May, Rollo. *Power and Innocence: A Search for the Sources of Violence.* New York: W. W. Norton, 1972. 283p.

282. Morton, Marian J. *The Terrors of Ideological Politics.* Cleveland: Press of Western Reserve University, 1972. 192p.

283. Nieburg, Harold L. *Political Violence: The Behavioral Process.* New York: St. Martin's Press, 1969. 184p.

284. O'Neill, Bard E., *et al,* eds. *Political Violence and Insurgency: A Comparative Approach.* Arvada, Colo.: Pheonix Press, 1974. 175p.

285. Rivers, Charles R., and Kenneth A. Switzer. *Violence.* Rochelle Park, N.J.: Hayden Press, 1976. 129p.

286. Selzer, Michael. *Terrorist Chic: An Exploration of Violence in the Seventies.* New York: Hawthorn, 1979. 224p.

287. Silberman, Charles E. *Criminal Violence, Criminal Justice.* New York: Random House, 1978. 540p.

288. Storr, Anthony. *Human Destructiveness.* New York: Basic Books, 1973. 127p.

Switzer, Kenneth A., jt. author. *See* Rivers, Charles R.

289. Toplin, Robert B. *Unchallenged Violence: An American Ordeal.* Westport, Conn.: Greenwood Press, 1975. 332p.

290. Usdine, Gene, ed. *Perspectives on Violence.* New York: Brunner-Mazel, 1972. 161p.

291. Von der Mehden, F. R. *Comparative Political Violence.* Englewood Cliffs, N.J.: Prentice-Hall, 1973. 124p.

292. Walter, Eugene V. *Terror and Resistance: A Study of Political Violence, with Case Studies of Some Primitive African Communities.* New York and London: Oxford University Press, 1969. 385p.

293. Wilber, Charles G., ed. *Contemporary Violence: A Multidisciplinary Examination.* Springfield, Ill.: C. C. Thomas, 1975. 163p.

Williamson, Arthur, jt. author. *See* Darby, John.

2. Articles

294. Abu-Lughad, Ibrahim. "Unconventional Violence and International Politics." *American Journal of International Law,* LXVII (November 1973), 100–103.

295. Arendt, Hannah. "Reflections on Violence." *Journal of International Affairs,* XXIII (Winter 1969), 1–35.

296. Azar, E. E. "Towards the Development of an Early Warning Model of International Violence." In: J. D. Ben-Dak, ed. *The Future of Collective Violence: Societal and International Perspectives.* Lund, Sweden: Studentlitteratur, 1974. pp. 145–164.

297. Ball-Rockeach, S. J. "Values and Violence: A Test of the Sub-Culture of Violence Thesis." *American Sociological Review,* XXXVIII (December 1973), 736–749.

298. Bell, J. Bowyer. "Trends on Terror: The Analysis of Political Violence." *World Politics,* XXIX (April 1977), 476–488.

299. Bylinsky, G. "New Clues to the Causes of Violence." *Fortune,* LXXXVII (January 1973), 134–138+.

300. Calvert, Peter. "Revolution: The Politics of Violence." *Political Studies,* XV (February 1967), 1–11.

301. Cameron, J. M. "Changing Patterns in Violence." *Medical Science Law,* XIII (October 1973), 261–264.

302. Carlton, David. "The Future of Political Substate Violence." In: Yonah Alexander, David Carlton, and Paul Wilkinson, eds. *Terrorism: Theory and Practice.* Boulder, Colo: Westview Press, 1979. Chpt. 9.

303. Cocozza, J. J., and H. J. Steadman. "Some Refinements in the Measurement and Prediction of Dangerous Behavior." *American Journal of Psychiatry,* CXXXI (September 1974), 1012–1014.

304. Cooper, Mark N. "A Reinterpretation of the Causes of Turmoil." *Comparative Political Studies,* VII (October 1974), 267–291.

305. Corning, Peter A. "Toward a General Theory of Violent Aggression." *Social Science Information,* XI (1972), 7–35.

306. Cressey, D. R. "A Confrontation of Violent Dynamics." *International Journal of Psychiatry,* X (September 1972), 109–130.

307. "Crimes by Women Are on the Rise All over the World." *U.S. News and World Report,* LXXIX (December 22, 1975), 49–51.

308. Drew, Paul. "Domestic Political Violence: Some Problems of Measurement." *Sociological Review,* I (February 1974), 5–25.

309. Feierabend, Ivo K., and Rosalind L. "The Comparative Study of Revolution and Violence." *Comparative Politics,* V (April 1973), 393–424.

310. ———. "Systemic Conditions of Political Agression: An Application of Frustration-Aggression Theory." In: Ivo K. Feierabend, Rosalind L. Feierabend, and Ted Robert Gurr, eds. *Anger, Violence, and Politics: Theories and Research.* Englewood Cliffs, N.J.: Prentice-Hall, 1972. pp. 136–183.

311. Firestone, Joseph M. "Continuities in the Theory of Violence." *Journal of Conflict Resolution,* XVIII (March 1974), 117–142.

312. Goodheart, E. "Revolution and Social Change: On the Rhetoric of Violence." *Current,* CXVIII (1970), 9–13.

26   *Violence*

313. Graham, H. D., and Ted Robert Gurr. "Violence in Perspective: An Essay Review." *Journal of Human Relations,* XX (Fall 1972), 494+.

314. Greenberg, Stanley B. "Social Differentiation and Political Violence." *Journal of Conflict Resolution,* XIX (March 1975), 161–184.

315. Gurr, Ted Robert. "The Calculus of Civil Conflict." *Journal of Social Issues,* XXVIII (Spring 1972), 27–47.

———, jt. author. *See* Graham, H. D.

316. Hacker, Frederick J. "Why Violent Crime Is Now in Fashion: An Interview." *U.S. News and World Report,* LXXXII (February 28, 1977), 57–58.

317. Hood, E. Ellsworth, "Violence and the Myth of Quantification." *International Philosophical Quarterly,* IX (December 1969), 590–600.

318. Hudson, Michael C. "Conditions of Political Violence and Instability: A Preliminary Test of Three Hypotheses." *Sage Professional Papers in Comparative Politics,* I (1970), 1–56.

319. Korpi, Walter. "Conflict, Power, and Relative Deprivation." *American Political Science Review,* LXVIII (December 1968), 1569–1578.

320. Laqueur, Walter. "Reflections on Violence." *Encounter,* XXXVIII (April 1972), 3–10.

321. Mantell, D. M. "The Potential for Violence in Germany." *Journal of Social Issues,* XXVII (Fall 1971), 101–112.

322. Mars, P. "The Nature of Political Violence." *Social and Economic Studies,* XXIV (June 1975), 221–238.

323. Miller, L. "Identity and Violence in Pursuit of the Causes of War and Organized Violence." *Israeli Annals of Psychiatry,* X (March 1972), 71–77.

324. Muller, E. N. "Test of a Partial Theory of Potential for Political Violence." *American Political Science Review,* LXVI (September 1972), 928–959.

325. O'Brien, Connor Cruise. "On Violence and Terror." *Dissent,* XXIV (Fall 1977), 433–436.

326. Ranly, B. W. "Defining Violence." *Thought,* XLVII (August 1972), 415–427.

327. Rose, T. "Violence and Political Control and Revolt." *International Review of History and Political Science,* V (Fall 1968), 106–141.

328. Ross, J. A. "Entropy and Violence: An Analysis of the Prospects for Postindustrial Society." *American Behavioral Scientist,* XX (March 1977), 457–476.

329. Sayers, J. E. "Violence and Unreason in Control." *Round Table,* LXIX (October 1969), 401–404.

330. Schneider, P. R., and A. L. "Social Mobilization, Political Institutions, Political Violence." *Comparative Political Studies,* IV (April 1971), 69–90.

331. Schwartz, M. M. "The Use of Force and the Dilemma of Violence." *Psychoanalytic Review,* LIX (1972–1973), 617–625.

332. Sperber, Manes. "Violence from Below." *Survey,* LXVIII (Summer 1972), 189–204.

333. Steiner, George. "The Many Faces of Violence: New Patterns of Aggression." *Atlas,* XXIII (January 1976), 29+.

334. Thompson, W. Scott. "Political Violence and the 'Correlation of Forces.'" *Orbis,* XIX (Winter 1976), 1270–1288.

335. "Violence in America: The Latest Theories and Research." *Today's Health,* LII (January 1974), 52–53.

336. "Violence: World-Wide Problem." *U. S. News and World Report,* LXIX (September 28, 1970), 24–26.

337. Wertham, F. "New Dimensions of Human Violence." *American Journal of Psychotherapy,* XXIII (July 1969), 374–380.

3. Documents, Papers, and Reports

338. Huntington, Samuel P. *Civil Violence and the Process of Development.* Adelphi Papers, no. 83. London: International Institute for Strategic Studies, 1971. 29p.

339. Mazrui, Ali A. *The Contemporary Case for Violence.* Adelphi Papers, no. 82. London: International Institute for Strategic Studies, 1971. 30p.

340. Miller, James A. "Political Violence Movements: An Interrogative, Integrative Systems Approach." Unpublished Ph.D. dissertation, The American University, 1976.

341. Mitchell, Edward J. *Relating Rebellion to the Environment: An Econometric Approach.* RAND Paper P-3726. Santa Monica, Calif.: RAND Corp., 1967. 8p.

342.   United States. Central Intelligence Agency. *Profile of Violence: An Analytical Model.* Research project. Washington, D. C., 1976. 55p.

343.   ———. Chamber of Commerce. Community and Regional Development Group. *Violence against Society.* Washington, D. C., 1971. 78p.

B. *Terrorism*

1. Books

344.   Alexander, Yonah, David Carlton, and Paul Wilkinson, eds. *Terrorism: Theory and Practice.* Boulder, Colo.: Westview Press, 1979. 320p.

345.   ———, and Seymour M. Finger, eds. *Terrorism: Interdisciplinary Perspectives.* New York: John Jay Press, 1977. 279p.

346.   ———, and Robert A. Friedlander, eds. *Self-Determination: National, Regional, and Global Dimensions.* Boulder, Colo.: Westview Press, 1974. 250p.

347.   Bassiouni, M. Cherif, ed. *International Terrorism and Political Crimes: Proceedings of the Third Conference on Terrorism and Political Crimes, Syracuse, Sicily, 1973.* Springfield, Ill.: C. C. Thomas, 1974. 594p.

348.   Beilenson, L. W. *Power through Subversion.* New York: Public Affairs Press, 1972. 310p.

349.   Bell, J. Bowyer. *Transnational Terror.* AEI-Hoover Institution Studies, no. 51. Stanford and Washington, D. C.: Hoover Institution and American Enterprise Institute for Public Policy Research, 1975. 91p.

350.   Bertelsen, Judy S., ed. *Nonstate Nations in International Politics: Comparative System Analysis.* New York: Praeger, 1976. 272p.

Carlton, David, jt editor. *See* Alexander, Yonah.

351.   ———, and Carlo Schaerf, eds. *International Terrorism and World Security: Proceedings of the International School on Disarmaments and Research on Conflict, Fifth Annual Meeting, Urbino, 1974.* New York: Wiley, 1975. 332p.

352.   Chaliland, Gerhard. *Revolution in the Third World.* Translated from the German. London: Penguin Books, 1978. 202p.

353.   Clinard, Marshall B. *Crime in Developing Countries: A Comparative Perspective.* New York: Wiley, 1973. 312p.

354.   Clutterbuck, Richard L. *Guerrillas and Terrorists.* London: Faber and Faber, 1977. 125p.

355. _____. *Living with Terrorism*. New Rochelle, N.Y.: Arlington House, 1975. 160p.

356. Dobson, Christopher, and Ronald Payne. *The Terrorists: Their Weapons, Leaders, and Tactics*. New York: Facts on File, 1979. 224p.

357. Eggers, William. *Terrorism: The Slaughter of Innocents*. Chatsworth, Calif.: Major Books, 1975. 192p.

Elias, Robert, jt author. *See* Hodges, Donald C.

358. Elliott, John D., and Leslie K. Gibson. *Contemporary Terrorism*. Gaithersburg, Md.: International Association of Chiefs of Police, 1978. 7p.

359. _____, eds. *Contemporary Terrorism: Selected Readings*. Gaithersburg, Md.: International Association of Chiefs of Police, 1978. 318p.

360. Ellis, John. *A Short History of Guerrilla Warfare*. New York: St. Martin's Press, 1976. 220p.

361. Fairbairn, Geoffrey. *Revolutionary Guerrilla Warfare: The Countryside Version*. Harmondsworth, Eng.: Penguin Books, 1974. 395p.

Ferguson, Yale H., jt. author. *See* Mansback, Richard W.

Finger, Seymour M., jt editor. *See* Alexander, Yonah.

Friedlander, Robert A., jt. editor. *See* Alexander, Yonah.

362. Gaucher, Roland. *The Terrorists: From Tsarist Russia to the O.A.S.* London: Secker & Warburg, 1968. 325p.

Gibson, Leslie K., jt. editor. *See* Elliott, John D.

363. Goode, Stephen. *Guerrilla Warfare and Terrorism*. New York: Franklin Watts, 1977. 152p.

364. Goodhart, Philip. *The Climate of Collapse: The Terrorist Threat to Britain and Her Allies*. Petersham, Surrey, Eng.: Foreign Affairs Publishing, 1975. 15p.

365. Green, L. C. *The Nature and Control of International Terrorism*. Calgary, Canada: University of Alberta, 1974. 56p.

366. Greene, Thomas H. *Comparative Revolutionary Movements*. Englewood Cliffs, N.J.: Prentice-Hall, 1974. 172p.

367. Hacker, Frederick J. *Crusaders, Criminals, Crazies: Terror and Terrorism in Our Time*. New York: W. W. Norton, 1977. 355p.

368. Hagopian, M. N. *The Phenomenon of Revolution*. New York: Dodd, Mead, 1975. 415p.

369. Hobsbawm, Eric J. *Revolutionaries.* New York: Pantheon, 1973. 278p.

370. Hodges, Donald C., Robert Elias, and Abu Shanab. *National Liberation Fronts, 1960–1970.* New York: Morrow, 1972. 350p.

371. Hyams, Edward S. *Terrorists and Terrorism.* New York: St. Martin's Press, 1974. 200p.

372. Klonis, N. I., pseud. *Guerrilla Warfare: Analysis and Projections.* New York: Robert Speller, 1972. 400p.

373. Kutner, Luis. *Due Process of Rebellion.* Chicago: Bardian House, 1974. 163p.

Lampert, Donald E., jt author. *See* Mansback, Richard W.

374. Laqueur, Walter Z. *Guerrilla: A History and Critical Study.* London: Weidenfeld and Nicolson, 1977. 462p.

375. _____ . *Terrorism.* Boston: Little, Brown, 1977. 277p.

376. _____ , ed. *The Guerrilla Reader: A Historical Anthology.* New York: New American Library, 1977. 246p.

377. _____ . *The Terrorism Reader: A Historical Anthology.* Philadelphia: Temple University Press, 1978. 291p.

378. Leonard, L. Larry. *Global Terrorism Confronts the Nations.* New York: New York University Press, 1979. 186p.

379. Livingston, Marius H., ed. *International Terrorism in the Contemporary World: Proceedings of the 1976 Glassboro State College International Symposium.* Contributions in Political Science, no. 3. Westport, Conn.: Greenwood Press, 1978. 522p.

380. Mansback, Richard W., Yale H. Ferguson, and Donald E. Lampert. *The Web of World Politics: Nonstate Actors in the Global World.* Englewood Cliffs, N.J.: Prentice-Hall, 1976. 326p.

381. O'Ballance, Edgar. *Language of Violence: The Blood Politics of Terrorism.* San Rafael, Calif.: Presidio Press, 1979. 350p.

382. Paine, Lauran B. *The Terrorists.* London: Hale, 1975. 176p.

383. Parry, Albert. *Terrorism: From Robespierre to Arafat.* New York: Vanguard Press, 1976. 624p.

Payne, Ronald, jt. author. *See* Dobson, Christopher.

384. Robinson, Donald, ed. *The Dirty Wars: Guerrilla Actions and Other Forms of Unconventional Warfare.* New York: Delacorte, 1968. 356p.

385.   Sarkesian, Sam C., ed. *Revolutionary Guerrilla Warfare.* Chicago: Precedent Publications, 1975. 623p.

Schaerf, Carlo, jt. editor. *See* Carlton, David.

386.   Schreiber, Jan E. *The Ultimate Weapon: Terrorists and World Order.* New York: Morrow, 1978. 218p.

387.   Schultz, D. O. *Subversive.* Springfield, Ill.: C. C. Thomas, 1973. 107p.

388.   Scott, Andrew M. *Insurgency.* Chapel Hill: University of North Carolina Press, 1970. 139p.

Shanab, Abu, jt. author. *See* Hodges, Donald C.

389.   Short, James F., Jr., ed. *Modern Criminals.* New Brunswick, N.J.: Transaction Books, 1973. 302p.

390.   Stohl, Michael, ed. *The Politics of Terrorism.* New York: Marcel Dekker, 1979. 419p.

391.   Taylor, David L. *Terrorism and Criminology: The Application of a Perspective.* West Lafayette, Ind.: Institute for the Study of Social Change, Department of Sociology and Anthropology, Purdue University, 1978. 33p.

392.   Watson, Francis M. *Political Terrorism: The Threat and the Response.* Washington, D. C.: Robert B. Luce, 1976. 248p.

393.   Wilkinson, Paul. *Political Terrorism.* New York: Wiley, 1975. 159p.

394.   ———. *Terrorism and the Liberal State.* New York: Wiley, 1978. 257p.

——— , jt. editor. *See* Alexander, Yonah.

2. Articles

395.   "Adding Up to an Epidemic." *Time,* CVI (November 3, 1975), 36+.

396.   Alexander, Yonah. "Some Perspectives on International Terrorism." *International Problems,* XIV (Fall 1975), 24–29.

397.   Anable, David. "Terrorism: Violence as Theater." *The Inter-Dependent,* III (January 1976), 1, 6.

398.   Bartos, Milan. "International Terrorism." *Review of International Affairs* (Belgrade), XXIII (April 1972), 25–26.

399.   Bell, J. Bowyer. "Contemporary Revolutionary Organizations." In: Robert O. Keohane and Joseph S. Nye, Jr., eds. *Transnational Relations and World Politics.* Cambridge: Harvard University Press, 1973. pp. 153–168.

400.   _____ . "Revolutionary Organizations: Special Cases and Imperfect Models." In: David Carlton and Carlo Schaerf, eds. *International Terrorism and World Security.* New York: Wiley, 1975. pp. 78–92.

401.   _____ . "Terror: An Overview." In: Marius H. Livingston, ed. *International Terrorism in the Contemporary World.* Westport, Conn.: Greenwood Press, 1978. pp. 36–43.

402.   _____ . "Transnational Terror and World Order." *South Atlantic Quarterly,* LXXIV (Autumn 1975), 404–417.

403.   _____ , et al. "Terrorism: A Debate." *New Republic,* CLXXIII (December 27, 1975), 12–15.

404.   Beres, Louis R. "Guerrillas, Terrorists, and Polarity: New Structural Models of World Politics." *Western Political Quarterly,* XXVII (December 1974), 624–636.

405.   Berry, F. Clifton, Jr. "Crime Many Not Pay, But Terrorism Has—So Far." *Armed Forces Journal International,* CXIII (August 1976), 18–19.

Booher, D. C., jt. author. *See* Stupach, Ronald J.

406.   Buckley, Alan D., ed. "International Terrorism." *Journal of International Affairs,* VII (Spring-Summer 1978), 1–163.

407.   Clutterbuck, Richard. "Living with Terrorism." *Police,* VII (August 1975), 12–14.

408.   _____ . "Two Typical Guerrilla Movements: The Irish Republican Army and the Tupamaros." *Canadian Defence Quarterly,* I (1972), 22+.

409.   Crozier, Brian. "Anatomy of Terrorism." *Nation,* CLXXXVIII (1959), 250–252.

A classic view.

410.   Cullinane, Maurice J. "Terrorism: A New Era of Criminality." *Terrorism,* I (1978), 119–124.

411.   Dickie-Clark, Hamish. "The Study of Conflict in South Africa and Northern Ireland." *Social Dynamics,* II (June 1976), 53–59.

412.   Douglas, J. D. "Terrorism: The Deadly Dance." *Christianity Today,* XXII (September 22, 1978), 10–11.

413.   Eckstein, Harry. "On the Etiology of Internal War." *History and Theory,* IV (1965), 133–163.

414.   Elliott, John D. "Transitions of Contemporary Terrorism." *Military Review,* LVII (May 1977), 3–15.

415.   Falk, Richard A. "Terror, Liberation Movements, and the Processes of Social Change." *American Journal of International Law,* LXIII (1969), 423–427.

416.   Fearey, Robert A. "Around the Globe—Outbreaks of Terror: An Interview." *U. S. News and World Report,* LXXIX (September 29, 1975), 76–79.

417.   _____. "International Terrorism: A Survey." In: William P. Lineberry, ed. *The Struggle against Terrorism.* Reference Shelf, v. 49, no. 3. New York: H. W. Wilson, 1977. pp. 83–95.

418.   _____. "International Terrorism: An Address." *Department of State Bulletin,* LXXIV (March 29, 1976), 394–403.

419.   "Introduction to International Terrorism." In: Marius H. Livingston, ed. *International Terrorism in the Contemporary World.* Westport, Conn.: Greenwood Press, 1978. pp. 25–35.

420.   "Focus on Terrorism." *Orbis,* XIX (Winter 1976), 1251–1343.

421.   Friedlander, Robert A. "The Origins of International Terrorism: A Micro-Legal-Historical Perspective." *Israel Yearbook on Human Rights,* VI (1976), 49–56.

422.   _____. "Terrorism." *Barrister,* II (Summer 1975), 10+.

423.   _____. "Terrorism and Political Violence: Some Preliminary Observations." *International Studies Notes,* II (Summer 1976), 4+.

424.   Friederich, C. J. "Opposition and Government by Violence." *Government and Opposition,* VII (January 1972), 3–19.

425.   Gellner, Ernest. "From the Revolution to Liberalization." *Government and Opposition,* XI (Summer 1976), 257–272.

426.   Hannay, William A. "International Terrorism: The Need for a Fresh Perspective." *International Lawyer,* VIII (February 1974), 268–284.

427.   Harrick, Philip J. "Terrorism—One of the Less Happy Phenomena of Our Times." *Department of State Newsletter,* CXCVIII (February 1978), 6–9.

428. Hersey, John. "The Year of the Triphammer, 1968." *Washington Post Magazine* (October 22, 1978), 14–47.

429. Hobsbawm, Eric J. "An Appraisal of Terrorism." *Canadian Dimension*, IX (Winter 1972), 11–14.

430. Holton, Gerald. "Reflections on Modern Terrorism." *Bulletin of the Atomic Scientists*, XXXII (November 1976), 8–9.

431. Howe, Irving. "The Return of Terror." *Dissent*, XXII (Summer 1975), 227–237.

432. _____. "The Ultimate Price of Random Terror." *Skeptic*, no. 11 (January-February 1976), 13–15, 58jbw—60.

433. Hutchinson, Martha C. "Transnational Terrorism and World Politics."*Jerusalem Journal of International Relations*, I (Winter 1975), 109–129.

434. "International Terrorism." In: *Great Decisions '79.*New York: Foreign Policy Association, 1979. Chpt. 8.

435. _____. *Senior Scholastic*, CIX (October 7, 1976), 22–25.

436. _____. *Stanford Journal of International Studies*, XII (Spring 1977), 1–163.

437. "Is the Terror Tide Rising?" *Senior Scholastic*, CII (April 23, 1973), 6–8.

438. Janke, Peter. "Transnational Terrorism." In: Royal United Service Institution for Defence Studies, eds. *R.U.S.I. and Brassey's Defence Yearbook, 1976–77*. Boulder, Colo: Westview Press, 1976. pp. 110–121.

439. Jenkins, Brian. "International Terrorism: A Balance Sheet." *Survival*, XVI (July-August 1975), 158–164.

440. _____. "International Terrorism: A New Mode of Conflict." In: David Carlton and Carlo Schaerf, eds. *International Terrorism and World Security.* New York: Wiley, 1975. pp. 13–49.

441. Johnson, Chalmers. "Terror." *Society*, XV (November 1977), 48–52.

442. Johnson, Paul. "The Age of Terror." *New Statesman and Nation*, LXXXVIII (November 29, 1974), 763–764.

443. Keller, John E. "Political Terrorism." *Law and Order*, XX (May 1973), 25+.

444.   Killrie, Nicholas N. "A New Look at Political Offenses and Terrorism." In: Simha F. Landau and Leslie Sebba, eds. *Criminology in Perspective: Essays in Honor of Israel Drapkin.* Lexington, Mass.: Lexington-Heath, 1977. Chpt. 6.

445.   Kissinger, Henry A. "Hijacking, Terrorism and War." *Department of State Bulletin,* LXXIII (September 8, 1975), 360–361.

446.   Knorr, Klaus. "Is International Coercion Waning or Rising?" *International Security,* I (Spring 1977), 92–110.

447.   Laqueur, Walter Z. "The Continuing Failure of Terrorism." *Harpers,* CCLIII (November 1976), 69–72+.

448.   _____. "The Futility of Terrorism." *Harpers,* CCLII (March 1976), 99–105.

449.   _____. "Guerrillas and Terrorists." *Commentary,* LVIII (October 1974), 40–48.

450.   _____. Terrorism: The Old Menace in a New Guise." *Current,* CCIV (July 1978), 31–35.

451.   Lasswell, Harold D. "Terrorism and the Political Process." *Terrorism,* I (1978), 255–264.

452.   Legum, Colin. "The Rise of Terrorism." *Current,* CXLVII (January 1973), 3–9.

453.   Leurdijk, J. Henk. "Summary of Proceedings: Our Violent Future." In: David Carlton and Carlo Schaerf, eds. *International Terrorism and World Security.* New York: Wiley, 1975. pp. 1–11.

454.   Livingston, G. D. "Political Terrorism: Past, Present, and Future." *Military Police Law Enforcement Journal,* II (Winter 1976), 34–39.

455.   Macomber, William B., Jr. "Deputy Under Secretary Macomber Discusses Terrorism in Interview on 'Today' Program." *Department of State Bulletin,* LXVIII (April 2, 1973), 399–402.

456.   "Map of Terrorism." *Assets Protection,* III (Summer 1978), 7–15.

457.   Maurer, Marvin. "The Ku Klux Klan and the National Liberation Front: Terrorism Applied to Achieve Diverse Goals." In: Marius H. Livingston, ed. *International Terrorism in the Contemporary World.* Westport, Conn.: Greenwood Press, 1978. pp. 131–152.

458.   May, William F. "Terrorism as Strategy and Ecstasy." *Social Research,* XLI (Summer 1974), 277–298.

Methvin, Eugene H., jt. author. *See* Strother, Robert S.

459.   Mickolus, Edward. "Transnational Terrorism." In: Michael Stohl, ed. *The Politics of Terrorism.* New York: Marcel Dekker, 1979. pp. 147–190.

460.   ———. "Trends in Transnational Terrorism." In: Marius H. Livingston, ed. *International Terrorism in the Contemporary World.* Westport, Conn.: Greenwood Press, 1978. pp. 44–76.

461.   Milte, Kerry. "Terrorism and International Order." *The Australian and New Zealand Journal of Ciminology,* VIII (June 1975), 101+.

462.   Moodie, Michael. "The Violent Theater of the Terrorist." *Defense and Foreign Affairs Digest,* VI (January 1978), 17–21.

463.   Moss, Robert. "International Terrorism and Western Societies." *International Journal,* XXVIII (Summer 1973), 418–430.

464.   Murphy, John F. "International Terrorism: From Definition to Measures Toward Suppression." In: *International Terrorism: Proceedings of an Intensive Panel at the 15th Annual Convention of the International Studies Association.* Milwaukee: Published for the International Studies Association by the Institute of World Affairs, University of Wisconsin, 1974. pp. 14–29.

465.   Neale, William D. "Terror: Oldest Weapon in the Arsenal." *Army,* XXIII (August 1973), 11–17.

466.   "New Look Rogue's Gallery." *Newsweek,* LXXXVII (January 5, 1976), 27–29.

467.   "New Reports Released on Terrorism." *Security Management,* XXII (August 1978), 24–26, 76–78.

468.   Nordic, Eric. "The Politics of Death." *Penthouse,* VIII (August 1973), 52+.

469.   North, David. "The Reign of Terror." *Macleans,* XCI (May 15, 1978), 61–63.

470.   Perlmutter, Peter. "Israeli, Irish, and Arab Terrorism." *Christian Century,* XCII (May 14, 1975), 487–488.

471.   Pfaff, William. "Reflections: Terrorism." *New Yorker,* LIII (September 18, 1978), 135–142.

472.   Plastrik, S. "On Terrorism." *Dissent,* XXI (Spring 1974), 143+.

473.   Possony, Stefan T. "Terrorism: A Global Concern." *Defense and Foreign Affairs Digest,* II (January 1973), 4–5.

474.   Preston, Paul. "Walking the Terrorist Tightrope." *Contemporary Review*, CCXXXIV (March 1979), 119–123.

475.   Radovanovic, Ljubomir. "The Problem of International Terrorism." *Review of International Affairs* (Belgrade), XXIII (October 1972), 6–8, 15–20.

476.   Ridenour, Robert. "Who Are the Terrorists and What Do They Want?" *Skeptic*, no. 11 (January-February 1976), 18–23.

477.   Romerstein, Herbert. "Transnational Threat." *National Review*, XXIX (November 25, 1977), 1364–1366.

478.   Rothstein, Andrew. "Terrorism: Some Plain Words." *Labour Monthly*, LV (September 1973), 413–417.

479.   Rubenstein, Murray. "When the Terrorists Strike." *Popular Mechanics*, CXLIX (March 1978), 90–93+.

480.   Russell, Charles A. "Transnational Terrorism." *Air University Review*, XXVII (January-February 1976), 26–35.

481.   Shaffer, Helen B. "Political Terrorism." *Editorial Research Reports*, I (May 13, 1970), 340–360.

482.   Simpson, Howard R. "Terror." *U.S. Naval Institute Proceedings*, XCVI (April 1970), 64–80.

483.   Sloan, Stephen. "International Terrorism: Academic Quest, Operational Art, and Policy Implications." *Journal of International Affairs*, VII (Spring-Summer 1978), 1–6.

484.   Smith, D. "Scenario Reality: A New Brand of Terrorism." *Nation*, CIX (March 30, 1974), 392–394.

485.   Smith, W. H. "International Terrorism: A Political Analysis." In: George W. Keeton and Georg Schwarzenberger, eds. *The Year Book of World Affairs, 1976*. Boulder, Colo.: Westview Press, 1976. pp. 138–157.

486.   Speck, D. H. "The Growing Problem of Terrorism." *Journal of California Law Enforcement*, X (January 1976), 88–92.

487.   "Spreading Political Terrorism in the Americas." *U.S. News and World Report*, LXXVIII (January 13, 1975), 19–20.

488.   Stencel, Sandra. "International Terrorism." *Editorial Research Reports*, VII (December 2, 1977), 911–932.

489.   Stiles, Dennis W. "Sovereignty and the New Violence." *Air University Review*, XXVII (July-August 1976), 89–95.

490. Stohl, Michael. "Myths and Realities of Political Terrorism." In: Michael Stohl, ed. *The Politics of Terrorism.* New York: Marcel Dekker, 1979. pp. 1–22.

491. Strother, Robert S., and Eugene H. Methvin. "Terrorism on the Rampage." *Reader's Digest,* CVII (November 1975), 73–77.

492. Stupach, Ronald J., and D. C. Booher. "Guerrilla Warfare: A Strategic Analysis in the Superpower Context." *Journal of Southeast Asia and the Far East,* I (November 2, 1970), 181–196.

493. Styles, George. "Terrorism: The Global War of the Seventies." *International Defense Review,* IX (August 1976), 594–596.

494. Syrkin, Marie. "Political Terrorism." *Midstream,* XVIII (September 1972), 3–11.

495. Taylor, Edmond. "Terrorists." *Horizon,* XV (Summer 1973), 58–65.

496. "Terrorism—Where Is It? What Is It?: Special Section." *Senior Scholastic,* CXI (February 8, 1979), 7–8+.

497. "Terrorist Acts against United Nations Missions." *U.N. Chronicle,* VIII (November 1971), 61–70.

498. Van Dalen, Robert. "Terrorism: Comment, Overview, and Some Speculations." *Military Police Law Enforcement Journal,* III (Winter 1976), 38–41.

499. "War without Boundaries." *Time,* CX (October 31, 1977), 28–31+.

500. Wilkinson, Paul. "Terrorist Movements." In: Yonah Alexander, David Carlton, and Paul Wilkinson, eds. *Terrorism: Theory and Practice.* Boulder, Colo.: Westview Press, 1979. Chpt. 5.

501. Wolf, John B. "Terrorist Manipulation of the Democratic Process." *Police Journal,* XLVIII (April-June 1975), 102–112.

502. _____ . _____ . In: Marius H. Livingston, ed. *International Terrorism in the Contemporary World.* Westport, Conn.: Greenwood Press, 1978. pp. 297–306.

503. "World Politics—New Style: Kidnapping, Hijacking, Bombing—Guerrilla Diplomacy." *U.S. News and World Report,* LXVII (September 22, 1969), 49–50.

504. "World Terrorism Flares Anew." *U.S. News and World Report,* LXXVIII (March 17, 1975), 25–26.

505. Zivic, John. "The Nonaligned and the Problem of International Terrorism." *Review of International Affairs* (Belgrade), XXIV (January 20, 1973), 6–8.

3.   Documents, Papers, and Reports

506. Bigney, Russell E., *et al. Exploration of the Nature of Future Warfare.* Carlisle Barracks, Pa.: U.S. Army War College, 1974. 106p.

507. Bite, Vita. *International Terrorism.* Issue Brief, no. IB74042. Washington, D.C.: Congressional Research Service, Library of Congress, 1975. 15p.

508. _____ . *International Terrorism in Its Historical Depth and Present Dimension, 1968–1975.* Washington, D.C.: Department of State, 1976. 36p.

509. Bouthol, Gaston. "On International Terrorism: Historical and Contemporary Aspects. 1968–1975." Unpublished paper, State Department Conference on International Terrorism in Retrospect and Prospect, 1975.

510. Brown, Marjorie A. "Terrorism." In: U.S. Congress. Joint Economic Committee. *The U.S. Role in a Changing World Political Economy—Major Issues for the 96th Congress: A Compendium of Papers.* 96th Cong., 1st sess. Washington, D.C.: U.S. Government Printing Office, 1979. pp. 225–248.

511. Condit, D. M. *Modern Revolutionary Warfare: An Analytical Overview.* Kensington, Md.: American Institute for Research, 1973. 134p.

512. Crozier, Brian. "International Terrorism." *Congressional Record,* CXXI (June 10, 1975), 18097–18100.

513. _____ . "Terrorism: The Problem in Perspective." Unpublished paper, Department of State Conference on International Terrorism in Retrospect and Prospect, 1976.

514. Fearey, Robert A. *Remarks before the Los Angeles World Affairs Council and the World Affairs Council of Orange County on International Terrorism.* Washington, D.C.: Office of the Special Assistant to the Secretary of State and Coordinator for Combatting Terrorism, Department of State, 1976. 15p.

515. Friedlander, Robert A. "Historical Perspectives on Terrorism." Unpublished paper, Conference on International Terrorism, Ralph Bunche Institute on the United Nations of the Graduate School and University Center of the City University of New York and the State University College at Oneonta of the State University of New York, 1976.

516.   Gurr, Ted Robert. "Some Characteristics of Contemporary Political Terrorism." Unpublished paper, Department of State Conference on International Terrorism in Retrospect and Prospect, 1976.

517.   Hutchinson, Martha C. "Implications of the Pattern of Transnational Terrorism." Unpublished paper, Convention of the International Studies Association, 1975.

518.   _____ . "Transnational Terrorism as a Policy Issue." Unpublished paper, Convention of the American Political Science Association, 1974.

519.   "International Terrorism." Unpublished proceedings of the Third Annual Conference of the Canadian Council of International Law, University of Ottawa, 1974.

520.   Jenkins, Brian. *International Terrorism: A New Kind of Warfare.* RAND Paper P-5261. Santa Monica, Calif.: RAND Corp., 1974. 13p.

521.   _____ . *International Terrorism: A New Mode of Conflict.* California Seminar on Arms Control and Foreign Policy Research Paper, no. 48, Los Angeles: Crescent Publications, 1975. 51p.

522.   _____ . "International Terrorism as a New Mode of Conflict." Unpublished paper, Convention of the International Studies Association, 1975.

523.   _____ . *Terrorism Works—Sometimes.* RAND Paper P-5217. Santa Monica, Calif.: RAND Corp., 1974. 9p.

524.   Johnson, Chalmers. "Perspectives on Terrorism." Unpublished paper, Department of State Conference on International Terrorism in Retrospect and Prospect, 1976.

525.   Karkashian, J. E. *The Problem of International Terrorism.* Washington, D.C.: Department of State, 1977. 4p.

526.   Methvin, Eugene H. "An Analysis of Paul Wilkinson, 'A Fatality of Illusions: Dominant Images of International Terrorism.'" Unpublished paper, Department of State Conference on International Terrorism in Retrospect and Prospect, 1976.

527.   Mickolus, Edward. *Codebook ITERATE* [International Terrorism: Attributes of Terrorist Events]. Ann Arbor, Mich.: Inter-University Consortium for Political and Social Research, University of Michigan, 1976. 57p.

528.   _____ . "Project ITERATE: Quantitative Studies of Transnational Terrorism." Unpublished paper, Convention of the Northeast Political Science Association, 1976.

529. _____ . "Statistical Approaches to the Study of Terrorism." Unpublished paper, Ralph Bunch Institute Conference on International Terrorism, 1976.

530. _____ . "Transnational Terrorism: Analysis of Terrorists, Events, and Environments." Unpublished Ph.D. dissertation, Yale University, 1979.

531. Milbank, David L. "International and Transnational Terrorism: Diagnosis and Prognosis." Unpublished paper, Department of State Conference on International Terrorism in Retrospect and Prospect, 1976.

532. _____ . _____ . Research Study. Washington, D.C.: Office of Political Research, Central Intelligence Agency, 1976. 46p.

533. Miller, James A. "Political Terrorism and Insurgency: An Interrogative Approach." Ralph Bunch Institute Conference on International Terrorism, 1976.

534. Munger, Murl D. *The Growing Utility of Political Terrorism.* Military Issues Research Memorandum. Carlisle Barracks, Pa.: Strategic Studies Institute, U.S. Army War College, 1977. 23p.

535. Pierre, Andrew J. "An Overview of the Causes of and Cures for International Terrorism." Unpublished paper, Convention of the International Studies Association, 1975.

536. Roberts, Kenneth E. *The Terror Trap.* Military Issues Research Memorandum. Carlisle Barracks, Pa.: Strategic Studies Institute, U.S. Army War College, 1975. 20p.

537. Shaw, Eric D., *et al. Analyzing Threats from Terrorism.* Washington, D.C.: CACI, 1976. 32p.

538. Stencel, Sandra. *International Terrorism.* Washington, D.C.: Editorial Research Reports, 1977. 22p.

539. Taylor, David L. "The Dimensions of the Effectiveness of Terrorism." Unpublished paper, Annual Meeting of the North Central Sociological Association, 1979.

540. "Terrorism as a Transnational Phenomenon and Its Impact on Security Assistance Programs." Unpublished paper, Workshop Number 2, Sixth Annual Security Assistance Symposim of the Foreign Area Officer Course, Civil Affairs and Security Assistance School, U.S. Army Institute for Military Assistance, 1974.

541. "Terrorism, Pre-Emption and Surprise." Unpublished proceedings, Symposium, Leonard Davis Institute of International Relations, Hebrew University, 1975.

542. United States. Central Intelligence Agency. *International Terrorism in 1977.* Washington, D.C., 1978.

543. _____. Congress. House. Committee on Foreign Affairs. Subcommittee on the Near East and South Asia. *International Terrorism: Hearings.* 93rd Cong., 2nd sess. Washington, D.C.: U.S. Government Printing Office, 1974. 219p.

544. _____. _____. _____. Committee on Internal Security. *Terrorism: A Staff Study.* 93rd Cong., 2nd sess. Washington, D.C.: U.S. Government Printing Office, 1974. 283p.

545. _____. _____. _____. _____. *Terrorism: Hearings.* 93rd Cong., 2nd sess. 4 pts. Washington, D.C.: U.S. Government Printing Office, 1974.

546. _____. _____. Senate. Committee on Foreign Relations. Subcommittee on Foreign Assistance. *International Terrorism: Hearings.* 95th Cong., 1st sess. Washington, D.C.: U.S. Government Printing Office, 1978. 93p.

547. _____. _____. _____. Committee on Public Works and Transportation, Subcommittee on Aviation. *International Terrorism: Hearings.* 95th Cong., 2nd sess. Washington D.C.: U.S. Government Printing Office, 1978. 392p.

548. _____. _____. _____. Committee on the Judiciary. Subcommittee to Investigate the Administration of the Internal Security Act and Other Internal Security Laws. *Terroristic Activities.* 93rd Cong., 2nd sess. to 94th Cong., 1st sess. 5 pts. Washington, D.C.: U.S. Government Printing Office, 1974–1975.

549. _____. Department of State. Foreign Service Institute. *Seminar on Terrorism: Washington Program.* Washington, D.C., 1978. 10p.

550. _____. National Advisory Commission on Criminal Justice Standards and Goals. Task Force on Disorders and Terrorism. *Disorders and Terrorism: Report.* Washington, D.C.: U.S. Government Printing Office, 1977. 661p.

551. Wilkinson, Paul. "A Fatality of Illusions: Dominant Images of International Terrorism." Unpublished paper, Department of State Conference on International Terrorism in Retrospect and Prospect, 1976.

III/Philosophy and Psychology of Terrorism

Introduction

What sorts of ideology are employed by terrorists to justify their actions? What are the teachings of violent men or radical thinkers who believe they can effect political change by the extranormal shedding of blood? The citations in subsection A provide general bibliographic guidance to the philosophies and doctrines of terrorism in the 1968–1979 period. Additional information will be found among the general works cited in section II:B above as well as in the specific geographical subsections in VIII below.

Is the mind of the terrorist deviant? Are terrorists sick or crazy? How can a person think in a manner which will allow him to perform a blood deed? The citations in subsection B provide general bibliographic charting of studies which have addressed these questions. Additional information relative to this part will be found among the citations in section II above and in sections IV and VIII below.

A. Philosophy of Terrorism

1. Books

552. Bell, J. Bowyer. *The Myth of the Guerrilla: Revolutionary Theory and Malpractice.* New York: Knopf, 1971. 285p.

553. _____ . *On Revolt: Strategies of National Liberation.* Cambridge: Center for International Affairs, Harvard University, 1976. 287p.

554. Blackman, Morris J., and Ronald G. Hellman, eds. *Terms of Conflict: Ideology in Latin American Politics.* Inter-American Politics Series, v. 1. Philadelphia: Institute for the Study of Human Issues, 1977. 275p.

555. Burton, Anthony. *Revolutionary Violence: The Theories.* New York: Crane, Russak, 1978. 147p.

556. Calvert, Peter *A Study of Revolution.* Oxford, Eng.: At the Clarenden Press, 1970. 249p.

557. Cohan, A. S. *Theories of Revolution: An Introduction.* New York: Wiley, 1976. 228p.

558. Cranston, Maurice W. *The New Left: Six Critical Essays.* New York: The Library Press, 1971. 208p.

559. Crozier, Brian. *A Theory of Conflict.* New York: Scribners, 1974. 245p.

560. Debray, Regis. *Strategy for Revolution.* New York: Monthly Review Press, 1969. 256p.

561. Ferreira, J. C. *Carlos Marighella.* Havana: Tricontinental, 1970.

562. Grundy, Kenneth W. *The Ideologies of Violence.* Columbus, Ohio: Merrill, 1974. 117p.

563. Guillen, Abraham. *Philosophy of the Urban Guerrilla: The Revolutionary Writings.* Translated and edited by Donald C. Hodges. New York: Morrow, 1973. 305p.

564. Hachey, Thomas, ed. *Voices of Revolution: Rebels and Rhetoric.* Hinsdale, Ill.: Dryden Press, 1973. 385p.

Hellman, Ronald G., jt. author. *See* Blackman, Morris J.

Hodges, Donald C., editor. *See* Guillen, Abraham.

565. Huberman, Leo, and Paul M. Sweezy, eds. *Regis Debray and the Latin American Revolution.* New York: Monthly Review Press, 1968. 138p.

566.   Kelly, R. J. *New Political Crimes and the Emergence of Revolutionary-Nationalist Ideology.* Chicago: Rand-McNally, 1973.

567.   Leiser, B. M. *Terrorism, Guerrilla Warfare, and International Morality.* Stanford, Calif.: Stanford University Press, 1977. 14p.

568.   Merleau-Ponty, Maurice. *Humanism and Terror.* Translated from the French. Boston: Beacon Press, 1969. 189p.

569.   Schafer, Stephen. *The Political Criminal: The Problem of Morality and Crime.* New York: Free Press, 1974. 179p.

Sweezy, Paul M., jt. editor. *See* Huberman, Leo.

2.   Articles

Adler, J. H., jt. author. *See* Serge, D. V.

570.   Baxter, R. R. "A Skeptical Look at the Concept of Terrorism." *Akron Law Review,* VII (Spring 1978), 380–387.

571.   Cannon, M. D. "Terrorism: Its Ethical Implications for the Future." *Futurist,* XI (December 1977), 351–354.

572.   Deakin, Thomas J. "The Legacy of Carlos Marighella." *FBI Law Enforcement Bulletin,* XLIII (October 1974), 19–25.

573.   Debray, Regis. "Revolution in the Revolution?: Armed Struggle and Political Struggle in Latin America." *Monthly Review,* XIX (July-August 1967), 1–128.

574.   Demaitre, Edmund. "Terrorism and the Intellectuals: Reprinted from the *Washington Sunday Star,* April 15, 1973." *Congressional Record,* CXIX (April 17, 1973), 12660–12662.

575.   Fox, Kenneth O. "The Cuban Theory of Revolutionary War: The Faith, the Fallacies, and the Heresy." *Journal of the Royal United Service Institution for Defence Studies,* CXII (December 1977), 35–40.

576.   Friedlander, Robert A. "Sowing the Wing: Rebellion and Violence in Theory and Practice." *Denver Journal of International Law and Policy,* VI (Spring 1976), 83–93.

577.   _____ . "Terrorism and Political Violence: Do the Ends Justify the Means?" In: Marius H. Livingston, ed. *International Terrorism in the Contemporary World.* Westport, Conn.: Greenwood Press, 1978. pp. 316–325.

578.   Glantz, Oscar. "New Left Radicalism and Punitive Moralism." *Polity,* VII (Spring 1975), 281–303.

579. Hassel, Conrad V. "Terror—The Crime of the Privileged: An Examination and Prognosis." *Terrorism,* I (1978), 1–16.

580. Heindel, R. H. "Thoughts on Terrorism." *Intellect,* CVI (February 1978), 284–285.

581. Hook, Sidney. "The Ideology of Violence." *Encounter,* XXIV (April 1970), 26–38.

582. Iviansky, Ze'ev. "Individual Terror: Concept and Typology." *Journal of Contemporary History,* XII (January 1977), 43–63.

583. Kipling, R. E. "Is Terrorism Ever Justified?" *Skeptic,* no. 11 (January-February 1976), 34–36, 61–62.

584. Laqueur, Walter. "The Origins of Guerrilla Doctrine." *Journal of Contemporary History,* X (July 1975), 341–382.

585. Martz, John D. "Doctrine and Dilemmas of the Latin American New Left." *World Politics,* XXII (January 1970), 171–196.

586. Mohammed, Aziz. "Key Trends in the Liberation Process." *World Marxist Review,* XX (February 1977), 4–13.

587. "The Morality of Terrorism." *Newsweek,* LXXXIII (February 25, 1974), 21–22.

588. Neier, Aryeh. "Terror and the Sense of Justice." *Nation,* CCXXVI (March 25, 1978), 326–327.

589. O'Brien, Connor Cruise. "Liberty and Terror." *Encounter,* XLIX (October 1977), 34–41.

Plecher, G. K., jt. author. *See* Runkle, Gerald.

590. Possony, Stefan T. "The Genesis of Terrorism." *Defense and Foreign Affairs Digest,* VI (January 1978), 36–38.

591. Runkle, Gerald, and G. K. Plecher. "Is Violence Always Wrong?" *Journal of Politics,* XXXVIII (May 1976), 367–389; XXXIX (November 1977), 1055–1063.

592. Schulz, Richard. "Conceptualizing Political Terrorism: A Typology." *Journal of International Affairs,* VII (Spring-Summer 1978), 7–16.

593. Serge, D. V., and J. H. Adler. "The Ecology of Terrorism." *Encounter,* XL (February 1973), 17–24.

594. Talmon, J. L. "The Legacy of Georges Sorel: Marxism, Violence, Fascism." *Encounter,* XXXIV (February 1970), 47–60.

595. "Terrorism and Marxism." *Monthly Review,* XXIV (November 1972), 1–6.

596. Wagenlehner, Guenther. "Motivation for Political Terrorism in Germany." In: Marius H. Livingston, ed. *International Terrorism in the Contemporary World.* Westport, Conn.: Greenwood Press, 1978. pp. 195–205.

597. Wilkinson, Paul. "Social Scientific Theory and Civil Violence." In: Yonah Alexander, David Carlton, and Paul Wilkinson, eds. *Terrorism: Theory and Practice.* Boulder, Colo.: Westview Press, 1979. Chpt. 2.

598. Young, Robert, "Revolutionary Terrorism, Crime, and Morality." *Social Theory and Practice,* IV (Fall 1977), 287–320.

3.   Documents, Papers, and Reports

599. Horowitz, Irving L. "Unicorns and Terrorists." Unpublished paper, Department of State Conference on International Terrorism in Retrospect and Prospect, 1976.

B.   *Psychology of Terrorism*

1.   Books

600. Clinard, Marshall B., and R. F. Meier. *Sociology of Deviant Behavior.* 5th ed. New York: Holt, Rinehart & Winston, 1979. 613p.

601. Dowton, James V. *Rebel Leadership: Commitment and Charisma in the Revolutionary Process.* New York: Free Press, 1973. 306p.

602. Gurr, Ted Robert. *Why Men Rebel.* Princeton, N.J.: Princeton University Press, 1970. 421p.

603. Hampden-Turner, Charles. *Radical Man: The Process of Psycho-Social Development.* Cambridge, Eng.: Schenkman, 1970. 433p.

604. McKnight, Gerald. *The Mind of the Terrorist.* Indianapolis: Bobbs-Merrill, 1974. 182p.

Meier, R. F., jt. author. *See* Clinard, Marshall B.

605. Methvin, Eugene H. *The Rise of Radicalism: The Social Psychology of Messianic Extremism.* New Rochelle, N.Y.: Arlington House, 1973. 584p.

606. Toch, Hans. *Violent Men: An Inquiry into the Psychology of Violence.* Chicago: Aldine, 1969. 268p.

607.   Wolfenstein, E. Victor. *The Revolutionary Personality.* Princeton, N.J.: Princeton University Press, 1967. 330p.

2.   Articles

608.   Anable, David. "The New 'Theater of Fear': Reprinted from the *Christain Science Monitor,* December 19, 1975." In: William P. Lineberry, ed. *The Struggle against Terrorism.* Reference Shelf, v. 49, no. 3. New York: H. W. Wilson, 1977. pp. 41–46.

609.   _____ . "Terrorism: Violence as Theater." *Inter-Dependent,* III (January 1976), 1, 6.

610.   "Behind the Rise in Crime and Terror." *U.S. News and World Report,* LXXIII (November 13, 1972), 41–44+.

611.   "The Belfast Syndrome: Irish Violence Damages Psyches." *Science Digest,* LXXIV (September 1973), 26–27.

612.   Belz, Martin, *et al.* "Is There a Treatment for Terror?" *Psychology Today,* XI (October 1977), 54–56+.

613.   Calvert, Michael. "The Characteristics of Guerrilla Leaders and Their Rank and File." *The Practitioner,* CCXI (December 1973), 1–30.

614.   Carroll, Robert. "The Mind of Abu Daoud." *Newsweek,* LXXXIX (January 24, 1977), 45.

615.   Crawford, Thomas J., and Murray Naditch. "Relative Deprivation, Powerlessness, and Militancy: The Psychology of Social Protest." *Psychiatry,* XXXIII (May 1970), 208–223.

616.   Davis, R. "Aggression and Politics." *Australian and New Zealand Journal of Psychiatry,* V (June 1971), 101–105.

617.   Evseeff, G. S. "A Psychiatric Study of a Violent Mass Murderer." *Journal of Forensic Sciences,* XVII (July 1972), 371–376.

618.   Frank, J. D. "Some Psychological Determinants of Violence and Its Control." *Australian and New Zealand Journal of Psychiatry,* VI (September 1972), 158–164.

619.   Gamson, William A. "Violence and Political Power: The Meek Don't Make It." *Psychology Today,* VIII (July 1974), 35–41.

620.   Gault, W. B. "Some Remarks on Slaughter." *American Journal of Psychiatry,* CXXVIII (October 1971), 450–454.

621.   Geen, R. G. "Context Effects in Observed Violence." *Journal of Personal and Social Psychology,* XXV (January 1973), 145–150.

622. _____ . "Reactions to Aggression-Related Stimuli Following Reinforcement of Aggression." *Journal of Psychology,* LXXXIII (January 1973), 75–102.

623. Goldschmidt, Dietrich. "Psychological Stress: A German Case Study." In: Julian Nagel, ed. *Student Poser.* London: Merlin Press, 1969. pp. 59–70.

624. "The Growing Psychological Aspect of International Terrorism." *Defense and Foreign Affairs Digest,* VI (October 1978), 36–37.

625. Gurr, Ted Robert. "A Causal Model of Civil Strife: A Comparative Analysis—Using New Indices." *American Political Science Review,* LXVIII (Fall 1968), 1104–1124.

626. _____ . "Psychological Factors in Urban Violence." *World Politics,* XX (November 1968), 245–278.

627. _____ . _____ . *Terrorism,* I (1978), 265–276.

628. Holton, Gerald. "Reflections on Modern Terrorism." *Bulletin of the Atomic Scientists,* XXXII (November 1976), 8–9.

629. Ilfeld, F. W. "Overview of the Causes and Prevention of Violence." *Archives of General Psychiatry,* XX (June 1969), 675–689.

630. Kaplan, Abraham. "The Psychodynamics of Terrorism." *Terrorism,* I (1978), 237–254.

631. Kelman, Herbert C. "Israelis and Palestinians: Psychological Prerequisites for Mutual Acceptance." *Internal Security,* III (Summer 1978), 162–186.

632. _____ . "Violence without Moral Restraint: Reflections on the Dehumanization of Victims and Victimizers." *Journal of Social Issues,* XXIX (1973), 25–61.

633. Knauss, Peter R., and D. A. Strickland. "Political Disintegration and Latent Terrorism." In: Michael Stohl, ed. *The Politics of Terrorism.* New York: Marcel Dekker, 1979. pp. 77–118.

634. La Chard, Jeanne. "The Mind of the Terrorist." *Listener,* XCIII (June 5, 1975), 722–723.

Leirnger, C., jt. author. *See* Lincoln, A.

635. Lincoln, A., and C. Leirnger. "Observers' Evaluations of the Victim and the Attacker in an Aggressive Incident." *Journal of Personality and Social Psychology,* XXII (May 1972), 202–210.

636. "The Lone Assassin." *Human Relations,* IV (September 1976), 43+.

637. Lupsha, Peter. "Explanation of Political Violence: Some Psychological Theories." *Politics and Society,* II (1971), 88–104.

638. Lyons, H. A. "Violence in Belfast: A Review of the Psychological Effects." *Public Health,* LXXXVII (September 1973), 231–238.

639. Matthews, A. S. "The Terrors of Terrorism." *South African Law Journal,* XLI (August 1974), 381+.

640. Middendorff, Wolfgang. "The Personality of the Terrorist." In: Marjorie Kravitz, ed. *International Summaries: A Collection of Selected Translations in Law Enforcement and Criminal Justice,* v. 3. Rockville, Md.: National Criminal Justice Reference Service, Law Enforcement Assistance Administration, Department of Justice, 1979. pp. 89–98.

Miller, Bowman H., jt. author. *See* Russell, Charles A.

641. Milte, Kerry L. "Terrorism: Political and Psychological Considerations." *Australian and New Zealand Journal of Criminology,* IX (June 1976), 89–94.

642. Moore, Robert. "Psychiatric Sequelae of the Belfast Riots." *British Journal of Psychiatry,* CXX (April 1972), 47+.

Moynahan, Brian, jt. author. *See* Watson, Peter.

643. Mueller, M. A. "Revolutionary Terrorist: A Character Analysis." *Military Police Law Enforcement Journal,* III (Fall 1976), 38–43.

Naditch, Murray, jt. author. *See* Crawford, Thomas J.

644. Ochberg, Frank. "The Victim of Terrorism: Psychiatric Considerations." *Terrorism,* I (1978), 147–168.

645. Odling-Smee, Winifred. "Victims of Belfast's Violence." *Nursing Times,* XXXIX (September 6, 1973), 1143–1146.

646. O'Malley, P. P. "Attempted Suicide before and after the Communal Violence in Belfast, August 1969: A Preliminary Study." *Journal of the British Medical Association,* LXV (March 4, 1972), 109–113.

647. Pepitone, Albert. "The Social Psychology of Violence." *International Journal of Group Tensions,* II (1972), 19–32.

648. Petzel, T. P. "Perception of Violence as a Function of Levels of Hostility." *Journal of Consulting Clinical Psychology,* XLI (August 1973), 35–36.

649. Pisano, Robert, and S. P. Taylor. "Reduction of Physical Aggression: The Effects of Four Strategies." *Journal of Personality and Social Psychology,* XIX (August 1971), 237–242.

650.   Russell, Charles A., and Bowman H. Miller. "[Composite] Profile of a Terrorist." *Military Review,* LVII (August 1977), 21–34.

651.   ———. ———. *Terrorism,* I (1978), 17–34.

652.   Ryter, Stephen L. "Terror as a Psychological Weapon." *The Review,* no. 16 (May-June 1966), 21, 145–150.

653.   Sabetta, A. R. "Transnational Terror: Causes and Implications for Response." *Stanford Journal of International Studies,* XII (Spring 1977), 147–156.

654.   Scharff, W. R., and R. S. Schlottman. "The Effects of Verbal Reports of Violence on Aggression." *Journal of Psychology,* LXXXIV (July 1973), 283–290.

Schlottman, R. S., jt. author. *See* Scharff, W. R.

655.   Scott, J. P. "The Control of Violence." *Conditional Reflex,* VI (April-June 1971), 63–66.

656.   Scott, P. D. "Victims of Violence." *Nursing Times,* LXX (July 4, 1970), 1036–1037.

657.   Slomich, Sidney J. "Social Psychopathology of Political Assassination." *Bulletin of the Atomic Scientists,* XXV (March 1969), 9–12.

658.   "Social Causes of Social Conflict in Connection with So-Called 'Political Criminality' [in West Germany]." In: National Criminal Justice Reference Service, eds. *International Summaries: A Collection of Selected Translations in Law Enforcement and Criminal Justice,* v. 1. Rockville, Md.: NCJRS, Law Enforcement Assistance Administration, Department of Defense, 1978. pp. 215–225.

659.   Spiegel, J. P. "The Dynamics of Violent Confrontation." *International Journal of Psychiatry,* X (September 1972), 93–108.

660.   Strauss, Harlan. "Revolutionary Types." *Journal of Conflict Resolution,* XIV (1973), 307+.

Strickland, D. A., jt. author. *See* Knauss, Peter R.

661.   Tan, E. S. "Psychiatric Sequelae to a Civil Disturbance." *British Journal of Psychiatry,* CXXII (January 1973), 57–63.

662.   Targ, Harry R. "Societal Structure and Revolutionary Terrorism: A Preliminary Investigation." In: Michael Stohl, ed. *The Politics of Terrorism.* New York: Marcel Dekker, 1979. pp. 119–146.

Taylor, S. P., Jt. author. *See* Pisano, Robert.

663.   Watson, Peter, and Brian Moynahan. "The Mind of the Terrorist." *Sunday Times-Spectrum,* (August 19, 1973), 8+.

664. Westermeyer, John. "On the Epidemicity of Amok Violence." *Archives of General Psychiatry,* XXVIII (June 1973), 873–876.

665. "What Makes a Skyjacker?" *Science Digest,* LXXI (January 1972), 21–22.

666. Wilkins, J. L., *et al.* "Personality Type: Reports of Violence and Aggressive Behavior." *Journal of Personality and Social Psychology,* XXX (August 1973), 243–247.

667. Zawodney, J. K. "Internal Organization Problems and the Sources of Tension as Catalysts of Violence." *Terrorism,* I (1978), 277–285.

3.   Documents, Papers, and Reports

668. Horowitz, Irving L. *Political Terrorism and Personal Deviance.* Research Study SR/RNAS-5. Washington, D.C.: Department of State, 1973. 10p.

669. Kelly, Clarence M. *Terrorism: A Phenomenon of Sickness.* Claremont, Calif.: Claremont Men's College, 1974. 4p.

IV/Terrorist Tactics

Introduction

Acts of terrorism, while different in practice from case to case, tend to fall into four general groups: air piracy, bombing, assassination, and kidnapping. The citations in subsection A treat these tactics in a general manner. Those in subsections B–E examine specifically the operational literature of air piracy and hijacking, assassination, hostage-taking and kidnapping, and that subcategory of terrorism, urban guerrilla warfare. Information on the general tactic of bombing will be found in section V:A below. Additional citations relative to these operations in specific countries will be found in sections VI–VIII below.

A. General Works

1. Books

670. Methvin, Eugene H. *The Riot Makers: The Technology of Social Demolition.* New Rochelle, N.Y.: Arlington House, 1970. 587p.

671. Momboisse, R. M. *Blueprint for Revolution: The Rebel, the Party, the Techniques of Revolt.* Springfield, Ill.: C. C. Thomas, 1970. 336p.

2. Articles

672. Bell, J. Bowyer. "Guerrilla Analysis: Present Directions." *Military Affairs,* XXXVII (December 1973), 155–157.

673. Clarke, Gerald. "When Terrorists Become Respectable: *Time* Essay." *Time,* CIV (November 25, 1974), 44–45.

674. Friedrich, C. J. "The Uses of Terror." *Problems of Communism,* XIX (November 1970), 46–48.

675. Fromkin, David. "The Strategy of Terrorism." *Foreign Affairs,* LIII (July 1975), 683–698.

676. Giroud, Alberto Bayo. "One Hundred Fifty Questions to a Guerrilla." In: Jay Mallin, ed. *Terror and Urban Guerrillas: A Study of Tactics and Documents.* Coral Gables, Fla.: University of Miami Press, 1971. pp. 117–163.

677. Hoover, J. Edgar. "The Revolutionary-Guerrilla Attacks Law Enforcement and Democratic Society: An Analysis of the Destructive Power of the Fanatical Few." *Albany Law Review,* XXXV (Fall 1971), 1–19.

678. Jay, Martin. "The Politics of Terror." *Partisan Review,* XXXVIII (1971), 95–103.

679. Latey, Maurice. "Violence as a Political Weapon." *NATO's Fifteen Nations,* XVI (December 1971-January 1972), 65–71.

680. Mallin, Jay. "Terrorism as a Military Weapon." *Air University Review,* XXVIII (January-February 1977), 54–64.

681. _____ . _____ . In: Marius H. Livingston, ed. *International Terrorism in the Contemporary World.* Westport, Conn.: Greenwood Press, 1978. pp. 389–401.

682. _____ . "Terrorism as a Political Weapon." *Air University Review,* XXII (July-August 1971), 45–52.

683. _____ . "Terrorism in Revolutionary Warfare." *Strategic Review,* II (Fall 1974), 48–55.

684.   Monks, M. R. "Guerrilla Warfare as a Political Weapon." *Hawk*, no. 34 (February 1973), 55–60.

685.   Moss, Norman. "The Politics of Terror." *Illustrated London News*, CCLXIV (April 1976), 31–32.

686.   O'Ballance, Edgar. "Terrorism: The New Growth Form of Warfare." In: Marius H. Livingston, ed. *International Terrorism in the Contemporary World*. Westport, Conn.: Greenwood Press, 1978. pp. 415–423.

687.   Pierre, Andrew J. "The Politics of International Terrorism." *Orbis*, XIX (Winter 1976), 1251–1269.

688.   "The Politics of Terror." *Time*, CIII (March 4, 1974), 11–15.

689.   Popper, F. J. "Internal War as a Stimulant of Political Development." *Comparative Political Studies*, III (January 1971), 413+.

690.   Price, H. Edward, Jr. "Strategy and Tactics of Revolutionary Terrorism." *Comparative Studies of Sociology and History*, XIX (January 1977), 52–66.

691.   Silverman, Jerry M. "Terror in Insurgency Warfare." *Military Review*, L (October 1970), 61–67.

692.   "Tactic of Terror: Arab Commandos." *Nation*, CCVIII (March 3, 1969), 258–259.

693.   "Terror Tactics." *Nation*, CCXVIII (June 1, 1974), 674–675.

694.   "Terrorism Is Developing into a Form of Total War." *U.S. News and World Report*, LXXIII (December 11, 1972), 49–50.

695.   "Terrorists' Goal: Sabotage Peace at All Costs." *U.S. News and World Report*, LXXVI (May 27, 1974), 31–32.

696.   Thornton, Thomas P. "Terror as a Weapon of Political Agitation." In: Harry Eckstein, ed. *Internal War: Problems and Approaches*. New York: Free Press, 1964. pp. 71–99.

697.   Van Dalen, Robert. "Terror as a Political Weapon." *Military Police Law Enforcement Journal*, II (Spring 1975), 21–26.

B. Air Piracy and Hijacking

1. Books

698.   Arey, James A. *The Sky Pirates*. New York: Scribners, 1972. 360p.

699.   Clyne, Peter. *An Anatomy of Skyjacking*. London: Abelard-Schuman, 1973. 200p.

700.   Hubbard, David G. *The Skyjacker: His Flights of Fancy.* New York: Macmillan, 1971. 262p.

701.   _____. *The Skyjackers.* New York: Collier Books, 1973. 317p.

702.   Joyner, Nancy D. *Aerial Hijacking as an International Crime.* Dobbs Ferry, N.Y.: Oceana, 1974. 344p.

703.   Phillips, David. *Skyjack: The Story of Air Piracy.* London: Harrap, 1973. 288p.

2. Articles

704.   Aggarwala, Narinder. "Political Aspects of Skyjacking." *International Conciliation,* no. 585 (November 1971), 7–21.

705.   _____, et al. "Air Hijacking, an International Perspective." *International Conciliation,* no. 585 (November 1971), 1–82.

706.   "Aircraft Hijacking: A Status Report." *Air Line Pilot,* VIII (August 1970), 26, 38–39.

707.   "Anatomy of a Skyjacker." *Time,* XCIV (December 5, 1969), 67–68+.

708.   "Arab Guerrillas Adopt Air Piracy as a Tactic." *Aviation Week and Space Technology,* XCIII (September 14, 1970), 33+.

709.   Armbrister, Trevor. "Code 3100: Skyjacker Aboard." *Reader's Digest,* CI (September 1972), 101–105.

710.   Barrie, G. N. "Crimes Committed Aboard Aircraft." *South African Law Journal,* LXXXIII (1968), 203+.

711.   Beristain, A. "Terrorism and Aircraft Hijackings." *International Journal of Criminology and Penology,* II (November 1974), 347–389.

712.   Buckley, William F., Jr. "The Skyjacker Problem." *National Review,* XXIV (September 29, 1972), 1082–1083.

713.   Denaro, Jacob. "Inflight Crimes." *Journal of Air Law and Commerce,* XXXV (1969), 171+.

714.   "Dilemma of the Airlines." *Newsweek,* LXXV (March 9, 1970), 33–34+.

715.   Elten, J. A. "This Is a Hijacking!" *Reader's Digest,* XCIX (July 1971), 213–217+.

716.   Evans, Alona E. "Aircraft Hijacking: Its Cause and Cure." *American Journal of International Law,* LXIII (October 1969), 695–710.

717. _____. "Report on Aircraft Hijacking in the United States." *Criminal Law Bulletin,* X (September 1974), 589–604.

718. Fick, Ronald L., *et al.* "Aircraft Hijacking: Criminal and Civil Aspects." *University of Florida Law Review,* XX (1969), 20+.

719. "Forcible Diversion of Civil Aircraft in Flight." *U.N. Chronicle,* VII (January 1970), 173–174.

720. Hawkins, Geoffrey. "Skyjacking." *Australian Journal of Forensic Sciences,* VII (June 1975), 157–168.

721. "Hijacking in the Skies: 48 Planes This Year—So Far." *U.S. News and World Report,* LXVII (September 22, 1969), 50.

722. Jacobson, Peter M. "From Piracy on the High Seas to Piracy in the High Skies: A Study of Aircraft Hijacking." *Cornell International Law Journal,* V (1972), 161+.

723. Kissinger, Henry A. "Hijacking, Terrorism, and War." *Department of State Bulletin,* LXXIII (September 8, 1975), 360–361.

724. Martin, Peter. "The Unlawful Seizure of Aircraft." *The Law Society's Gazette,* LXVI (1969), 714+.

725. Perret, Robert-Louis. "Air Transport Terrorism: Assigning the Guilt." *Interavia,* XXX (July 1975), 803–807.

726. Steelman, Herbert. "International Terrorism vis-à-vis Air Hijacking." *Southwestern University Law Review,* IX (1977), 85–110.

727. Sunderberg, Jacob W. F. "Lawful and Unlawful Seizure of Aircraft." *Terrorism,* I (1978), 423–440.

728. Turner, J. S. G. "Piracy in the Air." *Naval War College Review,* XXII (1969), 86–116.

729. "The Ugly New Airborne Game of Extortion." *Newsweek,* LXXIX (March 20, 1972), 22–23.

730. Wilson, R. A. "Terrorism, Air Piracy, and Hijacking." *Australian Journal of Forensic Sciences,* VII (June 1975), 169–174.

731. Wurfel, Seymour W. "Aircraft Piracy: Crime or Fun?" *William and Mary Law Review,* LXXVIII (Spring 1969), 820–873.

3. Documents, Papers, and Reports

732. Burris, Joseph B. *A Study of Aerial Hijacking.* Maxwell AFB, Ala.: Air Command and Staff College, Air University, 1972. 39p.

733.   Oberg, Duane C. *The Air Force and the Aerial Pirate.* Maxwell AFB, Ala.: Air Command and Staff College, Air University, 1973. 48p.

734.   Stokes, R. E. "Hijacking." Unpublished paper, Human Relations Symposium, Toronto, 1970.

735.   Turi, Robert T., *et al. Descriptive Study of Aircraft Hijackings.* Criminal Justice Monographs, v. 3, no. 5. Huntsville, Tex.: Institute of Contemporary Corrections and the Behavior Sciences, Sam Houston State University, 1972. 171p.

736.   United States. Congress. House. Committee on Foreign Affairs. *Aircraft Hijacking: Hearings.* 91st Cong., 2nd sess. Washington, D.C.: U.S. Government Printing Office, 1970. 199p.

737.   _____. _____. _____. Committee on Public Works and Transportation. Subcommittee on Aviation. *Aircraft Piracy–International Terrorism: Hearings.* 96th Cong., 1st sess. Washington, D.C.: U.S. Government Printing Office, 1979. 437p.

738.   _____. _____. Senate. Committee on Commerce. *Crimes Committed Aboard Aircraft: Report.* 92nd Cong., 2nd sess. Washington, D.C.: U.S. Government Printing Office, 1972. 10p.

739.   _____. _____. _____. Committee on Finances. *Skyjacking: Hearings.* 91st Cong., 2nd sess. Washington, D.C.: U.S. Government Printing Office, 1970. 26p.

740.   _____. Federal Aviation Administration. *Hijacking: Selected Readings* [February 1969–December 1970]. Washington, D.C., 1971. 53p.

741.   _____. _____. Task Force on Deterrence of Air Piracy. *Hijack Reference Data.* Washington, D.C., 1970. 29p.

742.   White, Edward T. *Terrorism in Civil Aviation: A Perennial World Problem.* Maxwell AFB, Ala.: Air Command and Staff College, Air University, 1974. 59p.

C. Assassinations

1. Books

743.   *Assassinations: The Murders That Changed History.* London: Marshall Cavendish, 1975. 65p.

744.   Camellion, Richard. *Assassination: Theory and Practice.* Boulder, Colo.: Paladin Press, 1977. 161p.

745. Crotty, William J., ed. *Assassinations and the Political Order.* New York: Harper & Row, 1971. 562p.

———, jt. author. *See* Kirkham, James F.

746. Ellis, Albert, and John Gullo. *Murder and Assassination.* New York: Lyle Stuart, 1971. 200p.

Gullo, John, jt. author. *See* Ellis, Albert.

747. Havens, Murray C. *The Politics of Assassination.* Englewood Cliffs, N.J.: Prentice-Hall, 1970. 174p.

748. Hurwood, Bernhardt J. *Society and the Assassin: A Background Book on Political Murder.* New York: Parent's Magazine Press, 1970. 240p.

749. Hyams, Edward. *Killing No Murder.* London: Panther, 1970. 251p.

750. Kirkham, James F., Sheldon Levy, and William J. Crotty. *Assassination and Political Violence: A Staff Report to the National Commission on the Causes and Prevention of Violence.* Washington, D.C.: U.S. Government Printing Office, 1969. 580p.

Levy, Sheldon, jt. author. *See* Kirkham, James F.

751. Paine, Lauren. *The Assassins' World.* New York: Taplinger, 1975. 208p.

752. Rapoport, David C. *Assassination and Terrorism.* Toronto: Canadian Broadcasting Corporation. CBC Learning Systems, 1971. 88p.

753. Wilson, Colin. *Order of Assassins: The Psychology of Murder.* London: Rupert Hart-Davis, 1972. 242p.

2. Articles

754. "Assassination: An Endless Nightmare." *U.S. News and World Report,* LXXIX (October 6, 1975), 17–21.

755. "Assassination as Foreign Policy." *Time,* CV (June 23, 1975), 8–9.

756. Crozier, Brian. "What Terrorists Hope to Gain by Murdering Americans: An Interview." *U.S. News and World Report.* LXXX (June 28, 1976), 33–34.

757. Danto, Arthur C. "Logical Portrait of the Assassin." *Social Research,* XLI (August 1974), 426–438.

758. Gross, Feliks. "Political Assassination." In: Marius H. Livingston, ed. *International Terrorism in the Contemporary World.* Westport, Conn.: Greenwood Press, 1978. pp. 307–315.

759.   Kaplan, John. "The Assassins." *Stanford Law Review*, IX (May 1967), 1110–1151.

760.   "Killing Cops: The New Terror Tactic." *U.S. News and World Report*, LXIX (August 31, 1970), 11–13.

761.   Leiden, Carl. "Assassination in the Middle East." *Trans-Action*, VI (May 1969), 20–23.

762.   McWilliams, W. C. "The Politics of Assassination." *Commonweal*, CII (July 18, 1975), 265–267.

763.   Mazrui, Ali A. "Thoughts on Assassination in Africa." *Political Science Quarterly*, LXXXIII (March 1968), 40–52.

764.   Waltzer, Michael. "The New Terrorists: Random Murder." *New Republic*, CLXXIII (August 30, 1975), 12–14.

765.   Weeks, Albert L. "Terrorism: The Deadly Tradition." *Freedom at Issue*, VIII (May-June 1978), 3+.

3. Documents, Papers, and Reports

766.   *The Police Officer: Primary Target of the Urban Guerrilla.* Washington, D.C.: Federal Bureau of Investigation, 1972. 3p.

D. Hostage and Kidnapping Incidents

1. Books

767.   Baumann, Carol E. *The Diplomatic Kidnappings: A Revolutionary Tactic of Urban Terrorism.* The Hague: Nijhoff, 1973. 182p.

768.   Cassidy, William L. *Political Kidnapping: An Introductory Overview.* Boulder, Colo.: Sycamore Island Books, 1978. 47p.

Goldblatt, Burt, jt. author. *See* Messick, Hank.

769.   Messick, Hank, and Burt Goldblatt. *Kidnapping: The Illustrated History.* New York: Dial Press, 1974. 206p.

770.   Ochberg, Frank, ed. *Victims of Terrorism.* Boulder, Colo.: Westview Press, 1979. 200p.

2. Articles

771.   Baumann, Carol E. "The Diplomatic Kidnappings: An Overview." In: *International Terrorism: Proceedings of an Intensive Panel at the 15th Annual Convention of the International Studies Association.* Milwaukee: Institute of World Affairs, University of Wisconsin, 1974. pp. 30–44.

772. Berman, Claire. "The Growing Spectre of Executive Kidnapping." *TWA Ambassador.* VIII (August 1976), 22–25.

773. Bristow, A. P. "Preliminary [Statistical] Research on Hostage Situations." *Law and Order,* XXV (March 1977), 73–77.

774. Clutterbuck, Richard. "Kidnapping." *Army Quarterly,* CIV (October 1974), 529–534.

775. "Diplomacy by Terror [Kidnappings]: Is It Getting Out of Control?" *U.S. News and World Report,* LXIX (August 24, 1970), 22–23.

776. Fitzgerald, Bruce D. "The Analytical Foundations of Extortionate Terrorism." *Terrorism,* I (1978), 347–362.

777. Hayter, William. "The Politics of Kidnapping." *Interplay,* IV (January 1971), 14–16.

778. "Hostage Dilemma." *Time,* CVI (October 20, 1975), 50+.

779. Hubbard, David. "Extortion Threats: The Possibility of Analysis." *Assets Protection,* I (Summer 1975), 17–19.

780. "Kidnapping: A World-Wide Increase." *Time,* CVI (August 25, 1975), 13.

781. "Kidnapping Diplomats: What's Back of the Terrorist Tactics." *U.S. News and World Report,* LXVIII (April 20, 1970), 22–23.

782. Lang, Daniel. "A Reporter at Large: Bank Drama." *New Yorker,* XLIX (November 25, 1974), 56–126.

783. Marshall, Edward. "Kidnapping Epidemic: A Form of Political Terrorism." *New Republic.* CLXX (April 6, 1974), 15–16.

784. Means, John. "Political Kidnapping and Terrorism." *North American Review,* CCLV (Winter 1970), 16–19.

785. Najmuddin, Dilshad. "The Kidnapping of Diplomatic Personnel." *Police Chief,* XL (February 1973), 18–23.

786. Plate, Thomas. "Kidnapping: The Growing Threat to All." *Good Housekeeping,* CLXXXI (November 1975), 60+.

787. Poulantzas, N. "Some Problems of International Law Connected with Urban Guerrilla Warfare: The Kidnapping of Members of Diplomatic Missions, Consular Offices, and Other Foreign Personnel." *Annals of International Studies,* III (1972), 137+.

788. Souchon, Henri. "Hostage-Taking: Its Evolution and Significance." *International Criminal Police Review,* no. 299 (June-July 1976), 168–173.

789.   Sponsler, T. H. "International Kidnapping." *International Lawyer,* V (1970), 27–52.

790.   Stechel, Ira. "Terrorist Kidnapping of Diplomatic Personnel." *Cornell International Law Journal,* V (Spring 1972), 187–217.

791.   Stratton, J. G. "The Terrorist Act of Hostage-Taking: A View of Violence and the Perpetrators." *Journal of Police Science and Administration,* VI (March and June 1978), 1–9, 123–134.

792.   Vayrynen, Raimo. "Some Aspects of the Theory and Strategy of Kidnapping." *Instant Research on Peace and Violence,* I (1971), 3+.

793.   Winchester, J. H. "Kidnapping Unlimited." *Reader's Digest,* CV (July 1974), 70–74.

794.   Wohlstetter, Roberta. "Kidnapping to Win Friends and Influence People." *Survey,* XX (Autumn 1974), 1–40.

3. Documents, Papers, and Reports

795.   Arenberg, G. S. *Hostage.* Washington, D.C.: National Police and Fire Fighters Association [1978?]. 32p.

796.   Blacksten, Ric. *Hostage Studies.* Arlington, Va.: Ketron, 1974. 24p.

797.   "Hostage Taking, Parts 1 and 2." In: National Criminal Justice Reference Service. *International Summaries: A Collection of Selected Translations in Law Enforcement and Criminal Justice,* v. 1. Rockville, Md.: NCJRS, Law Enforcement Assistance Administration, Department of Justice, 1978. pp. 51–68.

798.   Jenkins, Brian. *Terrorism and Kidnapping.* RAND Paper P-5255. Santa Monica, Calif.: RAND Corp., 1974. 8p.

799.   _____ , et al. *Numbered Lives: Some Statistical Observations from 1977 International Hostage Episodes.* RAND Paper P-5905. Santa Monica, Calif.: RAND Corp., 1977. 47p.

800.   Middendorff, Wolfgang. *New Developments in the Taking of Hostages and Kidnapping: A Summary.* Washington, D.C.: National Criminal Justice Reference Service Translations, 1975. 9p.

801.   Murphy, John F. "The Threat and Use of Force against Internationally Protected Persons and Diplomatic Facilities." Unpublished paper, Ralph Bunch Institute Conference on International Terrorism, 1976.

802.   United States, Congress, House. Committee on Internal Security. *Political Kidnappings, 1968–1973: A Staff Study.* 93rd Cong., 1st sess. Washington, D.C.: U.S. Government Printing Office, 1973. 61p.

E.   Urban Guerrilla Warfare: General Works

1. Books

803.   Burton, Anthony M. *Urban Terrorism: Theory, Practice, and Response.* New York: Free Press, 1975. 259p.

804.   Clutterbuck, Richard L. *Protest and the Urban Guerrilla.* New York: Abelard-Schuman, 1974. 309p.

805.   Mallin, Jay, ed. *Terror and Urban Guerrillas: A Study of Tactics and Documents.* Coral Gables, Fla.: University of Miami Press, 1971. 176p.

806.   Moss, Robert. *Urban Guerrillas: The New Face of Political Violence.* London: Maurice Temple Smith, 1972. 288p.

Published simultaneously in America by the New York firm of Coward-McCann.

807.   Oppenheimer, Martin. *The Urban Guerrilla.* Chicago: Quadrangle Books, 1969. 188p.

2. Articles

808.   Black, Robert J. "A Change in Tactics: The Urban Insurgent." *Air University Review,* XXIII (January–February 1972), 50–58.

809.   Caine, P. D. "Urban Guerrilla Warfare." *Military Review,* L (February 1970), 73–78.

810.   "The City as a Battlefield: A Global Concern." *Time,* XCVI (November 2, 1970), 19–22+.

811.   Clutterbuck, Richard L. "Police and Urban Terrorism." *Police Journal,* XLVIII (July–September 1975), 204–214.

812.   Coates, Joseph F. "Urban Violence: The Pattern of Disorder." *Annals of the American Academy of Political and Social Sciences,* CDV (January 1973), 25–40.

813.   Crowley, Fred R. "Insurgency in the Urban Area." *Marine Corps Gazette,* LVI (February 1972), 55–56.

814.   Faleroni, Alberto D. "What Is an Urban Guerrilla?" *Military Review,* XLVII (January 1967), 94–96.

815.   Grabosky, P. N. "The Urban Context of Political Terrorism." In: Michael Stohl, ed. *The Politics of Terrorism.* New York: Marcel Dekker, 1979. pp. 51–76.

816.   Griessman, B. E. "Toward an Understanding of Urban Unrest and Rioting." *Journal of Human Relations,* XVI (Summer 1968), 315–332.

817.   Harrigan, Anthony. "Combat in Cities." *Military Review,* XLVI (May 1966), 26–30.

818.   Harsch, J. C., *et al.* "Revolution and Social Change: Toward an Urban Guerrilla Movement." *Current,* CXVIII (1970), 13–26.

819.   Horchem, Hans Josef. "Patterns of the 'Urban Guerrilla.'" In: Walter Z. Laqueur, ed. *The Terrorism Reader: A Historical Anthology.* Philadelphia: Temple University Press, 1978. pp. 246–251.

820.   Howard, A. J. "Urban Guerrilla Warfare in a Democratic Society." *Medicine, Science, and the Law,* XII (October 1972), 231–243.

821.   Karber, Philip A. "Urban Terrorism: Baseline Data and a Conceptual Framework." *Social Science Quarterly,* LII (December 1971), 521–533.

822.   Lamont, Norman. "The Urban Guerrilla." *Crossbow,* XIV (April 1971), 32–33.

823.   Lerner, Max, *et al.* "Toward an Urban Guerrilla Movement?" *Current,* CXVIII (May 1970), 13–18.

824.   Mack, Andrew. "The Non-Strategy of Urban Guerrilla Warfare." In: J. Niejing, ed. *Urban Guerrilla: Studies on the Theory, Strategy, and Practice of Political Violence in Modern Societies.* Rotterdam, Holland: University of Rotterdam Press, 1974. pp. 22–45.

825.   Marighella, Carlos. "Minimanual of the Urban Guerrilla." In: Jay Mallin, ed. *Terror and Urban Guerrillas: A Study of Tactics and Documents.* Coral Gables, Fla.: University of Miami Press, 1971. pp. 67–116.

826.   Martinez-Codo, Enrique. "The Urban Guerrilla." *Military Review,* LI (August 1971), 3–10.

827.   Meier, R. L. "Some Thoughts on Conflict and Violence in the Urban Settlement." *American Behavioral Scientist,* X (January 1966), 11–12.

828.   Moore, John R. "Future War May Take the Form of Urban Terrorism." *Marine Corps Gazette,* LXIII (June 1979), 49–53.

829.   Moss, Robert. "Urban Guerrilla Warfare." In: Jackson Susman, ed. *Crime and Justice, 1971–1972: An A.M.S. Anthology.* New York: AMS, 1974. pp. 405–427.

830.   Peterson, Harries-Clichy. "Urban Guerrilla Warfare." *Military Review,* LII (March 1972), 82–89.

831.   Schlaak, Thomas M. "The Essence of Future Guerrilla Warfare: Urban Combat." *Marine Corps Gazette,* LX (December 1976), 18–26.

832. Teitler, G. "The Urban Guerrillas as a Revolutionary Phenomenon and as a Recruiting Problem." In: J. Niejing, ed. *Urban Guerrilla: Studies on the Theory, Strategy, and Practice of Political Violence in Modern Societies.* Rotterdam, Holland: University of Rotterdam Press, 1974. pp. 111–127.

833. Tinker, Hugh. "Can Urban Guerrilla Warfare Succeed?" *Current,* CXXIX (May 1971), 52–57.

834. "Trends in Urban Guerrilla Tactics." *FBI Law Enforcement Bulletin,* XLII (July 1973), 3–7.

835. Wolf, John B. "Organization and Management Practices of Urban Terrorist Groups." *Terrorism,* I (1978), 169–186.

836. _____. "Urban Terrorist Operations." *Police Journal,* XLIX (October-December, 1976), 277–284.

3. Documents, Papers, and Reports

837. Jenkins, Brian. *Soldiers Versus Gunmen: The Challenge of Urban Guerrilla Warfare.* RAND Paper P-5182. Santa Monica, Calif.: RAND Corp., 1974. 10p.

838. _____. *An Urban Strategy for Guerrillas and Governments.* RAND Paper P-4670/1. Santa Monica, Calif.: RAND Corp., 1972. 13p.

839. Moss, Robert. *Urban Guerrilla Warfare.* Adelphi Papers, no. 79. London: International Institute for Strategic Studies, 1971. 22p.

840. Roberts, Kenneth E. *Urban Guerrillas in the Americas.* Washington, D.C.: Systems Consultants, 1976. 29p.

841. *We Shall Fight in the Street.* Boulder, Colo.: Paladin Press, 1979. 68p.

V/Terrorist Armaments

Introduction

Terrorism, like many other violent crimes, could not succeed without the availability of arms necessary to kill, explode, or commandeer. The references in subsection A examine conventional armaments and explosives available to terrorists and cover the few general citations available on the tactic of bombing. Subsection B lists the abundant items concerning the potential threat of terrorists ever obtaining or manufacturing nuclear weapons. Additional citations relative to this section will be found among the works noted in section II:B above.

A. Conventional Arms: Guns, Bombs, and Bombings

1. Books

842. Archer, Denis. *Jane's Pocket Book of Rifles and Light Machine Guns.* New York: Collier Books, 1977. 231p.

Christensen, Devon, editor. *See* Truby, J. David.

843. Ezell, Edward C. *Small Arms of the World.* 11th rev. ed. Harrisburg, Pa.: Stackpole Books, 1977. 671p.

844. Glackin, James. *Elements of Explosive Production.* Boulder, Colo.: Paladin Press, 1979. 60p.

845. Hogg, Ian V., and John W. Weeks. *Military Small Arms of the 20th Century.* New York: Hippocrene Books, 1977. 284p.

846. Holmes, Bill. *Home Workshop Guns for Defense and Resistance.* 2 vols. Boulder, Colo.: Paladin Press, 1978–1979.

847. Minnery, John, and J. David Truby. *Improvised Modified Firearms.* Boulder, Colo: Paladin Press, 1975. 140p.

848. Powell, William. *The Anarchist Cookbook.* New York: Lyle Stuart, 1971. 160p.

849. Stoffell, Joseph. *Explosives and Homemade Bombs.* 2nd ed. Springfield, Ill.: C. C. Thomas, 1972. 304p.

850. Truby, J. David. *How Terrorists Kill: The Complete Terrorist Arsenal.* Edited by Devon Christensen. Boulder, Colo.: Paladin Press, 1978. 87p.

———, jt. author. *See* Minnery, John.

851. *Typical Foreign Unconventional Warfare Weapons.* Boulder, Colo.: Paladin Press, 1979. 54p.

Weeks, John W., jt. author. *See* Hogg, Ian V.

2. Articles

852. "And Now, Mail-a-Death: Letter Bombs Mailed to Israeli Diplomatic Offices." *Time,* C (October 2, 1972), 28+.

853. "Fake Bombs New Hijack Concern." *Aviation Week and Space Technology,* CV (September 20, 1976), 32.

854. Gertz, Dwight L. "Terrorist Weapons and the Terrorist Threat." *U.S. Naval Institute Proceedings,* CI (October 1975), 113–114.

855. "Letter Bombs: How to Recognize Them." *TIG Brief,* XXV (December 14, 1973), 15–16.

72   *Conventional Arms: Guns, Bombs, and Bombings*

856. McGuire, Patrick. "Target for Terrorists: An Assortment of Bombers Zero in on Business." *Conference Board Record,* VIII (August 1971), 2–8.

857. "New Arab Terror—Murder by Mail: Pencil-Shaped Bombs in Envelopes." *Newsweek,* LXXX (October 2, 1972), 30–31.

858. Styles, S. G. "The Car Bomb." *Journal of the Forensic Science Society,* XCIII (April 1975), 93–97.

859. "Terror Bombing: Rising Technique of Violence." *U.S. News and World Report,* LXVIII (March 23, 1970), 26–27.

3. Documents, Papers, and Reports

860. Elliott, John D. "Transitions of Contemporary Terrorism Related to Changes in Technology." Unpublished paper, NASA Summer Faculty Institute, 1976.

861. Frankfort Arsenal. *Improvised Munitions/Black Books.* 2 vols. Boulder, Colo.: Paladin Press, 1979.

862. *Improvised Weapons of the American Underground.* Boulder, Colo.: Paladin Press, 1979. 20p.

863. Jenkins, Brian. *High Technology Terrorism and Surrogate War: The Impact of New Technology on Low-Level Violence.* RAND Paper P-5339. Santa Monica, Calif.: RAND Corp., 1975. 26p.

864. Mengel, R. William. *Terrorism and New Technologies of Destruction.* Vienna, Va.: B.D.M. Corp., 1976. 35p.

865. United States. Army. *Boobytraps.* FM-5-13. Boulder, Colo.: Paladin Press, 1979. 133p.

866. _____. _____. *Explosives and Demolitions.* FM 5-25. Washington, D.C.: U.S. Government Printing Office, 1967. 188p.

867. _____. _____. *Incendiaries.* TM 31-201-1. Boulder, Colo.: Paladin Press, 1979. 150p.

868. _____. _____. *Unconventional Warfare Devices and Techniques.* TM 31-200-1. Boulder, Colo.: Paladin Press, 1979. 234p.

869. _____. Congress. Senate. Committee on the Judiciary. Subcommittee to Investigate the Administration of the Internal Security Act and Other Internal Secutiry Laws. *Terroristic Activity, Part VII: Terrorist Bombings—Hearings.* 94th Cong., 1st sess. Washington, D.C.: U.S. Government Printing Office 1975. 121p.

870. _____ . Federal Aviation Administration. Civil Aviation Security Service. *Explosives Aboard Aircraft* [1949–1979]. Washington, D.C., 1979. 20p.

B. *The Nuclear Threat*

1. Books

871. Curtis, Richard, and Elizabeth Hogan. *Perils of the Peaceful Atom.* London: Gollancz, 1970. 274p.

872. Compert, David C., *et al. Nuclear Weapons and World Politics: Alternatives for the Future.* New York: McGraw-Hill, 1977. 370p.

873. Greenberg, Martin H., and Augustus R. Norton, eds. *Studies in Nuclear Terrorism.* Boston: G. K. Hall, 1979. 250p.

Hogan, Elizabeth, jt. author. *See* Curtis, Richard.

Norton, Augustus R., jt. editor. *See* Greenberg, Martin H.

874. Phillips, John A., with David Michaels. *Mushroom: The Story of the A-Bomb Kid.* New York: Morrow, 1978. 287p.

875. Wohlstetter, Albert, *et al. Moving toward Life in a Nuclear Armed Crowd!* Los Angeles: Heuristics Press, 1976. 110p.

2. Articles

876. Adelson, Alan M. "Please Don't Steal the Atomic Bomb." *Esquire,* (May 1969), 130–133, 144.

877. "Backyard A-Bombs." *Time,* CV (November 27, 1972), 14.

878. Barnet, Richard J. "Ultimate Terrorism." *Progressive,* XLIII (February 1979), 14–19.

879. Beres, Louis R. "The Threat of Nuclear Terrorism in the Middle East." *Current History,* LXX (January 1976), 1–15.

880. _____ . "The Threat of Palestinian Nuclear Terrorism in the Middle East." *International Problems,* XV (Fall 1976), 48–56.

881. Blair, D. G. and G. D. Brewer. "The Terrorist Threat to World Nuclear Programs." *Journal of Conflict Resolution,* XXI (September 1977), 379–403.

Brewer, G. D., jt. author. *See* Blair, D. G.

882. Cohen, Bernard L. "The Potentialities of Terrorism." *Bulletin of the Atomic Scientists,* XXXII (June 1976), 34–35.

883. Comey, David D. "The Perfect Trojan Horse: The Threat of Nuclear Terrorism." *Bulletin of the Atomic Scientists,* XXXII (June 1976), 33–34.

884. Conrad, Thomas M. "Do-It-Yourself A-Bomb." *Commonweal,* (July 25, 1969), 455–457.

885. ———. "Radioactive Malevolence." *Bulletin of the Atomic Scientists,* XXX (February 1974), 16–20.

886. DeNike, L. Douglas. "Nuclear Terrorism." *Sierra Club Bulletin,* (November-December 1975), *passim.*

887. ———. "Radioactive Malevolence." *Science and Public Affairs,* XXX (February 1974), 16–20.

888. Dumas, L. J. "National Security and the Arms Race." In: David Carlton and Carlo Schaerf, eds. *International Terrorism and World Security.* New York: Wiley, 1975. pp. 158–164.

889. Dunn, Lewis. "Nuclear 'Gray Marketeering.'" *International Security,* I (Winter 1977), 107–118.

890. Ebon, Martin. "Apocalyptic Terrorists." *Humanist,* XXXVIII (November 1978), 26–29.

891. Feld, Bernard. "The Menace of Fission Power Economy." *Science and Public Affairs,* XXX (April 1974), 32–34.

892. Flood, Michael. "Nuclear Sabotage." *Bulletin of the Atomic Scientists,* XXXII (October 1976), 29–38; XXXIII (January 1977), 6+.

893. Frank, Forrest R. "Nuclear Terrorism and the Escalation of International Conflict." *Naval War College Review,* XXIX (Fall 1976), 12–27.

894. Ingram, Timothy H. "Nuclear Hijacking Now within the Grasp of any Bright Lunatic." *Washington Monthly,* IV (January 1973), 20–28.

895. Janke, Peter. "Nuclear Terrorism." In: Royal United Service Institution for Defence Studies, eds. *RUSI and Brassey's Defence Yearbook, 1977–78.* Boulder, Colo.: Westview Press, 1977. pp. 103–112.

896. Klevens, Edward H. "The Plutonium Connection and a Small Case of Blackmail." *American Journal of Physics,* XLIV (April 1976), 406–407.

897. Krieger, David M. "Nuclear Power: A Trojan Horse for Terrorists." In: B. Jasani, ed. *Nuclear Proliferation Problems.* Cambridge, Mass.: Published by MIT Press for the Stockholm International Peace Research Institute, 1974. pp. 168–186.

898. _____."Terrorists and Nuclear Technology." *Bulletin of the Atomic Scientists,* XXXI (June 1975), 28–34.

899. _____. "What Happens If... ?: Terrorists, Revolutionaries, and Nuclear Weapons." *Annuals of the American Academy of Political and Social Science,* CDXXX (March 1977), 44–57.

900. _____. "When Terrorists Go Nuclear." *Congressional Record,* CXX (July 1, 1974), 21943–21944.

901. Lapp, Ralph E. "The Ultimate Blackmail." *New York Times Magazine,* (February 4, 1973), 13+.

902. Mengel, R. William. "The Impact of Nuclear Terrorism on the Military's Role in Society." In: Marius H. Livingston, ed. *International Terrorism in the Contemporary World.* Westport, Conn.: Greenwood Press, 1978. pp. 402–414.

903. Mullen, Robert K. "Mass Destruction and Terrorism." *Journal of International Affairs,* VII (Spring-Summer 1978), 63–89.

904. Norman, Lloyd. "Our Nuclear Weapons Sites: Next Target of Terrorists?" *Army,* XXVII (June 1977), 28–31.

905. Norton, Augustus R. "Nuclear Terrorism and the Middle East." *Military Review,* LVI (April 1976), 3–11.

906. _____. "Terrorists, Atoms, and the Future: Understanding the Threat." *Naval War College Review,* XXXII (May-June 1979), 30–50.

907. "*Nova*—The Plutonium Connection: Reprinting of the Transcript." *Congressional Record,* CXXI (March 11, 1975), 3620+.

908. O'Toole, Thomas. "Spread of Plutonium Worries A-Scientists: Reprinted from the *Washington Post,* June 23, 1974." *Congressional Record,* CXX (July 1, 1974), 21942–21943.

909. Perry, H. Allen. "The Threat of Nuclear Blackmail." *American Legion Magazine,* XCVIII (May 1975), 8–11+.

910. Ponte, Lowell. "Better Do as We Say: This is an Atomic Bomb and We're Not Fooling." *Penthouse,* VII (February 1972), *passim.*

911. Ribicoff, Abraham. "The Threat of Nuclear Theft and Sabotage." *Congressional Record,* CXX (April 30, 1974), 6621–6630.

912. Rosenbaum, David M. "Nuclear Terror." *International Security,* I (Winter 1977), 140–161.

913. Salamon, Benjamin. "Nuclear Power Plants and International Politics." *Millennium,* IV (Winter 1975–1976), 200–219.

914.   Shapley, Deborah. "Plutonium Reactor Proliferation Threatens a Nuclear Black Market." *Science,* CLXXII (April 9, 1971), 143–146.

915.   Taylor, Theodore B. "Diversion by Non-Governmental Organizations." In: Mason Willrich, ed. *International Safeguards and the Nuclear Industry.* Baltimore, Md.: John Hopkins Press, 1973. pp. 176–199.

————, jt. author. *See* Willrich, Mason.

916.   Willrich, Mason. "Terrorists Keep Out: The Problem of Safeguarding Nuclear Materials in a World of Malfunctioning People." *Bulletin of the Atomic Scientists,* XXXI (May 1975), 12–16.

917.   ————, and Theodore B. Taylor. "Nuclear Theft." *Survival,* XVI (July-August 1974), 186–191.

918.   Wohlstetter, Albert. "Terror on a Grand Scale." *Survival,* XVII (May-June 1976), 98–104.

919.   Woods, G. D. "The Possible Criminal Use of Atomic or Biochemical Materials." *Australian and New Zealand Journal of Criminology,* VIII (June 1975), 113–123.

3. Documents, Papers, and Reports

920.   Beres, Louis R. "The Nuclear Threat of Terrorism." Unpublished paper, North American Peace Science Conference Annual Meeting, 1975.

921.   Berkowitz, B. J., *et al. Superviolence: The Civil Threat of Mass-Destructive Weapons.* Santa Barbara, Calif.: ADCON Corp., 1972.

922.   Bigney, Russell E., *et al. Exploration of the Nature of Future Warfare.* Carlisle Barracks, Pa.: Strategic Studies Institute, U.S. Army War College, 1974. 106p.

923.   Billington, G. R. *Nuclear Terrorism.* Maxwell AFB, Ala.: Air War College, Air University, 1975. 46p.

924.   Blair, Bruce. "A Proposal for Analyzing the Terrorist Threat to U.S. Nuclear Programs." Unpublished paper, Department of Administrative Science, Yale University, 1976.

925.   Burnham, E. *The Threat to Licensed Nuclear Facilities.* MITRE Technical Report MTR-7022. McLean, Va.: MITRE Corp., 1975. 223p.

926.   Cohen, Bernard L. *The Hazards of Plutonium Dispersal.* Oak Ridge, Tenn.: Institute for Energy Analysis, 1975.

927.   DeLeon, Peter, *et al. Attributes of Potential Criminal Adversaries of U.S. Nuclear Programs.* RAND Report R-2225-SL. Santa Monica, Calif.: RAND Corp., 1978. 73p.

928. DeNike, L. Douglas. "Nuclear Hijacking and Human Malice." Unpublished paper, University of Southern California School of Medicine, 1972.

929. _____. "The Vulnerability to Antisocial Interventions of Nuclear Power Plants and Their Auxiliary Activities." Unpublished testimony, Los Angeles Department of Water and Power, 1974.

930. Dunn, Lewis, *et al. Routes to Nuclear Weapons: Aspects of Purchase or Theft.* Croton-on-Hudson, N.Y.: Hudson Institute, 1977.

931. Feiveson, Harold A. "Latent Proliferation: The International Security Implications of Civilian Nuclear Power." Unpublished Ph.D. dissertation, Princeton University, 1972.

932. Hutchinson, Marth C. "Defining Future Threat: Terrorists and Nuclear Proliferation." Unpublished paper, Ralph Bunch Institute Conference on International Terrorism, 1976.

933. _____. "Terrorism and the Diffusion of Nuclear Power." Unpublished paper, 17th Annual Convention of the International Studies Association, 1976.

934. Jenkins, Brian. *The Potential for Nuclear Terrorism.* RAND Paper P-5876. Santa Monica, Calif.: RAND Corp., 1977. 11p.

935. _____. *Will Terrorists Go Nuclear?* RAND Paper P-5541. Santa Monica, Calif.: RAND Corp., 1975. 10p.

936. Kinderman, E. M. "Plutonium: Home-Made Bombs." In: U.S. Congress. Senate. Committee on Government Operations. *Peaceful Nuclear Exports and Weapons Proliferation: Hearings.* 94th Cong., 1st sess. Washington, D.C.: U.S. Government Printing Office, 1975. pp. 25–26+.

937. Mabry, Robert C., Jr. "Nuclear Theft: Real and Imagined Danger." Unpublished M.A. thesis, U.S. Naval Postgraduate School, 1976.

938. Matson, Eric K. *Terrorists Armed with Nuclear Weapons.* Maxwell AFB, Ala.: Air Command and Staff College, Air University, 1976. 50p.

939. Mengel, R. William, *et al. Analysis of the Terrorist Threat to the Commercial Nuclear Industry.* Vienna, Va.: BDM Corp., 1975.

940. Mullen, Robert K. *The International Clandestine Nuclear Threat.* Santa Barbara, Calif.: Mission Research Corp., 1975.

941. "Nuclear Theft and Terrorism: Discussion Group Report." In: *Sixteenth Strategy for Peace Conference Report.* Muscatine, Iowa: Stanley Foundation, 1975. pp. 33–40.

942. Quester, George. "What's New on Nuclear Proliferation." In: U.S. Congress. House. Committee on International Relations. Subcommittee on International Security and Scientific Affairs. *Nuclear Proliferation—Future U.S. Foreign Policy Implications: Hearings.* 94th Cong., 1st sess. Washington, D.C.: U.S. Government Printing Office, 1975. pp. 476–499.

943. Taylor, Theodore B., *et al. Preliminary Survey of Non-National Nuclear Threats.* Stanford Research Institute Technical Note SSC-TN-5205-83. Stanford, Calif.: Stanford Research Institute, 1968.

VI/Domestic and International Support For and Countermeasures Against Terrorism

Introduction

Hard as it may be for some readers to believe, certain nations, out of expediency or conviction, have from time to time supported certain terrorist activities. Examples of support include supplying arms and training and providing asylum. The Soviets and Libyans have long been associated with the Palestinian cause, while some American groups have provided gun money for the IRA. The citations in subsection A treat these and other acts of national support for terrorism.

During the last decade, countries have adopted various measures, based on differing theories, to forewarn and provide against terrorist acts. The materials in subsection B treat in a general fashion those intelligence and security activities, specifically as they relate to civil aviation, bombings, hostages and personnel, especially those of the business community and the nuclear field.

Many authorities doubt that terrorism would be as successful as it currently appears to be without the widespread attention given by the print and electronic media. The references in subsection C deal specifically with this question and give food for thought to all students of our topic and of journalism.

Additional references relative to this section will be found in sections II:B and III above and VIII below.

A. Domestic and International Support of Terrorism

1. Books

944. Barron, John. *KGB: The Secret Work of Soviet Secret Agents.* New York: Reader's Digest Press; dist. by E. P. Dutton, 1973. 462p.

Deacon, Richard, pseud. *See* McCormick, Donald.

945. Freedman, Robert O. *Soviet Policy Toward the Middle East Since 1970.* Rev ed. New York: Praeger, 1978. 400p.

946. Greig, Ian. *The Communist Challenge to Africa.* Sandton, South Africa: Southern Africa Freedom Foundation, 1977. 384p.

947. McCormick, Donald. *The Chinese Secret Service.* By Richard Deacon, pseud. New York: Taplinger, 1974. 523p.

948. Rubinstein, Alvin Z., ed. *Soviet and Chinese Influence in the Third World.* New York: Praeger, 1975. 246p.

2. Articles

949. Abu-Jaber, Faiz S. "Soviet Attitude toward Arab Revolutions." *Middle East Forum* (Winter 1971), 41–65.

950. Adie, W. A. C. "China, Israel, and the Arabs." *Conflict Studies,* no. 12 (May 1971), 1–18.

951. Borodin, Nikolai. "The Palestinian Resistance Movement: A Soviet View." *New Middle East,* no. 21 (December 1972), 27–28.

952. Cooley, John K. "China and the Palestinians." *Journal of Palestine Studies,* I (Winter 1972), 19–34.

953. Crozier, Brian. "New Light on Soviet Subversion." *Soviet Analyst,* III (April 11, 1974), 1–3.

954. Deming, Angus. "The American Connection [to the IRA]." *Newsweek,* LXXXVI (December 1, 1975), 52+.

955. ———. "Arming the IRA." *Newsweek,* LXXIX (March 6, 1972), 47+.

956. ———. "The Cuban Connection: Coordination of the United Revolutionary Organizations." *Newsweek,* LXXXVIII (November 1, 1976), 53–54.

957. Evans, Medford. "Conspiracy: The New World Order Isn't New." *American Opinion,* XVII (December 1974), 47–52+.

958. "Exile Bombers: [Cuban] Co-ordination of the United Revolutionary Organizations." *Time,* CVIII (November 1, 1976), 60+.

959. Fisher, Desmond. "Exporting Death to Ireland: Arms Purchased with American Donations." *Commonweal,* CIV (June 10 and August 5, 1977), 356–358, 500–502.

960. Fox, R. W. "Algeria, Israel, and al Fatah." *Commonweal,* XCII (May 8, July 10, September 25, 1970), 184–185, 331+, 475+; XCIII (October 23, 1970), 83+.

961. Freedman, Robert O. "Soviet Policy toward International Terrorism." In: Yonah Alexander, ed. *International Terrorism: National, Regional, and Global Perspectives.* New York: Praeger, 1976. pp. 115–147.

962. Friedlander, Robert A. "Reflections on Terrorist Havens." *Naval War College Review,* XXXII (March-April 1979), 59–67.

963. Holley, Charles. "Why Libya Exports Chaos." *Atlas,* XXIII (November 1976), 14–16.

964. Hotz, Robert. "Libyan-Financed Hijackers." *Aviation Week and Space Technology,* CV (August 30, 1976), 9.

965. Jabber, Fuad. "The Arab Regimes and the Palestinian Revolution, 1967–1971." *Journal of Palestine Studies,* II (Winter 1973), 79–101.

966. Mallin, Jay. "Phases of Subversion: The Castro Drive on Latin America." *Air University Review,* XXV (November-December 1973), 54–62.

967. Romaniecki, Leon. "The Soviet Union and International Terrorism." *Soviet Studies,* XXVI (July 1974), 417–440.

968. Rositzke, Harry. "The KGB's Broadening Horizons." *Problems of Communism,* XXIV (May 1975), 43–45.

969. Schapiro, Leonard. "The Soviet Union and the PLO." *Survey,* XXIII (Summer 1978), 193–207.

970. Thom, William G. "Trends in Soviet Support for African Liberation." *Air University Review,* XXV (July-August 1974), 36–43.

971. Vicinic, Milan. "The Responsibility of States for Acts of International Terrorism." *Review of International Affairs* (Belgrade), XXIII (1972), 11+.

972. Whetton, Lawrence L. "Changing Soviet Attitudes towards Arab Radical Movements." *New Middle East,* no. 18 (March 1970), 20–27.

973. Yodfat, Alexander. "The Soviet Union and the Palestine Guerrillas." *Mizan,* XI (January-February 1969), 8–17.

3. Documents, Papers, and Reports

974. Israel. Ministry of Foreign Affairs. Division of Information. *Accessories to Terror: The Responsibility of Arab Governments for the Organization of Terrorist Activities.* Middle East Information Series, v. 25. Jerusalem, 1973.

975. Kirkpatrick, Lyman B., Jr., and Howland H. Sargeant. *Soviet Political Warfare Techniques: Espionage and Propaganda in the 1970's.* Strategy Paper, no. 11. New York: National Strategy Information Center, 1972. 82p.

976. Ma'oz, Moshe. *Soviet and Chinese Relations with the Palestinian Guerrilla Organizations.* Jerusalem Papers on Peace Problems, no. 4. Jerusalem: Hebrew University, 1974. 35p.

977. Morgan, William D. *The U.S.S.R. and the Palestinian Question.* Report no. 124. Washington, D.C.: Industrial College of the Armed Forces, 1975. 61p.

978. Nelson, Harold D. "Military Assistance." In: *Algeria: A Country Study.* DA Pam 550–44. Washington, D.C.: Published for Foreign Area Studies, The American University, by the U.S. Government Printing Office, 1979. pp. 283–289.

979. Norton, Augustus R. *Moscow and the Palestinians: A New Tool of Soviet Policy in the Middle East.* Coral Gables, Fla.: Center for Advanced International Studies, University of Miami, 1974. 26p.

980. Riollot, Jean. *The Soviet Attitude toward the Palestinian Organizations.* New York: Radio Liberty Committee, 1970. 7p.

981. Romaniecki, Leon. *Arab Terrorists in the Middle East and the Soviet Union.* Jerusalem: Soviet and East European Research Center, Hebrew University, 1973.

Sargeant, Howland H., jt. author. *See* Kirkpatrick, Lyman B., Jr.

982. United States. Central Intelligence Agency. "International Communist Front Organizations." In: U.S. Congress. House. Permanent Select Committee on Intelligence. *The CIA and the Media: Hearings.* 95th Cong., 1st and 2nd sess. Washington, D.C.: U.S. Government Printing Office, 1978. pp. 560–625.

983. _____ . _____ . National Foreign Assessment Center. *Communist Aid to the Less Developed Countries of the Free World, 1976.* ER 77-10296. Washington, D.C.: Document Expediting Service, Exchange and Gift Division, Library of Congress, 1977. 37p.

984. _____. Congress. Senate. Committee on the Judiciary. Sub-committee to Investigate the Administration of the Internal Security Act and Other Internal Security Laws. *Terroristic Activity, Part VI: The Cuban Connection in Puerto Rico—Hearings.* 94th Cong., 1st sess. Washington, D.C.: U.S. Government Printing Office, 1975. 177p.

985. _____. _____. _____. _____. _____. *Terroristic Activity, Part IX: Interlocks between Communism and Terrorism—Hearings.* 94th Cong., 2nd sess. Washington, D.C.: U.S. Government Printing Office, 1976. 97p.

B. Domestic and International Countermeasures Against Terrorism

1. General Works

a. Books

986. Bell, J. Bowyer. *A Time of Terror: How Democratic Societies Respond to Revolutionary Terrorism.* New York: Basic Books, 1978. 292p.

987. Buckman, Peter. *The Limits of Protest.* Indianapolis: Bobbs-Merrill, 1970. 288p.

988. Cohen, Eliot A. *Commandos and Politicians: Elite Military Units in Modern Democracies* [U.S., Britain, France, Israel]. Studies in International Affairs, no. 40. Cambridge: Center for International Affairs, Harvard University, 1978. 136p.

989. Evans, Peter. *The Police Revolution.* London: Pitman, 1973. 192p.

990. Kitson, Frank. *Low-Intensity Operations: Subversion, Insurgency, Peace-Keeping.* Hamden, Conn.: Archon Books, 1974. 208p.

991. Moss, Robert, *Counter Terrorism.* London: Economist Brief Books, 1972. 64p.

b. Articles

992. Ahmad, Eqbal. "Revolutionary War and Counterinsurgency." *Journal of International Affairs,* XXV (Winter 1971), 1–47.

993. Alesevich, Eugene. "Police Terrorism." In: Marius H. Livingston, ed. *International Terrorism in the Contemporary World.* Westport, Conn.: Greenwood Press, 1978. pp. 269–275.

994. Allbach, D. M. "Countering Special Threat Situations." *Military Police Law Enforcement Journal,* II (Summer 1975), 34–40.

995.   Anable, David. "Tackling an International Problem." *Current,* CLXXX (February 1976), 57–60.

996.   *"Atlas* Survey: Controlling Terrorism." *Atlas,* XXV (July 1978), 10–12.

997.   Barclay, C. N. "Countermeasures against the Urban Guerrilla." *Military Review,* LII (January 1972), 83–90.

998.   Beaumont, Roger A. "Military Elite Forces: Surrogate War, Terrorism, and the New Battlefield." *Parameters,* IX (March 1979), 17–29.

999.   Bell, J. Bowyer. "Dealing with Terrorist Acts." *Intellect,* CIV (May 1976), 551+.

1000.   Black, Harold, and Marvin J. Labes. "Guerrilla Warfare: An Analogy to Police-Criminal Interaction." *American Journal of Orthopsychiatry,* XXXVII (July 1967), 666–670.

1001.   Blishchenko, Igor P. "International Violence as a Special Problem of the Fight against Crime." *International Review of Criminal Policy,* no. 32 (1976), 8–13.

1002.   Bobrow, Davis B. "Preparing for Unwanted Events: Instances of International Political Terrorism." *Terrorism,* I (1978), 397–422.

1003.   Bowett, Derek. "Reprisals Involving Recourse to Armed Force." *American Journal of International Law,* LXVI (January 1971), 1–36.

1004.   Burnham, James. "Antiterror Problems." *National Review,* XXVI (March 29, 1974), 365+.

1005.   _____ . "Assessing the Terrorism Trade-Off." *National Review,* XXV (January 5, 1973), 22+.

1006.   Cherry, William A. "Countermeasures against the Barricaded Gunman: Theory and Techniques." *Law and Order,* XXII (October 1974), 12–14.

1007.   "Clearer Than Ever—No Sure Way to Handle Global Terrorists: Who They Are, What They've Done." *U.S. News and World Report,* LXXX (January 5, 1976), 27–28.

1008.   Clifford, W. "New and Special Problems of Crime: National and Transnational." *International Review of Criminal Policy,* no. 32 (1976), 3–7.

1009.   Conley, Michael C. "The Strategy of Communist-Directed Insurgency and the Conduct of Counterinsurgency." *Naval War College Review,* XXI (July 1969), 73–79.

86   *Domestic and International Countermeasures Against Terrorism*

1010. Conquest, Robert. "Thwarting Terrorism." *Alternative,* X (October 1976), 22–24.

1011. "Curbing Terrorism: A Symposium." *Atlas,* XXV (January 1978), 31–37.

1012. Del Grosso, D. S., and John C. Short. "A Concept for Anti-Terrorist Operations." *Marine Corps Gazette,* LXIII (June 1979), 54–59.

1013. Derriennic, Jean-Pierre. "The Nature of Terrorism and the Effective Response." *International Perspectives, III* (May-June 1975), 7–10.

1014. Gavzer, Bernard. "The Terrorists: How the Free World Can Fight Back." *Parade Magazine,* (May 20, 1979), 4–7.

1015. Gregory, F. "Protest and Violence: The Police Response." *Conflict Studies,* no. 75 (June 1976), 1–20.

1016. Grondona, Mariano. "Reconciling International Security and Human Rights." *International Security,* III (Summer 1978), 3–16.

1017. Gude, Edward W. "Dealing with Worldwide Terror." *Society,* X (January 1973), 9+.

1018. Heilbrunn, Otto. "When the Counterinsurgents Cannot Win." *Journal of the Royal United Service Institution for Defence Studies,* CXIV (1969), 55–58.

1019. Hillard, J. Z. "Countersubversive Operations in Urban Areas." *Military Review,* XLVI (June 1966), 12–19; XLVII (September 1967, 27–35.

1020. Horowitz, Irving . "Can Democracy Cope with Terrorism?" *Civil Liberties Review,* IV (May-June 1977), 29–32+.

1021. _____ . "Civil Liberties Dangers in Anti-Terrorist Policies." *Civil Liberties Review,* IV (March-April 1977), 25–32.

1022. _____ . "Political Terrorism and State Power." *Journal of Political and Military Sociology,* I (Spring 1973), 145–157.

1023. Institute for the Study of Conflict. "Terrorism Can Be Stopped." *Skeptic,* no. 11 (January-February 1976), 44–49.

1024. Javits, Jacob K. "International Terrorism: Apathy Exacerbates the Problem." *Terrorism,* I (1978), 111–118.

1025. Kahn, Ely J. "Profiles: The Views of Richard L. Clutterbuck." *New Yorker,* LIV (June 12, 1978), 37–40+.

1026.   Karkashian, J. E. "Dealing with International Terrorism." *Department of State Bulletin,* LXXVII (October 31, 1977), 605–609.

1027.   Kutner, Luis. "Constructive Notice: A Proposal to End International Terrorism." *New York Law Forum,* XIX (1973), 325–350.

Labes, Marvin J., jt. author. *See* Black, Harold.

1028.   Legum, Colin. "How to Curb International Terrorism." *Current Histgory,* CXLVII (January 1973), 3–9.

1029.   Levy, S. G. "Governmental Injustice and Attitudes toward Political Violence." In: J. D. Ben-Dak, ed. *The Future of Collective Violence: Societal and International Perspectives.* Lund, Sweden: Studentlitteratur, 1974. pp. 57–79.

1030.   Martinez-Codo, Enrique. "Continental Defense and Counterinsurgency." *Military Review,* L (April 1970), 71–74.

1031.   Nepote, John. "INTERPOL and Organized Crime." *Australian Police Journal,* XXIX (October 1975), 253–266.

1032.   O'Brien, Connor Cruise. "Liberty or Terror?" *International Security,* II (Fall 1977), 56–67.

1033.   Paust, Jordan J. "Approach to Decision with Regard to Terrorism." *Akron Law Review,* VII (Spring 1978), 397–403.

1034.   Pierre, Andrew J. "Coping with International Terrorism." *Survival,* XVIII (March-April 1976), 60–67.

1035.   Possony, Stefan T. "Coping with Terrorism." *Defense and Foreign Affairs Digest,* II (February 1973), 6–7.

1036.   Rosen, Steven J. "Measures against International Terrorism." In: David Carlton and Carlo Schaef, eds. *International Terrorism and World Security.* New York: Wiley, 1975. pp 60–68.

Short, John C., jt. author. *See* Del Grosso, C. S.

1037.   Sloan, Stephen. "Non-Territorial Terrorism: An Empirical Approach to Policy Formation." *Conflict,* I (1978), 131–144.

————, jt. author. *See* Wise, Charles.

1038.   Terekhov, Vladimir. "International Terrorism and the Fight against It." *New Times* (Moscow), no. 11 (March 1974), 20–22.

1039.   "Terrorism: What Can Be Done?" *National Review,* XXVI (March 15, 1974), 303+.

88   *Domestic and International Countermeasures Against Terrorism*

1040. "U.S. Business Throws Billions into the Fight against Terrorists." *U.S. News and World Report*, LXXXIII (November 21, 1977), 24–26.

1041. Wahl, Jonathan. "Responses to Terrorism: Self-Defense or Reprisal?" *International Problems*, XII (June 1973), 25–34.

1042. "What Can Be Done about Terrorism?" *Time*, CXI (May 1, 1978), 30–31+.

1043. Wilkinson, Paul. "Terrorism: The International Response." *World Today*, XXXIV (January 1978), 5–13.

1044. ———. "Terrorism Versus Liberal Democracy: The Problems of Response." *Conflict Studies*, no. 67 (January 1976), 1–19.

1045. Wise, Charles, and Stephen Sloan. "Countering Terrorism: The U.S. and Israeli Approach." *Middle East Review*, IX (Spring 1977), 55–59.

1046. Wolf, John B. "Controlling Political Terrorism in a Free Society." *Orbis*, XIX (Winter 1976), 1289–1308.

1047. Zivic, John. "The Nonaligned and the Problem of International Terrorism." *Review of International Affairs* (Belgrade), XXIV (January 20, 1973), 6–8.

c. Documents, Papers, and Reports

1048. Bramskill Police College. *Study of Public Order in Six EEC* [European Economic Community] *Countries: Belgium, Denmark, France, Holland, Italy, and West Germany.* 11th Service Course. Hampshire, Eng., 1974. 105p.

1049. Green, L. C. *The Nature and Control of International Terrorism.* Occasional Paper, no. 1. Atlanta, Ga.: Department of Political Science, University of Atlanta, 1974. 56p.

1050. Gregory, F. *Protest and Violence—the Police Response: A Comparative Analysis of Democratic Methods* [in France, West Germany, Italy, Japan, the United Kingdom, and the United States]. London: Institute for the Study of Conflict, 1976. 15p.

1051. Gude, Edward W. "Some Rough Notes on Response to Terrorism." Unpublished paper, Department of State Conference on Terrorism. 1972.

1052. Hutchinson, Martha C. "Transnational Terrorism as a Policy Issue." Unpublished paper, Annual Convention of the American Political Science Association, 1974.

1053. International Criminal Police Organization. *INTERPOL— 50th Anniversary, 1923–1973.* Paris, 1973. 88p.

1054. Israel. Ministry of Foreign Affairs. *Efforts Continue to Check Arab Terrorism.* Washington, D.C.: Embassy of Israel, 1973.

1055. Mallin, Jay. "Terror and the Military." Unpublished paper, 7th National Security Affairs Conference, National War College, 1974.

1056. Mickolus, Edward F. "International Terrorism: Review and Projection." Unpublished paper, Probe International, Inc., Conference on Terrorism and the American Corporation, 1976.

1057. Phillips, Charles D. *Counterterror Campaign: The Road to Success.* Carlisle Barracks, Pa.: Strategic Studies Institute, U.S. Army War College, 1975. 24p.

1058. Pierre, Andrew J. "Summary of Comments at Conference on International Terrorism." Unpublished paper, Department of State Conference on Terrorism in Retrospect and Prospect, 1976.

1059. Roberts, Kenneth E. *Terrorism and the Military Response.* Carlisle Barracks, Pa.: Strategic Studies Institute, U.S. Army War College, 1975. 19p.

1060. Shepherd, T. E., *et al. Exercise Europa* [Anti-terrorism in Belgium, West Germany, Italy, and Holland]. 12th Senior Command Course. Hampshire, Eng.: Bramskill Police College, 1975. 60p.

1061. University of Iowa. Institute of Public Affairs. *Terrorism: The Problem and the Question of Controls.* Iowa City [1975?]. [1p.]

2. Intelligence and Security

a. Books

1062. Bouza, A. V. *Police Intelligence: The Operations of an* [New York City Police Department Bureau of Special Services] *Investigative Unit.* New York: AMS Press, 1976. 192p.

1063. Colby, William E., with Peter Forbath. *Honorable Men: My Life in the CIA.* New York: Simon and Schuster, 1978. 493p.

1064. Greenwood, Colin. *Police Tactics in Armed Operations.* Boulder, Colo.: Paladin Press, 1979. 320p.

1065. Phillips, David A. *The Night Watch: 25 Years of Peculiar Service.* New York: Atheneum, 1977. 309p.

b. Articles

1066. "Aftermath of the Kidnappings: The Relationship of Terrorism and Increased Intelligence Activities." *Nation,* CCXVIII (March 9, 1974), 292+.

1067. "'All the Inefficiencies of Any Intelligence Service': The Biggest Threat Is Terrorism." *Armed Forces Journal International,* CXI (October 1973), 46–48.

1068. Arms, Ed. "The CIA Octopus Engulfs Terrorists." *Encore,* VII (July 10, 1978), 12+.

1069. Babcock, James H. "Intelligence and National Security." *Signal,* XXXIII (November-December 1978), 16–18+.

1070. Bennett, Robert K. "The Terrorists among Us: An Intelligence Report." *Reader's Digest,* XCIX (October 1971), 115–120.

1071. Bevilacqua, A. C. "Intelligence and Insurgency." *Marine Corps Gazette,* LX (January 1976), 40–46.

1072. Bottom, N. R., Jr. "Security Intelligence." *Security Management,* XX (July 1976), 36–39.

1073. Colby, Jonathan E. "The Developing International Law on Gathering and Sharing Security Intelligence." *Yale Studies in World Public Order,* I (1974), 49–92.

1074. Cooper, H. H. A. "Terrorism and the Intelligence Function." In: Marius H. Livingston, ed. *International Terrorism in the Contemporary World.* Westport, Conn.: Greenwood Press, 1978. pp. 287–296.

1075. Copeland, Miles. "Unmentionable Uses of the CIA: Counterterrorist Activity." *National Review,* XXV (September 14, 1973), 990– 997.

1076. Estace, Harry F." Changing Intelligence Priorities." *Electronic Warfare/Defense Electronics,* X (November 1978), 35+.

1077. Galyean, T. E. "Acts of Terrorism and Combat by Irregular Forces: An Insurance 'War Risk.'" *California Western International Law Journal,* IV (1974), 314+.

1078. Gwynne-Jones, Alum. "World Nation-State Structure Makes Intelligence Essential: Reprinted from the *New York Times,* February 15, 1976." In: George Wittman, ed. *The Role of the American Intelligence Organizations.* Reference Shelf, v. 48, no. 5. New York: H. W. Wilson, 1976. pp. 91–95.

1079. McDouglas, Myres. "The Intelligence Function and World Public Order." *Temple Law Quarterly,* XLVI (Spring 1973), 365+.

1080.   Rositzke, Harry. "Terrorism." In: his *The CIA's Secret Operations: Espionage, Counterespionage, and Covert Operations.* New York: Reader's Digest Press, 1977. pp. 111–117.

1081.   Saxe-Fernandez, John. "From Counterinsurgency to Counterintelligence." In: Julio Cotler and Richard Fagan, eds. *Latin America and the United States: Changing Political Realities.* Stanford: Stanford University Press, 1974. pp. 347–360.

1082.   Weil, H. M. "Domestic and International Violence Forecasting Approach." *Futures,* VI (June 1974), 477–485.

c. Documents, Papers, and Reports

1083.   Becker, Louis, *et al. Terrorism: Information as a Tool for Control.* CRS Report 78-1655PR. Washington, D.C.: Congressional Research Service, Library of Congress, 1978. 237p.

1084.   Brewer, Gary D. *Existing in a World of Institutionalized Danger.* Technical Report, no. 102. New Haven: School of Organization and Management, Yale University, 1976. 56p.

1085.   Kelly, Clarence M. *Intelligence Investigations: Excerpts from Testimony before House Subcommittee on Appropriations, February 20, 1976.* Washington, D.C.: Federal Bureau of Investigation, 1976. 10p.

1086.   Kupperman, Robert H. *Facing Tomorrow's Terrorist Incident Today.* Washington, D.C.: Law Enforcement Assistance Administration, Department of Justice, 1977. 101p.

1087.   Private Security Advisory Council. *Prevention of Terroristic Crimes.* Boulder, Colo.: Paladin Press, 1978. 30p.

1088.   Shriver, Robert B., Jr. *Countering Terrorism on Military Installations: Final Report.* McLean, Va.: Science Applications, 1977. 562p.

1089.   United States. Congress. House. Committee on the Judiciary. Subcommittee on Civil Rights and Constitutional Rights. *FBI Counterintelligence Programs: Hearings.* 93rd Cong., 2nd sess. Washington, D.C.: U.S. Government Printing Office, 1974. 47p.

1090.   _____ . _____ . Senate. Committee on the Judiciary. Subcommittee to Investigate the Administration of the Internal Security Act and Other Internal Security Laws. *The Nationwide Drive against Law Enforcement Intelligence Operations: Hearings.* 94th Cong., 1st sess. Washington, D.C.: U.S. Government Printing Office, 1975. 46p.

1091.   _____ . Department of the Army. *Physical Security.* FM 19-30. Washington, D.C.: U.S. Goverment Printing Office, 1979. 513p.

3. Security Measures: Civil Aviation

a. Books

1092. Moore, Kenneth C. *Airport, Aircraft, and Airline Security.* Los Angeles: Security World Publishing, 1976. 374p.

1093. Rich, Elizabeth. *Flying Scared: Why We Are Being Skyjacked and How to Put a Stop to It.* New York: Stein & Day, 1972. 194p.

b. Articles

1094. "Air Guards to Ride Shotgun." *Senior Scholastic,* XCVII (September 28, 1970), 9–10.

1095. Air Law Group. "Hijacking: Why Governments Must Act." *Aeronautical Journal,* LXXIV (February 1970), 143–145.

1096. "Airlines Seek a Breakthrough: Preventions of Hijacking." *Science News,* XCIV (August 31, 1968), 204–205.

1097. "Airlines vs. Hijackers." *Newsweek,* LXXVI (October 26, 1970), 76–78.

1098. "Airport Security Searches and the Fourth Amendment." *Columbia Law Review,* LXXI (1971), 1039–1058.

1099. "Anti-Hijacking Moves Accelerate in Wake of Pilots' Work Stoppage." *Aviation Week and Space Technology,* XCVII (July 3, 1972), 7, 29–30.

1100. "As the War against Skyjackers Steps Up." *U.S. News and World Report,* LXIX (December 28, 1970), 15–16.

1101. Bell, Robert, G. "The U.S. Response to Terrorism against International Civil Aviation." *Orbis,* XIX (Winter 1976), 1326–1343.

1102. Boltwood, Charles E., *et al.* "Skyjacking, Airline Security, and Passenger Reactions: Toward a Complex Model for Prediction." *American Psychologist,* XXVII (June 1972), 539–545.

1103. Brower, Charles N. "Aircraft Hijacking and Sabotage: Initiative or Inertia?" *Department of State Bulletin,* LXVIII (June 18, 1973), 872–875.

1104. "Business Aircraft Security Tightened." *Aviation Week and Space Technology,* XCIX (October 8, 1973), 14–15.

1105. "Can the Skyjackers Be Thwarted?" *Newsweek,* LXXX (November 27, 1972), 21–23.

1106. Chauncey, Robert. "Deterrence: Certainty, Severity, and Skyjacking." *Criminology,* XII (February 1975), 467–473.

1107.   Clark, Lorne S. "The Struggle to Cure Hijacking." *International Perspective,* XLVII (January-February 1973), 47–51.

1108.   Coleman, H. J. "British Ponder Skymarshals on Transports." *Aviation Week and Space Technology,* CI (December 2, 1974), 28–29.

1109.   _____. "Hijack Policy Reflects a Conservative View." *Aviation Week and Space Technology,* XCII (April 13, 1970), 43+.

1110.   Cooper, M. R., *et al.* "Factor Analysis of Air Passenger Reactions to Skyjacking and Airport Security Measures as Related to Personal Characteristics and Alternatives to Flying." *Applied Psychology,* LIX (June 1974), 365–368.

1111.   Dailey, John T. "Some Psychological Contributions to Defense against Hijacking." *American Psychology,* XXX (February 1975), 161–165.

1112.   _____, *et al.* "Federal Aviation Administration's Behavioral Research Program for Defense against Hijacking." *Aviation, Space, and Environmental Medicine,* XLVI (April 1975), 423–427.

1113.   Davis, Benjamin O., Jr. "Tougher Tactics in the War against Plane Hijackers: An Interview." *U.S. News and World Report,* LXXIII (July 17, 1972), 26–28.

1114.   "Deterring Aircraft Terrorist Attacks and Compensating Victims." *University of Pennsylvania Law Review,* CXXV (May 1977), 1134–1165.

1115.   Doty, Laurence. "Anti-Hijacking Proposals Proliferate." *Aviation Week and Space Technology,* XCIII (September 21, 1970), 26–27.

1116.   "The Drive against Skyjackers." *U.S. News and World Report,* LXXIII (July 3, 1972), 11–13.

1117.   Evans, Alona E. "A Proposed Method of Control." *Journal of Air Law and Commerce,* XXXVII (1971), 161–182.

1118.   "FAA Studies Ways to End Hijacking." *American Aviation,* XXXII (March 17, 1969), 1–24.

1119.   Fenello, Michael J. "The Technical Prevention of Air Piracy." *International Conciliation,* no. 585 (November 1971), 28–51.

1120.   "The Fruitless War against Crime in the Air." *Life,* LXXIII (December 29, 1972), 81–82.

1121.   Horovitz, J. F. "Arab Terrorism and International Aviation: Deterrence Versus the Political Act." *Chitty's Law Journal,* XXIV (May 1976), 145–154.

1122. "How to Stop Air Piracy." *Newsweek,* LXXVI (September 21, 1970), 28–29.

1123. Hubbard, David G. "Bringing Skyjackers Down to Earth." *Time,* XCVIII (October 4, 1971), 64–65.

1124. "Is There Any Answer to Plane Hijackers?" *U.S. News and World Report,* LXVII (October 20, 1969), 34–35.

1125. Keller, John E. "Law Enforcement in Airport Security." *Law and Order,* XX (November 1972), 46+.

1126. Kraus, Douglas M. "Searching for Hijackers: Constitutionality, Costs, and Alternatives." *University of Chicago Law Review,* XL (Winter 1973), 383–420.

1127. Lissitsyn, Oliver J. "In-Flight Crime and U.S. Legislation." *American Journal of International Law,* LXVII (April 1973), 306–313.

1128. McArthur, W. J., *et al.* "Handling the Hijacker." *Aerospace Medicine,* XLIII (October 1972), 1118–1121.

1129. McNeil, Mark S. "Aerial Hijacking and the Protection of Diplomats." *Harvard International Law Journal,* XIV (1973), 595+.

1130. Marrett, John. "World Alert against Hijacking." *UNESCO Courier,* XXXI (April 1978), 22–23.

1131. Mason. B. J. "Grounding the Skyjacker: Benjamin O. Davis and the Sky Marshal Plan." *Ebony,* XXVIII (November 1972), 48–50+.

1132. Maxwell, B. "What Security?: Some Try Harder, That's All!" *Far Eastern Economic Review,* XCIX (January 20, 1978), 31+.

1133. Minor, W. W. "Skyjacking Crime-Control Models." *Journal of Criminal Law and Criminology,* LXVI (March 1975), 94–105.

1134. "Mogadishu's Aftermath: Lufthansa's Security Measures." *Time,* CX (November 28, 1977, 56.

1135. "New Traps for Skyjackers." *U.S. News and World Report,* LXXIV (January 15, 1973), 15–17.

1136. Nixon, Richard M. "Airplane Hijacking: Statement by the President." *Weekly Compilation of Presidential Documents,* VI (September 14, 1970), 1193–1194.

1137. "On the Aggressive Defense: El Al Security Measures." *Time,* CVIII (July 26, 1976), 40.

1138. "The Perilous War on the Skyjacker." *Life,* LXXIII (August 11, 1972), 26–31.

1139. "Protecting Airports from Terrorists." In: William P. Lineberry, ed. *The Struggle against Terrorism.* Reference Shelf, v. 49, no. 3. New York: H. W. Wilson, 1977. pp. 142–144.

1140. Reighard, H. L. "FAA Goal: Stop In-Flight Crime at the Gate." *Air Line Pilot,* XXXIX (1970), 18–20.

1141. Rein, Bert. "A Government Perspective." *Journal of Air Law and Commerce,* XXXVII (1971), 183–194.

1142. Schultz, Morton J. "How the Airlines Hope to Stop the Hijackers." *Popular Mechanics,* CXXXIII (May 1970), 83–85.

1143. _____ . "Terror in Our Skies: Can We Stop It?" *Popular Mechanics,* CXXXVIII (September 1972), 138–141+.

1144. Shaffer, Helen B. "Control of Skyjacking." *Editorial Research Reports,* I (January 1973), 67–84.

1145. Shepherd, Hugh. "Vermin in the Air: Is Their Summary Destruction in Law Justified?" *Contemporary Review,* CCXVII (November 1970), 236–239.

1146. "The Skyjacker and How to Stop Him." *Saturday Review of Literature,* LV (August 26, 1972), 46–52.

1147. "Skyjacking: What Causes It and a Way to End It." *U.S. News and World Report,* LXVI (February 17, 1969), 68–69.

1148. "Skyjackings—A Growing Menace: Can They Be Stopped?" *U.S. News and World Report,* LXXIII (November 27, 1972), 15–17.

Stewart, John T., jt. author. *See* Volpe, John A.

1149. "Stopping Skyjackers: The Drive to Get a Better U.S. System." *U.S. News and World Report,* LXVII (June 15, 1970), 31–32.

1150. "Stopping the Skyjacker: The War Shifts to the Ground." *U.S. News and World Report,* LXII (January 31, 1972), 33–34.

1151. "Terror Attacks on Air Travel: What Can Be Done?" *U.S. News and World Report,* LXIX (September 21, 1970), 17–19.

1152. Tillinghast, Charles C., Jr. "How to End Skyjacking: Interview with a Top [Airline] Executive." *U.S. News and World Report,* LXIX (October 12, 1970), 48–52.

1153. "Tougher Tactics in the War against Plane Hijackers." *U.S. News and World Report,* LXIII (July 17, 1972), 26–28.

1154. Trotter, R. J. "Psyching the Skyjacker." *Science News,* CI (February 12, 1972), 108–110.

1155. Villanova University. Symposium on Skyjacking. "Problems and Potential Solutions." *Villanova Law Review,* no. 18 (1973), 1–120.

1156. Volpe, John A., and John T. Stewart. "Aircraft Hijacking: Some Domestic Internal Responses." *Kentucky Law Journal,* LIX (Winter 1971), 273–318.

1157. Wahl, Paul. "How Science Will Foil the Skyjackers." *Popular Science,* CXCVII (November 1970), 58–60+.

1158. Watkins, H. D. "Anti-Hijacking Slips: Penalties Stiffen." *Aviation Week and Space Technology,* XCVII (July 17, 1972), 26–28.

1159. "When Armed Guards Ride Your Plane." *U.S. News and World Report,* LXIX (September 28, 1970), 22–23.

1160. Woolsey, J. P. "Prevention of Hijacking Switches from Passive to Active Measures." *Aviation Week and Space Technology,* XCIII (September 21, 1970), 29–30.

1161. Wright, Jim. "A Congressman Speaks: Airline Hijacking—A Time for Cautious Optimism." *Airways,* VI (June 1970), 20–25.

c. Documents, Papers, and Reports

1162. Cooper, Michael R., *et al.* "Passenger Attitudes toward Airline Security and the Threat of Skyjacking." Unpublished paper, 79th Annual Convention of the American Psychological Association, 1971.

1163. Obert, Duane C. *The Air Force and the Aerial Pirate.* Maxwell AFB, Ala.: Air Command and Staff College, Air University, 1973. 49p.

1164. Smith, R. C. "Handling Disturbed Passengers." Unpublished paper, Flight Safety Foundation Air Safety Seminar, 1971.

1165. United States. Congress. House. Committee on Ways and Means. *Administration Anti-Hijacking Proposals: Hearings.* 91st Cog., 2nd sess. Washington, D.C.: U.S. Government Printing Office, 1970. 47p.

1166. _____ . _____ . _____ . _____ . Subcommittee on Transportation and Aeronautics. *Aviation Safety and Aircraft Piracy: Hearings.* 91st Cong., 1st and 2nd sess. Washington, D.C.: U.S. Government Printing Office, 1970. 488p.

1167. _____ . _____ . Senate. Committee on Commerce. Subcommittee on Aviation. *The Administration's Emergency Anti-Hijacking Regulations: Hearings.* 93rd Cong., 1st sess. Washington, D.C.: U.S. Government Printing Office, 1973. 195p.

1168. _____ . Federal Aviation Administration. Civil Aviation Security Service. *Legal Status of Hijackers Summarized.* Washington, D.C., 1979. 6p.

1169. _____ . _____ . _____ . *Semiannual Report to Congress on the Effectiveness of the Civil Aviation Security Service.* Washington, D.C., 1972–.

4. Security Measures: Bombings

a. Books

1170. Chase, L. J., ed. *Bomb Threats, Bombings, and Civil Disturbances: A Guide for Facility Protection.* Corvallis, Oreg.: Continuing Education Publications, 1971. 105p.

1171. Lenz, Robert R. *Explosives and Bomb Disposal Guide.* Springfield, Ill.: C. C. Thomas, 1973. 320p.

1172. Macdonald, Peter G. *Stopping the Clock: Bomb Disposal in the World of Terrorism.* London: Hale, 1977. 159p.

b. Articles

1173. "Aides to the Detection of Explosives." *Security Gazette,* XVII (February 1975), 48–49, 61.

1174. "Can Airports Be Made Safe from Terror Bombings?" *U.S. News and World Report,* LXXX (January 12, 1976), 58.

1175. Cross, Richard F. "Bomb Protection Plans for Banks." *Bankers Magazine,* CLIV (Summer 1971), 83–88.

1176. Dodd, Norman L. "Send for Felix." *Military Review,* LVIII (March 1978), 46–55.

1177. "The Drive to Halt Terror Bombings." *U.S. News and World Report,* LXX (March 15, 1971), 17–19.

1178. Lyons, H. A. "Terrorists' Bombing and the Psychological Sequelae." *Journal of the British Medical Association,* LXVII (January 12, 1974), 15–19.

1179. McGuire, Patrick. "When Bombing Threatens." *Conference Board Record,* VIII (September 1971), 57–63.

1180. "Protection against Terrorist Bombers." *Assets Protection,* I (1976), 28–33.

1181. Ronayne, J. A. "Package Bombs and Their Investigation." *Indiana Police Journal,* (April 1961), 54+.

A classic.

1182. Styles, S. G. "Defeating the Terrorist Bomber." *International Defense Review,* X (February 1977), 121–122.

1183. "Who Are the Bomb Throwers?" *Society*, XI (September 1974), 7–8.

5. Security Measures: Hostage Personnel and Business

a. Books

1184. Alexander, Yonah, and Robert A. Kilmarx, eds. *Political Terrorism and Business: The Threat and the Response.* New York: Praeger, 1979.

1185. Bloomfield, L. M., and G. F. Fitzgerald. *Crimes against Internationally Protected Persons: Prevention and Punishment.* New York: Praeger, 1975. 290p.

1186. Clutterbuck, Richard L. *Kidnap and Ransom: The Response.* London and Boston: Faber & Faber, 1978. 192p.

1187. Cunningham, W. C. *Prevention of Terrorism: Security Guidelines for Business and Other Organizations.* McLean, Va.: Hallcrest Press, 1978. 108p.

1188. Fisher, A. James. *Security for Business and Industry.* Englewood Cliffs, N.J.: Prentice-Hall, 1979. 374p.

Fitzgerald, G. F., jt. author. *See* Bloomfield, L. M.

1189. Fuqua, Paul, and Jerry Wilson. *Terrorism: The Executive's Guide to Survival.* Houston: Gulf Publishing, 1978. 166p.

Kilmarx, Robert A., jt. editor. *See* Alexander, Yonah.

1190. Maher, George F. *Hostage: A Police Approach to a Contemporary Crisis.* Springfield, Ill.: C. C. Thomas, 1977. 90p.

1191. Reber, John. *Executive Protection Manual.* Schiller Park, Ill.: Motorola Teleprograms, 1978. 289p.

Wilson, Jerry, jt. author. *See* Fuqua, Paul.

b. Articles

1192. Adkins, E. H., Jr. "Protection of American Industrial Dignitaries and Facilities Overseas." *Security Management*, XVIII (July 1974, 14–16, 55.

1193. Beall, M. D. "Hostage Negotiations." *Military Police Law Enforcement Journal*, III (Fall 1976), 30–37.

1194. Bozakis, Christos L. "Terrorism and the Internationally Protected Person in the Light of the ILC's Draft Articles." *International and Comparative Law Quarterly*, XXII (1974), 32+.

1195.   Connelly, Sherryl. "Staying Alive as a Hostage." *Cincinnati Inquirer Magazine*, (April 29, 1979), 12–19.

1196.   Cooper, H. H. A. "The Terrorist and the Victim." *Victimology*, I (Summer 1976), 229–239.

1197.   Culley, J. A. "Hostage Negotiations." *FBI Law Enforcement Bulletin*, XLIII (October 1974), 10–14.

1198.   Davis, A. S. "Terrorism as a Security Management Problem." *Security Management*, XX (March 1976), 10–12.

1199.   DeBecker, George. "Protecting VIP's." *Counterforce*, I (March 1977), 11–14.

1200.   "Executive Protection." *Security Register*, I (1975), 15–19.

1201.   Fawcett, J. E. S. "Kidnappings vs. Government Protection." *World Today*, XXVI (September 1970), 359–362.

1202.   Fitzpatrick, T. K. "Movement Security." *Assets Protection*, III (Summer 1978), 16–24.

1203.   Gelb, Barbara. "A Cool-Headed Cop Who Saves Hostages." *New York Times Magazine* (April 17, 1977), 30–33, 39–91.

1204.   Grodsky, M. "The Protection of Dignitaries." *International Police Academy Review*, VI (October 1972), 1–6.

1205.   Hamer, John. "Protection of Diplomats." *Editorial Research Reports*, II (1973), 759+.

1206.   Hassel, Conrad V. "The Hostage Situation." *Police Chief*, XLII (September 1975), 55–58.

1207.   Hernon, Frederick E. "Executive Terrorism: Guidelines for Avoiding Kidnapping for Ransom." *Magazine of Banking Administration*, LIII (January 1977), 18–21.

1208.   Horobin, Anthony. "Hostage-Taking: Coping with a Crisis." *Police Review*, LXXXVII (September 29, 1978), 1438–1440.

1209.   Hoyt, Wade A. "Driving in the Age of Fear: The Scotti School of Defensive Driving." *New York Magazine*, XI (May 1, 1978), 45–46.

1210.   "Israel Refining Hostage Rescue Tactics." *Aviation Week and Space Technology*, CV (September 27, 1976), 17.

1211.   James, T. "Rescuing Hostages: To Deal or Not to Deal." *Time*, C (September 18, 1972), 28–29.

1212. Johnson, T. A. "Role for the Behavioral Scientist in Hostage-Negotiation Incidents." *Journal of Forensic Sciences,* XXIII (October 1978), 797–803.

1213. Lillich, Richard B. "State Responsibility for Injuries to Aliens Occasioned by Terrorists Activities." *American University Law Review,* XXVI (Winter 1977), 217–313.

1214. McClure. "Hostage Survival." *Conflict,* I (1978), 21–48.

1215. _____ . _____ . In: Marius H. Livingston, ed. *International Terrorism in the Contemporary World.* Westport, Conn.: Greenwood Press, 1978. pp. 276–281.

1216. McGuire, E. Patrick. "The Terrorist and the Corporation." *Across the Board,* XIV (May 1977), 11–19.

1217. Maher, George F. "Organizing a Team for Hostage Negotiations." *Police Chief,* XLIII (June 1976), 61–62.

1218. Mahoney, H. T. "After a Terrorist Attack: Business as Usual." *Security Management,* XIX (March 1975), 16–19.

1219. Mayer, A. J., *et al.* "Businessmen and Terrorism." *Newsweek,* XC (November 14, 1977), 82–84+.

1220. Mickolus, Edward. "Negotiating for Hostages: A Policy Dilemma." *Orbis,* XIX (Winter 1976), 1309–1326.

1221. Miller, Abraham H. "Hostage Negotiation and the Concept of Transference." In: Yonah Alexander, David Carlton, and Paul Wilkinson, eds. *Terrorism: Theory and Practice.* Boulder, Colo.: Westview Press, 1979. Chpt. 1.

1222. _____ . "Negotiations for Hostages: Implications of the Police Experience." *Terrorism,* I (1978), 125–146.

1223. Miller, Judith. 'Bargain with Terrorists?" *New York Times Magazine,* (July 18 and August 22, 1976), 7, 38–42, 77–78.

1224. O'Connor, F. X. "What to Do If You're Kidnapped: Leave Your Fingerprints Everywhere." *Saturday Evening Post,* CCXLVIII (May 1976), 6–9.

1225. "Patient Sieges: Dealing with Hostage-Takers." *Assets Protection,* I (1976), 21–27.

1226. Rayne, F. "Executive Protection and Terrorism." *Top Security,* I (October 1975), 225–229.

1227. Reber, J. R. "Hostage Survival." *Security Management,* XXXII (August 1978), 46–50.

1228.   Roquet, Claude, and Allen Rowe. "Task Force on Kidnapping." *External Affairs,* XXIII (1971), 6–11.

Rowe, Allen, jt. author. *See* Roquet, Claude.

1229.   Salewski, Wolfgang. "Conduct and Negotiations in Hostage Situations." In: Marjorie Kravitz, ed. *International Summaries: A Collection of Selected Translations in Law Enforcement and Criminal Justice,* v. 3. Rockville, Md.: National Criminal Justice Reference Service, Law Enforcement Assistance Administration, Department of Justice, 1979. pp. 99–104.

1230.   Scotti, T. "Countermeasures: Protective Driving." *Counterforce,* I (March 1977), 17–18.

1231.   Shaw, Paul. "Executive Protection." *Security Register,* I (February 1974), 15–19.

1232.   _____ . "Terrorism and Executive Protection." *Assets Protection,* I (1976), 8–13.

1233.   Singer, L. W. "A New Way to Face Terrorists: A Crisis Management System." *Security Management,* XXI (September 1977), 6–9, 11–14.

1234.   Stencel, Sandra. "How to Protect Yourself from Terrorism." *Skeptic,* no. 11 (January-February 1976), 37–42.

1235.   Stratton, J. G. "The Terrorist Act of Hostage-Taking: Considerations for Law Enforcement." *Journal of Police Science and Administration,* VI (June 1978), 123–134.

1236.   Train, John. "Executive Security." *Forbes,* CXXIII (June 25, 1979), 118–119.

1237.   Vandiver, J. V. "Extortion Investigation." *Assets Protection,* I (Summer 1975), 20–28.

1238.   Wackenhut, G. R. "Business Is the Target of Bombings and Bomb Hoaxes." *Office,* LXXIV (September 1971), 14–16+.

1239.   "Wages—and Profits—of Fear: Executive Protection." *Time,* CXII (July 10, 1978), 54–55+.

c. Documents, Papers, and Reports

1240.   Book, Don. "Hostage Defense Measures: A Training Program." Unpublished M.A. thesis, Sam Houston State University, 1977.

1241.   Burns International Investigation Bureau. *Executive Protection Handbook.* Miami, Fla., 1974. 26p.

1242. Connelly, Ralph W. "Third Party Involvement in International Terrorist Extortion." Unpublished M.A. thesis, U.S. Naval Postgraduate School, 1976.

1243. "Countermeasures to Combat Terrorism at Major Events." Unpublished paper, Department of State Senior Seminar in Foreign Policy, 1975.

1244. Jenkins, Brian. *Hostage Survival: Some Preliminary Observations.* RAND Paper P-5627. Santa Monica, Calif.: RAND Corp., 1976. 13p.

1245. _____. *Hostages and Their Captors: Friends and Lovers.* RAND Paper P-5519. Santa Monica, Calif.: RAND Corp., 1975. 3p.

1246. _____. *Should Corporations Be Prevented from Paying Ransom?* RAND paper P-5291. Santa Monica, Calif.: RAND Corp., 1974. 13p.

1247. _____. *Terrorists Seize Hostages in Arcadia—Laconia Commandos on Alert: A Scenario for Simulation in Negotiating with Terrorists Holding Hostages.* RAND Paper P-6339. Santa Monica, Calif.: RAND Corp., 1979. 9p.

1248. Mann, Clarence J. "International Terrorism and the Overseas Business Community." Unpublished paper, 15th Annual Convention of the International Studies Association, 1974.

1249. Needham, James P. *Standing Operating Procedures: Hostage Situations.* Ft. Leavenworth, Kans.: U.S. Army Command and Staff College, 1977. 43p.

1250. Organization of American States. Inter-American Juridical Committee. *Convention to Prevent and Punish the Acts of Terrorism Taking the Form of Crimes against Persons and Related Extortion That are of International Significance.* Washington, D.C., 1971. 18p.

1251. *Protecting Industrial-Business Facilities and Personnel from Terrorist Activities.* Rye, N.Y.: Reymont Associates, 1977. 18p.

1252. United States. Congress. House. Committee on Foreign Affairs. Subcommittee on Inter-American Affairs. *Safety of U.S. Diplomats: Hearings.* 91st Cong., 2nd sess. Washington, D.C.: U.S. Government Printing Office, 1971. 10p.

1253. _____. _____. Senate. Committee on the Judiciary. Subcommittee on Criminal Laws and Procedure. *Terrorist and His Victim: Hearings.* 95th Cong., 1st sess. Washington, D.C.: U.S. Government Printing Office, 1977. 33p.

1254. _____ . _____ . _____ . _____ . Subcommittee to Investigate the Administration of the Internal Security Act and Other Internal Security Laws. *Terroristic Activity, Part V: Hostage Defense—Hearings.* 94th Cong., 1st sess. Washington, D.C.: U.S. Government Printing Office, 1975. 57p.

1255. _____ . Department of Justice. Law Enforcement Assistance Administration. National Private Advisory Council. *Prevention of Terroristic Crimes: Security Guidelines for Business, Industry, and Other Organizations.* Washington, D.C.: U.S. Government Printing Office, 1976. 33p.

1256. _____ . Department of State. Foreign Service Institute. *Terrorism: Avoidance and Survival.* Washington, D.C.: U.S. Government Printing Office, 1979. 22p.

1257. _____ . General Services Administration. *Terrorism and the V.I.P.* Washington, D.C. [1977?]. 48p.

6. Security Measures: Nuclear

a. Books

Althoff, Philip, jt. editor. *See* Leachman, Robert A.

1258. Atlantic Council of the United States. Nuclear Fuels Policy Working Group. *Nuclear Power and Nuclear Weapons Proliferation: Report.* 2 vols. Boulder, Colo.: Westview Press, 1978.

1259. De Volpi, Alexander. *Proliferation, Plutonium, and Policy: Institutional and Technological Impediments to Nuclear Weapons Propagation.* New York: Pergamon Press, 1979. 361p.

1260. Greenwood, Ted, *et al. Nuclear Proliferation: Motivations, Capabilities, and Strategies for Control.* New York: McGraw-Hill, 1977. 210p.

1261. Inglis, David R. *Nuclear Energy: Its Physics and Its Social Challenge.* Reading, Mass.: Addison-Wesley, 1973. 395p.

1262. Larus, Joel. *Nuclear Weapons Safety and the Common Defense.* Columbus: Ohio State University Press, 1967. 171p.

1263. Leachman, Robert A., and Philip Althoff, eds. *Preventing Nuclear Theft: Guidelines for Industry and Government.* New York: Praeger, 1972. 377p.

1264. Lefever, Ernest W. *Nuclear Arms in the Third World: U.S. Policy Dilemma.* Washington, D.C.: Brookings Institution, 1979. 154p.

1265.   McPhee, John. *Curve of Binding Energy.* New York: Farrar, 1973. 232p.

1266.   Sanders, Benjamin. *Safeguards against Nuclear Proliferation.* Cambridge, Mass.: MIT Press, 1975. 114p.

Taylor, Theodore B., jt. author. *See* Willrich, Mason.

1267.   Willrich, Mason. *Global Politics of Nuclear Energy.* New York: Praeger, 1971. 204p.

1268.   _____ , ed. *Civil Nuclear Power and International Security.* New York: Praeger, 1971. 124p.

1269.   _____ . *International Safeguards and the Nuclear Industry.* Baltimore, Md.: Johns Hopkins Press, 1973. 302p.

1270.   _____ , and Theodore B. Taylor, *Nuclear Theft: Risks and Safeguards.* New York: Ballinger, 1974. 252p.

b. Articles

1271.   Buchanan, J. R., ed. "Safeguards against the Theft or Diversion of Nuclear Materials." *Nuclear Safety,* XV (September-October 1974), 513–619.

1272.   Cherico, P. "Security Requirements and Standards for Nuclear Power Plants." *Security Management,* XVIII (January 1975), 22–24.

1273.   Doub, William O., and Joseph M. Duker. "Making Nuclear Energy Safe and Secure." *Foreign Affairs,* LIII (February 1975), 756–772.

Duker, Joseph M., jt. author. *See* Doub, William O.

1274.   Frank, Forrest R. "An International Convention against Nuclear Theft." *Bulletin of the Atomic Scientists,* XXXI (December 1975), 51.

1275.   Fromm, Joseph. "100 Nations Grapple with a Nightmare: Uncontrolled A-Arms." *U.S. News and World Report,* LXXVIII (May 12, 1975), 67–68.

1276.   Gillette, Robert. "GAO Calls Security Lax at Nuclear Plants." *Science,* CXCIV (December 6, 1974), 906–907.

1277.   _____ . "Nuclear Safeguards: Holes in the Fence." *Science,* CXCIII (December 14, 1973), 1112–1114.

1278.   Kelly, O. "If Terrorists Go after U.S. Nuclear Bombs . . ." *U.S. News and World Report,* LXXXVI (March 12, 1979), 43–45.

1279. Szasz, Paul C. "International Atomic Energy Agency Safeguards." In: Mason Willrich, ed. *International Safeguards and the Nuclear Industry.* Baltimore, Md.: Johns Hopkins Press, 1973. pp. 73–141.

1280. Taylor, Theodore B. "International Safeguards of Non-Military Nuclear Technology, Part II: The Need for Nuclear Safeguards." *I.R.&T. Nuclear Journal,* I (February 1969), 1–15.

1281. "Treaty on the Non-Proliferation of Nuclear Weapons." *International Atomic Energy Agency Bulletin,* II (April 1975), 2–61.

c. Documents, Papers, and Reports

1282. Atomic Industries Forum. Public Affairs and Information Program. *Protecting Nuclear Power Plants.* Washington, D.C., 1978. 15p.

1283. California. Office of Emergency Services. *Nuclear Blackmail or Nuclear Threat: Emergency Response Plan.* Sacramento, Calif.: 1976. 40p.

1284. Corwin, Arthur J. *A Survey of Terrorist Capabilities, the Threat to Nuclear Resources, and Some Recommended Improvements for Defensive Security Posture.* Report AFIT-CI-77-66. Wright Patterson AFB, Ohio: U.S. Air Force Institute of Technology, 1977. 177p.

1285. International Atomic Energy Agency. "Safeguards [and] the Structure and Content of Agreements between the Agency and States Required in Connection with the Treaty on the Non-Proliferation of Nuclear Weapons." In: U.S. Congress. Senate. Committee on Government Operations. *Peaceful Nuclear Exports and Weapons Proliferation: Hearings.* 94th Cong., 1st sess. Washington, D.C.: U.S. Government Printing Office, 1975. pp. 732–788.

1286. Jenkins, Brian. *Terrorism and the Nuclear-Safeguards Issue.* RAND Paper P-5611. Santa Monica, Calif.: RAND Corp., 1976. 7p.

1287. United States. Congress. House. Committee on Foreign Affairs. Subcommittees on International Organizations and Movements and the Near East and South Asia. *U.S. Foreign Policy and the Export of Nuclear Technology to the Middle East: Hearings.* 93rd Cong., 2nd sess. Washington, D.C.: U.S. Government Printing Office, 1974. 333p.

1288. _____. _____. Office of Technology Assessment. *Nuclear Proliferation and Safeguards.* New York: Praeger, 1977. 270p.

1289. _____. Nuclear Regulatory Commission. "Rules for Physical Protection of Nuclear Plants and Materials." In: U.S. Congress. Senate. Committee on Government Operations. *Peaceful Nuclear Exports and Weapons Proliferation: Hearings.* 94th Cong., 1st sess. Washington, D.C.: U.S. Government Printing Office, 1975. pp. 356–361.

C. Terrorism and the News Media

1. Books

1290.   Lasswell, Harold D. *World Revolutionary Propaganda.* Westport, Conn.: Greenwood Press, 1973. 200p.

1291.   Snider, Marie, ed. *The Media and Terrorism: The Psychological Impact.* Newton, Kans.: Prairie View Press, 1978. 51p.

1292.   Winchester, Simon. *Northern Ireland in Crisis: Reporting the Ulster Troubles.* New York: Holmes & Meier, 1975. 256p.

2. Articles

1293.   Alexander, Yonah. "Communications Aspects of International Terrorism." *International Problems,* XVI (Spring 1977), 55–60.

1294.   _____. "Terrorism, the Media, and the Police." *Journal of International Studies,* VII (Spring-Summer 1978), 101–114.

1295.   _____. _____. *Police Studies,* I (June 1978), 45–52.

1296.   Bell, J. Bowyer. "Chroniclers of Violence in Northern Ireland: A Tragedy in Endless Acts." *Review of Politics,* XXXVIII (October 1976), 10–33.

1297.   _____. "'Chroniclers of Violence in Northern Ireland: The Analysis of Tragedy." *Review of Politics,* XXXVI (October 1974), 521–543.

1298.   _____. "Chroniclers of Violence in Northern Ireland: The First Wave Interpreted." *Review of Politics,* XXXIV (April 1972), 147–157.

1299.   _____. "Terrorist Scripts and Live-Action Spectaculars." *Columbia Journalism Review,* XVII (May 1978), 47–50.

1300.   Cooper, H. H. A. "Terrorism and the Media." *Chitty's Law Journal,* XXXIV (September 1976), 226–232.

1301.   Halloran, J. D. "Mass Communication: Symptom or Cause of Violence?" *International Social Science Journal,* XXX (Fall 1978), 816–833.

1302.   Heron, Paddy. "Television's Role in Reporting Ulster Violence." *Harrangue, a Political and Social Review* (Belfast), I (Summer 1974), 2+.

1303.   Hickey, Neil. "Terrorism and Television." *TV Guide,* XXIV (July 31–August 7, 1976), 2–6, 10–13.

1304.   Mosse, Hilde L. "The Media and Terrorism." In: Marius H. Livingston, ed. *International Terrorism in the Contemporary World.* Westport, Conn.: Greenwood Press, 1978. pp. 282–286.

1305.   Redlick, Amy S. "The Transnational Flow of Information as a Cause of Terrorism." In: Yonah Alexander, David Carlton, and Paul Wilkinson, eds. *Terrorism: Theory and Practice.* Boulder, Colo.: Westview Press, 1979. Chpt. 3.

3. Documents, Papers, and Reports

1306.   Field Enterprises, Inc. *The Media and Terrorism: A Seminar Sponsored by the Chicago Sun-Times and Chicago Daily News.* Chicago, 1977. 38p.

1307.   Mickolus, Edward. *Assessing the Degrees of Error in Public Reporting of Transnational Terrorism.* Washington, D.C.: Office of Political Research, Central Intelligence Agency, 1976.

VII/International Law and Terrorism

Introduction

The references in this section revolve around the international legal community's effort to codify laws, clear up jurisdictions, and put together conventions which would bind the world community together in law against the terrorist. Unfortunately, this approach has not in general met with success, first, because there is widespread difference as to what constitutes "terrorism" and, second, because many governments remain determined to provide sanctuary or to deal with terroristic activity on an *ad hoc* basis.

The materials in subsection A treat in a general manner the subject of international law and jurisdiction as it relates to terrorism. Those in subsection B focus on the work of international organizations, especially the United Nations, and provide citations to many international conventions, particularly those relating to protected (diplomatic) personnel. Subsection C gives the user a large body of literature on the most successful application of international agreements against terrorism, those concerning civil aviation.

Additional references relative to this section may be found in sections II:B and VI above.

A. International Law, Criminal Jurisdiction, and Terrorism

1. Books

1308. Bailey, Sydney D. *Prohibitions and Restraints in War.* London and New York: Oxford University Press, 1972. 194p.

1309. Bassiouni, M. Cherif. *International Extradition and World Public Order.* Dobbs Ferry, N.Y.: Oceana, 1974. 630p.

1310. _____ , and Ved P. Nanda, eds. *A Treatise on International Criminal Law.* Springfield, Ill.: C. C. Thomas, 1973. 751p.

1311. Bond, James E. *The Rules of Riot: Internal Conflict and the Law of War.* Princeton, N.J.: Princeton University Press, 1974. 280p.

1312. Crelinsten, Ronald D. *Terrorism and Criminal Justice: An International Perspective, Derived from the Conference on "The Impact of Terrorism and Skyjacking an Operations of Criminal Justice Systems," Rochester, Michigan, Febraury 1976.* Boston: Lexington-Heath Books, 1978. 131p.

1313. Evans, Alona E., and John F. Murphy, eds. *Legal Aspects of International Terrorism.* Boston: Published for the American Society of International Law by D. C. Heath, 1978. 690p.

1314. Meron, Theodor. *Some Legal Aspects of Arab Terrorists' Claim to Privileged Combatancy.* New York: Sabra Books, 1978. 38p.

Murphy, John F., jt. editor. *See* Evans, Alona E.

Nanda, Ved P., jt. editor. *See* Bassiouni, M. Cherif.

1315. Shearer, I. A. *Extradition in International Law.* Dobbs Ferry, N.Y.: Oceana, 1971. 283p.

2. Articles

1316. Abu-Lughad, Ibrahim. "Unconventional Violence and International Law." *American Journal of International Law,* LXVII (November 1973), 100–104.

1317. American Bar Association. Section on International Law. "Council Resolution on International Terrorism." *Vista,* VIII (April 1973), 53–56.

1318. Bassiouni, M. Cherif. "Methodological Options for International Legal Control of Terrorism." In: M. Cherif Bassiouni, ed. *International Terrorism and Political Crimes: Proceedings of the Third Conference on Terrorism and Political Crimes, Syracuse, Sicily, 1973.* Springfield, Ill.: C. C. Thomas, 1974. pp. 485–492.

1319. Blischenko, Igor P. "Combatting Terrorism by International Law." *Soviet Law and Government,* XIV (Winter 1975–1976), 81–96.

1320. Bond, James E. "Application of the Law of War to Internal Conflict." *Georgia Journal of International and Comparative Law,* III (1973), 345–384.

1321. Cantrell, Charles L. "Political Offense Exemption in International Extradition: A Comparison of the United States, Great Britain, and the Republic of Ireland." *Marquette Law Review,* LX (1977), 777–824.

1322. Cochard, Renata. "Terrorism and Extradition in Belgian Law." In: Marjorie Kravitz, ed. *International Summaries: A Collection of Selected Translations in Law Enforcement and Criminal Justice,* v. 3. Rockville, Md.: National Criminal Justice Reference Service, Law Enforcement Assistance Administration, Department of Justice, 1979. pp. 139–146.

1323. DeSchutter, Bart. "Problems of Jurisdiction in the International Control and Repression of Terrorism." In: M. Cherif Bassiouni, ed. *International Terrorism and Political Crimes: Proceedings of the Third Conference on Terrorism and Political Crimes, Syracuse, Sicily, 1973.* Springfield, Ill.: C. C. Thomas, 1974. pp. 377–390.

1324. Evans, Alona E. "Terrorism and Political Crimes in International Law." *American Society of International Law Proceedings,* XII (1973), 87–110.

1325. "Extraterritorial Jurisdiction and Jurisdiction Following Forcible Abduction: A New Israeli Precedent in International Law." *Michigan Law Review,* LXXII (April 1974), 1087–1113.

1326. Franck, Thomas M. "International Legal Action concerning Terrorism." *Terrorism,* I (1978), 187–198.

1327. Friedlander, Robert A. "Coping with Terrorism: What Is to Be Done?" *Ohio Northern University Law Review,* V (Spring 1978), 432–443.

1328. _____ . "Terrorism and International Law: What Is Being Done?" *Rutgers-Camden Law Journal,* VIII (Spring 1977), 383–392.

1329. _____ . "Terrorism: What's behind Our Passive Acceptance of Transnational Mugging?" *Barrister,* II (Summer 1975), 10–71.

1330. Ginossar, S. "Outlawing Terrorism." *Israel Law Review,* XIII (Spring 1979), 150–159.

1331. Gross, Leo. "International Terrorism and International Criminal Jurisdiction." *American Journal of International Law,* LXVII (July 1973), 508–511.

1332. Johnson, R. J. "Conflict Avoidance through Acceptable Decisions." *Journal of Human Relations,* XXVII (Winter 1974), 71+.

1333. Killrie, Nicholas. "Reconciling the Irreconcilable: The Quest for International Agreement over Political Crime and Terrorism." In: Arthur S. Banks, ed. *Year Book of World Affairs, 1978.* Boulder, Colo.: Westview Press, 1978. pp. 208–236.

1334. Lador-Lederer, J. J. "A Legal Approach to International Terrorism." *Israel Law Review,* IX (April 1974), 194–220.

1335. "Law and the Suppression of Terrorism." In: National Criminal Justice Reference Service. *International Summaries: A Collection of Selected Translations in Law Enforcement and Criminal Justice,* v. 1. Rockville, Md.: National Criminal Justice Reference Service, Law Enforcement Assistance Administration, Department of Justice, 1978. pp. 23–38.

1336. Lawrence, William. "The Status under International Law of Recent Guerrilla Movements in Latin America." *International Lawyer,* VII (1973), 409+.

1337. Legros, Pierre. "The Idea of Terrorism in Comparative Law." In: Marjorie Kravitz, ed. *International Summaries: A Collection of Selected Translations in Law Enforcement and Criminal Justice,* v. 3. Rockville, Md.: National Criminal Justice Reference Service, Law Enforcement Assistance Administration, Department of Justice, 1979. pp. 115–122.

Lowell, Cym H., jt. author. *See* Pye, A. Kenneth.

1338. Malawer, Stuart S. "United States Foreign Policy and International Law: The Jordanian Civil War and Air Piracy." *International Problems,* X (1971), 31–40.

1339. Mallison, William T., Jr., and Sally V. "'The Concept of Public Purpose Terror in International Law." *Journal of Palestine Studies,* IV (Winter 1975), 36–51.

1340. _____ . "The Concept of Public Purpose Terror in International Law: Doctrines of the Santions to Reduce the Destruction of Human and Material Values." *Howard Law Journal,* XVIII (1973), 12–28.

1341. Marchant, Daniel. "Abductions Effected outside National Territory." *Bulletin of the International Commission of Jurists,* VII (Winter 1966), 243–268.

1342. Mattson, M. K. "The Taking and Killing of Hostages: Coercion and Reprisal in International Law." *Notre Dame Lawyer,* LIV (October 1978), 131–148.

1343.   Milte, Kerry L. "Extradition and the Terrorist." *Australian and New Zealand Journal of Criminology,* XI (June 1978), 89–94.

1344.   Minor, W. W. "Political Crime, Political Justice, and Political Prisoners." *Criminology,* XII (February 1975), 385–398.

1345.   Moore, John N. "Towards Legal Restraints on International Terrorism." *American Society of International Law Proceedings,* XII (1973), 88–94.

1346.   Murphy, John F. "International Legal Controls of International Terrorism: Performance and Prospects." *Illinois Bar Journal,* LXIII (April 1975), 444+.

1347.   _____ . "Professor [Leo] Gross's Comments on International Terrorism and International Criminal Jurisdiction." *American Journal of International Law,* LXVIII (April 1974), 306+.

1348.   Palmer, B. "Codification of Terrorism as an International Crime." In: M. Cherif Bassiouni, ed. *International Terrorism and Political Crimes: Proceedings of the Third Conference on Terrorism and Political Crimes, Syracuse, Sicily, 1973.* Springfield, Ill.: C. C. Thomas, 1974. pp. 507–518.

1349.   Paust, Jordan J. "A Survey of Possible Legal Responses to International Terrorism: Prevention, Punishment and Cooperative Action." *Georgia Journal of International and Comparative Law,* V (1975), 431–469.

1350.   _____ . "Terrorism and the International Law of War." *Military Law Review,* LXIV (1974), 1–36.

1351.   Pye, A. Kenneth, and Cym H. Lowell. "The Criminal Process during Civil Disorder." *Duke Law Journal,* III (August 1975), 581–690.

1352.   Silver, Isidore. "Toward a Theory of the Political Defense." *Catholic Lawyer,* XVIII (1972), 206–236.

1353.   Sliwowski, George. "Legal Aspects of Terrorism." In: David Carlton and Carlo Schaerf, eds. *International Terrorism and World Security.* New York: Wiley, 1975. pp. 69–77.

1354.   Stevenson, John R. "International Law and the Export of Terrorism." *Department of State Bulletin,* LXVII (December 4, 1972), 645–652.

1355.   _____ . _____ . *The Record of the Association of the Bar of the City of New York,* XXVII (December 1972), 716–729.

1356.   Sundberg, J. W. F. "The Case for an International Criminal Court." *Journal of Air Law and Commerce,* XXXVII (1971), 211–227.

1357. Taulbee, J. L. "Retaliation and Irregular Warfare in Contemporary International Law." *International Lawyer,* VII (January 1973), 195–204.

1358. "Terrorism and Political Crimes in International Law." *American Journal of International Law,* LXVII (November 1973), 87–111.

1359. Tharp, Paul A., Jr. "The Laws of War as a Potential Legal Regime for the Control of Terrorist Activities." *Journal of International Affairs,* VII (Sring-Summer 1978), 91–100.

1360. Thornton, Thomas P. "Terrorism and the Death Penalty." *America,* CXXXV (December 11, 1976), 410–412.

1361. Tiewul, S. A. "Terrorism: A Step towards International Control." *Howard International Law Journal,* XIV (Summer 1973), 585–595.

1362. Toman, J. "Terrorism and the Regulation of Armed Conflict." In: M. Cherif Bassiouni, ed. *International Terrorism and Political Crimes: Proceedings of the Third Conference on Terrorism and Political Crimes, Syracuse, Sicily, 1973.* Springfield, Ill.: C. C. Thomas, 1974. pp. 133–154.

1363. United States. Department of State. "The Role of International Law in Combatting Terrorism." *Current Foreign Policy,* no. 8689 (January 1973), 1–9.

1364. Weis, Peter. "Asylum and Terrorism." *International Commission of Jurists Review,* XVIII (December 1977), 37–43.

1365. Wortley, B. A. "Political Crime in English Law and International Law." In: Humphrey Waldock and R. Y. Jennings, eds. *British Yearbook of International Law, 1971.* London and New York: Oxford University Press, 1973. pp. 219–253.

1366. Zlataric, B. "History of International Terrorism and Its Legal Control." In: M. Cherif Bassiouni, ed. *International Terrorism and Political Crimes: Proceedings of the Third Conference on Terrorism and Political Crimes, Syracuse, Sicily, 1973.* Springfield, Ill.: C. C. Thomas, 1974. pp. 474–484.

3. Documents, Papers, and Reports

1367. Crelingsten, Ronald D., ed. *Impact of Terrorism and Skyjacking on the Operations of the Criminal Justice System.* Montreal: International Center for Comparative Criminology, University of Montreal, 1976. 260p.

1368. Lockwood, Bert B., Jr. "The Utility of International Law in Dealing with International Terrorism." Unpublished paper, Annual Convention of the International Studies Association, 1975.

1369. Rubin, Alfred P. "International Terrorism and International Law." Unpublished paper, Ralph Bunch Institute Conference on International Terrorism, 1976.

B. International Organizations, Conventions, and Terrorism

1. Books

1370. Howley, Dennis C. *The U.N. and the Palestinians.* New York: Exposition Press, 1975. 168p.

1371. Kelly, George A., and Linda B. Miller. *Internal War and International Systems: Perspectives on Methods.* Cambridge: Center for International Affairs, Harvard University, 1969. 40p.

Miller, Linda B., jt. author. *See* Kelly, George A.

1372. Thant, U. *View from the U.N.* Garden City, N.Y.: Doubleday, 1978. 508p.

2. Articles

1373. Bennett, W. Tapley. "U.S. Gives Views in Security Council Debate on Israeli Rescue of Hijacking Victims at Entebbe: Statement." *Department of State Bulletin,* LXXV (August 2, 1976), 181–186.

1374. _____. "U.S. Initiatives in the United Nations to Combat International Terrorism." *International Lawyer,* VII (1973), 753–759.

1375. _____. "U.S. Votes against U.N. General Assembly Resolution Calling for a Study of Terrorism." *Department of State Bulletin,* LXVIII (January 22, 1973), 81–94.

1376. Brach, Richard S. "The Inter-American Convention on the Kidnapping of Diplomats." *Columbia Journal of Transnational Law,* X (1971), 392–412.

1377. Buckley, William F., Jr. "Closing Day—Terrorism." In: *U.N. Journal: A Delegate's Odyssey.* New York: Putnam, 1974. pp. 247–252.

Carbonneau, Thomas, E., jt. author. *See* Lillich, Richard B.

1378. Corves, Erich. "International Cooperation in the Field of International Political Terrorism." *Terrorism,* I (1978), 199–211.

1379. Council of Europe. "European Convention on the Suppression of Terrorism." *International Legal Materials,* XV (November 1976), 1272–1276.

1380. Finger, S. M. "International Terrorism and the United Nations." In: Yonah Alexander, ed. *International Terrorism: National, Regional, and Global Perspectives.* New York: Praeger, 1976. pp. 323–348.

1381. Franck, Thomas M., and Bert B. Lockwood, Jr. "Preliminary Thoughts toward an International Convention on Terrorism." *American Journal of International Law,* LXVIII (January 1974), 69–90.

1382. Hoveyda, Fereydown. "The Problem of International Terrorism at the United Nations." *Terrorism,* I (1978), 71–84.

1383. Jack, H. A. "Hostages, Hijacking, and the Security Council: Reaction to the Entebbe Raid." *America,* CXXXV (September 4, 1976), 94–97.

1384. _____ . "Terrorism: Another U.N. Failure." *America,* CXXIX (October 20, 1973), 282–286.

1385. Jova, J. J. "O.A.S. Asked to Consider the Problem of Kidnapping." *Department of State Bulletin,* LXII (May 25, 1970), 662.

1386. Korey, William. "Moral Bankruptcy at the U.N." *Midstream,* XIX (February 1973), 34–42.

1387. Lagoni, Rainer. "The United Nations and International Terrorism." In: Marjorie Kravitz, ed. *International Summaries: A Collection of Selected Translations in Law Enforcement and Criminal Justice,* v. 3. Rockville, Md.: National Criminal Justice Reference Service, Law Enforcement Assistance Administration, Department of Justice, 1979. pp. 157–164.

1388. Lahey, K. A. "Control of Terrorism through a Broader Interpretation of Article 3 of the Four Geneva Conventions of 1949." In: M. Cherif Bassiouni, ed. *International Terrorism and Political Crimes: Proceedings of the Third Conference on Terrorism and Political Crimes, Syracuse, Sicily, 1973.* Springfield, Ill.: C. C. Thomas, 1974. pp. 191–200.

1389. Leigh, Monroe. "The United Nations: How Should It Deal with Terrorism?" *Department of State Newsletter,* CLXXXVI (January 1977), 28–29.

1390. _____ . "U.S. Calls for Responsible Measures against International Terrorism." *Department of State Bulletin,* LXXVI (January 24, 1977), 75–77.

1391. Lillich, Richard B., and Thomas E. Carbonneau. "The 1976 Terrorism Amendment to the Foreign Assistance Act of 1961." *Journal of International Law and Economy,* II (Spring 1977), 223–236.

Lockwood, Bert B., Jr., jt. author. *See* Franck, Thomas M.

1392. Murphy, John F. "United Nations Proposals on the Control and Repression of Terrorism." In: M. Cherif Bassiouni, ed. *International Terrorism and Political Crimes: Proceedings of the Third Conference on Terrorism and Political Crimes, Syracuse, Sicily, 1973.* Springfield, Ill.: C. C. Thomas, 1974. pp. 493–506.

1393. Organization of American States. "Convention to Prevent and Punish Acts of Terrorism Taking the Form of Crimes against Persons and Related Extortion That Are of International Significance." *American Journal of International Law,* LXV (October 1971), 898–901.

1394. _____. "Draft Convention for the Prevention and Punishment of Certain Acts of International Terrorism." *Department of State Bulletin,* LXVII (October 16, 1972), 431–433.

1395. _____. "First Special Session of the O.A.S. General Assembly Held in Washington: Text of O.A.S. Resolution on Terrorism." *Department of State Bulletin,* LXIII (July 27, 1970), 115–119.

1396. _____. "Third Special Session of the O.A.S. General Assembly Adopts Measures on Kidnapping and Terrorism: Text of Convention and Resolution." *Department of State Bulletin,* LXVII (February 22, 1971), 228–234.

1397. Parks, W. Hays. "1977 Protocols to the Geneva Convention of 1949." *Naval War College Review,* XXXI (Fall 1978), 17–27.

1398. Smith, Monique, and John Stone. "International Conventions on Terrorism: A Selected Review." In: Marjorie Kravitz, ed. *International Summaries: A Collection of Selected Translations in Law Enforcement and Criminal Justice,* v. 3. Rockville, Md.: National Criminal Justice Reference Service, Law Enforcement Assistance Administration, Department of Justice, 1979. pp. 165–172.

Stone, John, jt. author. *See* Smith, Monique.

1399. "Terrorism: The Proposed U.N. Draft Convention." *Georgia Journal of International and Comparative Law,* III (Spring 1973), 430–447.

1400. Travers, Patrick J. "The Legal Effect of United Nations Action in Support of the Palestine Liberation Organization and the National Liberation Movements of Africa." *Harvard International Law Journal,* XVII (Summer 1976), 561–580.

1401. "U.N. Deadlocks on Hijacking, [Entebbe] Rescue." *Aviation Week and Space Technology,* CV (July 19, 1976), 241–242.

1402. "U.S. Presses Other Nations to Curb Terror Attacks." *U.S. News and World Report,* LXXIII (October 9, 1972), 26–27.

1403. United Nations. Ad hoc Committee on International Terrorism. "Committee on Terrorism Submits Summary of Views to [General] Assembly." *U.N. Chronicle,* XIV (April 1977), 54.

1404. _____. General Assembly, "Convention to Prevent and Punish Crimes against Internationally Protected Persons, including Diplomatic Agents." *Department of State Bulletin,* LXX (December 1973), 91–95.

1405. _____. _____. "Draft Convention for the Prevention and Punishment of Certain Acts of International Terrorism." *Department of State Bulletin,* LXVII (October 26, 1972), 431–433.

1406. _____. Security Council. "Council Fails to Adopt Draft Resolution after Considering Uganda Hijacking Issue." *U.N. Chronicle,* XIII (August 1976), 15–21+.

1407. "Vindication for the Israelis: The U.N. Debate on Entebbe Rescue." *Time,* CVIII (July 26, 1976), 39–40.

1408. Waldheim, Kurt. "Secretary-General Calls for Urgent Attention to the Question of International Terrorism: Excerpts from Press Conference, September 16, 1976." *U.N. Chronicle,* XIII (October 1976), 40–42.

3. Documents, Papers, and Reports

1409. United Nations. General Assembly. Ad hoc Committee on International Terrorism. *Observations of States Submitted in Accordance with Assembly Resolution 3034.* New York, 1973. 45p.

1410. _____. _____. _____. *Report.* New York, 1973. 34p.

1411. _____. _____. _____. _____. New York, 1977. 54p.

1412. _____. Social Defense Research Institute. *Torture and Hostage Taking.* Translated from the Italian. Rockville, Md.: National Criminal Justice Reference Service, Law Enforcement Assistance Administration, Department of Justice, 1971. 8p.

1413. United States. Department of State. Bureau of Public Affairs. *U.S. Efforts to Combat Terrorism.* P-520. Washington, D.C., 1973. Unpaged.

C. International Law and Aerial Hijacking

1. Books

1414. Agrawala, S. K. *Aircraft Hijacking and International Law.* Tripathi, India: Oceana, 1973. 242p.

1415.   McWhinney, Edward. *The Illegal Diversion of Aircraft and International Law.* Leyden: Sijthoff, 1975. 123p.

1416.   _____ , ed. *Aerial Piracy and International Law.* Dobbs Ferry, N.Y.: Oceana, 1971. 213p.

2. Articles

1417.   Abramovsky, Abraham. "Multilateral Conventions for the Suppression of Unlawful Seizure and Interference with Aircraft." *Columbia Journal of Transnational Law,* XIII (1974), 381–405; XIV (1975), 268–300, 451–484.

1418.   "Aerial Hijacking: Convention for the Suppression of the Unlawful Seizure of Aircraft." *American Journal of International Law,* LXV (April 1971), 440–447.

1419.   "Antihijack Parley Studies Sanctions." *Aviation Week and Space Technology,* CIX (August 7, 1978), 39+.

1420.   Barrie, G. N. "Crimes Committed Aboard Aircraft." *South African Law Journal,* LXXXIV (1968), 203–208.

1421.   Bell, Robert G. "The U.S. Response to Terrorism against International Civil Aviation." *Orbis,* XIX (Winter 1976), 1326–1343.

1422.   Bidinger, Jerome R., and Roman A. Bninski. "A Legal Response to Terrorist Hijacking and Insurance Liability." *Law and Policy in International Business,* VI (Fall 1974), 1167–1210.

Bninski, Roman A., jt. author. *See* Bidinger, Jerome R.

1423.   Bohlke, Gary L. "Crimes Aboard Aircraft: Jurisdictional Considerations." *Journal of International Law and Economics,* V (January 1971), 139–167.

1424.   Boyle, Robert P. "International Act to Combat Aircraft Hijacking." *Lawyer of the Americas,* IV (1972), 460–473.

1425.   Bradford, A. L. "Legal Ramifications of Hijacking Airplanes." *American Bar Association Journal,* XLVIII (1962), 1034–1039.

A classic study.

1426.   "The Brazilian Hijacking Law (October 20, 1969)." *International Legal Materials,* IX (January 1970), 180–184.

1427.   Brooks, Roy L. "Skyjacking and Refugees: The Effect of the Hague Convention upon Asylum." *Harvard International Law Journal,* XVI (Winter 1975), 93–112.

1428. Brower, Charles N. "Department [of State] Urges Senate Advice and Consent to Ratification of Montreal Convention on Aviation Sabotage." *Department of State Bulletin,* XLVII (October 16, 1972), 444–448.

1429. Chaturvedi, S. C. "Hijacking and the Law." *Indian Journal of International Law,* XI (1971), 89–105.

1430. "The Cuban Hijacking Law (September 16, 1969)." *International Legal Materials,* VIII (November 1969), 1175–1177.

1431. Dinstein, Yoram. "Criminal Jurisdiction over Aircraft Hijacking." *Israel Law Review,* VII (1972), 195–206.

1432. Emmanuelli, Claude. "Legal Aspects of Aerial Terrorism: Piecemeal vs. the Comprehensive Approach." *Journal of International Law and Economics,* X (August-December 1975), 503–518.

1433. Evans, Alona E. "The Law and Aircraft Hijacking." *Syracuse Journal of International Law and Commerce,* II (1973), 265–274.

1434. Feller, S. Z. "Comment on Criminal Jurisdiction over Aircraft Hijacking." *Israel Law Review,* VII (1972), 207–214.

1435. FitzGerald, Gerald F. "Concerted Action against States Found in Default of Their International Obligations in Respect of Unlawful Interference with International Civil Aviation." In: C. B. Bourne, ed. *Canadian Yearbook of International Law, 1972.* Vancouver, British Columbia: University of British Columbia Press, 1973. pp. 261–277.

1436. _____ . "The London Draft Convention on Acts of Unlawful Interference against International Civil Aviation." In: Edward W. McWhinney, ed. *Aerial Piracy and International Law.* Leyden: Sijthoff, 1971. pp 36–54.

1437. _____ . "Recent Proposals for Concerted Action against States in Respect of Unlawful Interference in International Civil Aviation." *Journal of Air Law and Commerce,* XL (1974), 161+.

1438. _____ . "Toward Legal Suppression of Acts against Civil Aviation." *International Conciliation,* no. 585 (November 1971), 42–82.

1439. Forsberg, Oscar. "I.F.A.L.P.A. Position and Report on Hijacking." *Air Line Pilot,* XXXIX (July 1970), 42–46.

1440. Friedlander, Robert A. "Banishing Fear from the Skies: A Statutory Proposal." *Duquesne Law Review,* XVI (1978), 283+.

Fuller, David O., Jr., jt. author. *See* Hirsch, Arthur I.

1441.   Hijacking and Justice." *Commonweal*, XCVII (March 2, 1973), 491–492.

1442.   Hirsch, Arthur I., and David O. Fuller, Jr. "Aircraft Piracy and Extradition." *New York Law Forum*, XVI (Spring 1970), 392–419.

1443.   Horlick, Gary N. "The Developing Law of Air Hijacking." *Harvard International Law Journal*, XII (Winter 1971), 33–70.

1444.   _____ . "The Public and Private International Response to Aircraft Hijacking." *Vanderbilt Journal of Transnational Law*, VI (Fall 1972), 144–185.

1445.   International Civil Aviation Organization. Assembly. "Convention for the Suppression of Unlawful Seizure of Aircraft." *International Legal Materials*, X (January 1971), 133–136.

1446.   _____ . _____ . "Convention on Aviation Sabotage Adopted by Montreal Conference: Statement." *Department of State Bulletin*, LXV (October 25, 1971), 464–468.

1447.   _____ . _____ . "Draft Convention on the Unlawful Seizure of Aircraft (March 1970)." *International Legal Materials*, IX (July 1970), 669–672.

1448.   _____ . _____ . "Draft Proposals on the Unlawful Seizure of Aircraft." *International Legal Materials*, VIII (March 1969), 245–257.

1449.   _____ . _____ . "Draft Proposals on the Unlawful Seizure of Aircraft." *International Legal Materials*, IX (January 1970), 68–79.

1450.   _____ . _____ . "Proposals concerning Hijacking and Unlawful Interference with Civil Aviation." *International Legal Materials*, XII (March 1973), 377–391.

1451.   _____ . _____ . "Proposals concerning Unlawful Interference against International Civil Aviation." *International Legal Materials*, IX (November 1970), 1183–1217.

1452.   Johnson, L. D. "The Aviation Crimes Acts of 1972." *New Zealand University Law Review*, V (1973), 305+.

1453.   Khan, Rahmatullah. "Hijacking and International Law." *Africa Quarterly*, X (1971), 398–403.

1454.   Lissitzyn, Oliver J. "In-Flight Crime and United States Legislation." *American Journal of International Law*, LXVII (April 1973), 306–313.

1455.   _____ . "International Control of Aerial Hijacking: The Role of Values and Interests." *American Society of International Law Proceedings*, (1973), 80–86.

1456.   Loy, Frank E. "Some International Approaches to Dealing with the Hijacking of Aircraft." *International Lawyer,* IV (April 1970), 444–452.

1457.   Lynn, Robert H. "Air Hijacking as a Political Crime—Who Should Judge?" *California Western International Law Journal,* II (1971), 2+.

1458.   McClintock, Michael C. "Skyjacking: Its Domestic, Civil, and Criminal Ramifications." *Journal of Air Law and Commerce,* XXXIX (Winter 1973), 29–80.

1459.   McKeithen, R. N. Smith. "Prospects for the Prevention of Aircraft Hijackings through Law." *Columbia Journal of Transnational Law,* IX (1970), 60–80.

1460.   McMahon, John P. "Air Hijacking: Extradition as a Deterrent." *Georgetown Law Journal,* LVIII (June 1970), 1135–1152.

1461.   McWhinney, Edward W., *et al.* "New Developments on the Law of International Aviation: The Control of Aerial Hijacking." *American Journal of International Law,* LXV (September 1971), 71–96.

1462.   Sushman, Malik. "Legal Aspects of the Problem of Unlawful Seizure of Aircraft." *Indian Journal of International Law,* IX (1969), 61+.

1463.   Malmborg, K. E. "New Developments in the Law of International Aviation: The Control of Aerial Hijacking." *American Society of International Law Proceedings,* (1971), 75–80.

1464.   Mankiewicz, R. H. "The 1970 Hague Convention." *Journal of Air Law and Commerce,* XXXVII (1971), 195–210.

1465.   Perret, Robert-Louis. "Punishment of Aerial Piracy: New Developments." *Interavia,* XXXI (June 1976), 545.

1466.   Rafat, Amir. "The Control of Aircraft Hijacking: The Law of International Civil Aviation." *World Affairs,* CXXXIV (Fall 1971), 143–156.

1467.   Rogers, William P. "United States and Cuba Reach Agreement on Hijacking: Text of Note, February 15, 1973." *Department of State Bulletin,* LXVIII (March 5, 1973), 260–262.

1468.   Rosenfield, Stanley B. "Air Piracy: Is It Time to Relax Our Security?" *New England Law Review,* IX (1973), 81+.

1469.   Ruppenthal, K. M. "World Law and the Hijackers." *Nation,* CCVIII (February 3, 1969), 144–146.

1470.   Samuels, Alec. "The Legal Problems: An Introduction." *Journal of Air Law and Commerce,* XXXVII (1971), 163–170.

1471.   Sarkav, A. K. "The International Air Law and Safety of Civil Aviation." *Indian Journal of International Law,* XII (April 1972), 200–208.

1472.   Schneider, L. E. "Senate Unit Bulwarks Hague Bill." *Aviation Week and Space Technology,* XCVII (August 14, 1972), 22–23.

1473.   Sharp, J. M. "Canada and the Hijacking of Aircraft." *Manitoba Law Journal,* V (1973), 451+.

1474.   Sheehan, William M. "Hijacking and World Law." *World Federalist,* XVI (January-February 1970), 14–15+.

1475.   Shepard, Ira M. "Air Piracy: The Role of the International Federation of Airline Pilots' Association." *Cornell International Law Journal,* III (Winter 1970), 79–91.

1476.   Shubber, Sami. "Aircraft Hijacking under the Hague Convention 1970: A New Regime?" *International and Comparative Law Quarterly,* XXII (October 1973), 687–726.

1477.   _____. "Aircraft Hijacking under the Hague Convention upon Asylum." *Harvard International Law Journal,* XVI (1973), 93+.

1478.   _____. "Is Hijacking of Aircraft 'Piracy' in International Law?" In: *British Yearbook of International Law, 1968–1969.* London: Oxford University Press, 1970. pp. 193–204.

1479.   "Skyjack Pact: U.S. and Cuba." *Newsweek,* LXXXI (February 26, 1973), 36+.

1480.   Smith, Chester L. "The Probable Necessity of an International Prison in Solving Aircraft Hijacking." *International Lawyer,* V (1971), 269+.

1481.   Stephen, John E. "Going South: Air Piracy and Unlawful Interference with Air Commerce." *International Lawyer,* IV (1970), 433+.

1482.   Sushman, Malik. "Legal Aspects of the Problem of the Unlawful Seizure of Aircraft." *Indian Journal of International Law,* IX (1969), 61–71.

1483.   "Symposium on the Unlawful Seizure of Aircraft: Approaches to the Legal Problems." *Journal of Air Law and Commerce,* XXXVII (1971), 162–233.

1484.   "U.S. Asks Quick, Positive Action Implementing [U.N.] Anti-hijack Vote." *Aviation Week and Space Technology,* CVII (November 14, 1977), 15–16.

1485. "U.S.-Cuban Agreement on Hijacking: Text." *Current History,* LXVI (January 1974), 34+.

1486. United Nations. General Assembly. "Assembly Condemns Acts of Aerial Hijacking." *U.N. Chronicle,* XIV (December 1977), 23–26.

1487. "Unlawful Interference with International Civil Aviation: Exchange of Letters between President Nixon and the President of the International Civil Aviation Association." *Weekly Compilation of Presidential Documents,* VI (August 17, 1970), 1061–1063.

1488. Van Panhuys, Haro F. "Aircraft Hijacking and International Law." *Columbia Journal of Transnational Law,* IX (1970), 1+.

1489. Volpe, John A. "United States Proposal on the Unlawful Seizure of Aircraft for Blackmail Purposes Adopted by I.C.A.O. Council: Statement with Texts." *Department of State Bulletin,* LXIII (October 1, 1970), 449–453.

1490. _____ , et al, "I.C.A.O. Special Subcommittee Meets at Washington." *Department of State Bulletin,* LXVII (October 2, 1972), 357–364.

1491. Wetmore, W. C. "U.N. Spurs Antihijacking Drive: U.N. Hijacking Resolution Terms Detailed." *Aviation Week and Space Technology,* CVII (November 14, 1977), 14–15.

1492. White, Gillian M. E. "The Hague Convention for the Suppression of Unlawful Seizure of Aircraft." *International Commission of Jurists Review,* VI (1971), 38–45.

1493. Yammoto, Soji. "The Japanese Enactment for the Suppression of Unlawful Seizure of Aircraft and International Law." *Japanese Annual of International Law,* XIII (1971), 70–80.

3. Documents, Papers, and Reports

1494. "Convention for the Suppression of Unlawful Acts against the Safety of Civil Aviation (Montreal, 1971)." In: U.S. Department of State. *U.S. Treaties and Other International Agreements,* v. 24, pt. 1. Washington, D.C.: U.S. Government Printing Office, 1973. pp. 565–602.

1495. "Convention for the Suppression of Unlawful Seizure of Aircraft (Hague, 1970)." In: U.S. Department of State. *U.S. Treaties and Other International Agreements,* v. 22, pt. 2. Washington, D.C.: U.S. Government Printing Office, 1971. pp. 1641–1684.

1496. Gist, Francis J. "The Aircraft Hijacker and International Law." Unpublished M.A. thesis, McGill University, 1968.

1497.   International Civil Aviation Organization. Assembly. *Convention for the Suppression of Unlawful Acts against the Safety of Civil Aviation, Signed at Montreal on 2 3 September 1971.* Montreal, 1971. 28p.

1498.   _____ . _____ . *Documentation Related to the Assembly of the I.C.A.O. Assembly: 17th Session, Extraordinary.* 5 pts. Montreal, 1970.

1499.   Israel. Ministry of Foreign Affairs. *The I.C.A.O. and Arab Terrorist Operations: A Record of Resolutions.* Jerusalem, 1973.

1500.   "Piracy: Sea and Air." Unpublished paper, 54th Conference of the International Law Association, 1971.

1501.   United States. Congress. House. Committee on Foreign Affairs. Subcommittee on Inter-American Affairs. *Hijacking Accord between the United States and Cuba: Hearings.* 93rd Cong., 1st sess. Washington, D.C.: U.S. Government Printing Office, 1973. 18p.

1502.   _____ . _____ . _____ . Committee on Internal Security. *Anti-Hijacking Act of 1973: Hearings.* 93rd Cong., 1st sess. 2 pts. Washington, D.C.: U.S. Government Printing Office, 1973.

1503.   _____ . _____ . Senate. Committee on Commerce. *Convention on Offenses and Certain Other Acts Committed on Board Aircraft: Hearings.* 91st Cong., 2nd sess. Washington, D.C.: U.S. Government Printing Office, 1970. 23p.

1504.   _____ . _____ . _____ . _____ . Subcommittee on Aviation. *Anti-Hijacking Act of 1971: Hearings.* 92nd Cong., 2nd sess. Washington, D.C.: U.S. Government Printing Office, 1972. 144p.

1505.   _____ . _____ . _____ . _____ . _____ . *Anti-Hijacking Act of 1971: Report.* 92nd Cong., 2nd sess. Washington, D.C.: U.S. Government Printing Office, 1972. 12p.

1506.   _____ . _____ . _____ . Committee on Foreign Relations. *Aircraft Hijacking Convention: Hearings.* 92nd Cong., 1st sess. Washington, D.C.: U.S. Government Printing Office, 1971. 99p.

VIII/Terrorism Around the World, 1968–1980

Introduction

Perhaps the simplest thing one can say about terrorism in these days is that it is a worldwide phenomenon. Although closed societies seem not to have suffered as much as open ones, terrorists have struck in every corner of the globe.

The references in this section, the largest in the book, provide the user with sources on both domestic and international terrorism by geographic area. After a look at evidence supporting the existence of terrorist networks, the reader may examine subsections which circle the world from Europe to North America. Here the reader will find references to the alphabet-soup of terrorist organizations, to the PLO, the IRA, the RAF, the FLQ, the SLA and other terror bands such as the Tupamaros and Weathermen. Here also are citations to the deeds, the Munich and Lod massacres, the IRA bombing of London and the murder of Lord Mountbatten, and political kidnappings in Latin America. Additionally, the reader can find information on local countermeasures in specific cases, such as the Dutch Marines versus the South Mollucans and the FBI versus the Weathermen, and transnational responses such as the Israeli rescue at Entebbe.

Additional materials relative to this section are found in all of the previous sections, especially II:B and IV.

A. Terrorist Networks

1. Books

1507. Demaris, Ovid. *Brothers in Blood: The International Terrorist Network.* New York: Scribners, 1977. 441p.

1508. Dobson, Christopher, and Ronald Payne. *The Carlos* [Ilich Ramirez Sanchez] *Complex: A Study in Terror.* New York: G. P. Putnam, 1977. 254p.

Payne, Ronald, jt. author. *See* Dobson, Christopher.

2. Articles

1509. Beres, Louis R. "Guerrillas, Terrorists, and Polarity: New Structural Models of World Politics." *Western Political Quarterly,* XXVII (December 1974), 624–626.

1510. Carroll, Robert. "Terror Incorporated." *Newsweek,* LXXXVI (July 14, 1975), 40+.

1511. Clutterbuck, Richard. "Terrorist International." *Army Quarterly,* CIV (January 1974), 154–159.

1512. "Five Faces of World Terrorism." *U.S. News and World Report,* LXXXIV (May 22, 1978), 31.

1513. "The German Connection: Links between the Red Brigades and the Red Army Faction." *Time,* CXII (August 28, 1978), 33.

1514. "Political Terrorist Groups." *Assets Protection,* II (Spring 1977), 45–47.

1515. Sterling, Claire. "Terrorist Network." *Atlantic,* CCXLII (November 1978), 37–43+; CCXLIII (March 1979), 34+.

1516. "Talking Quietly: Bonn-PLO Dialogue." *Time,* CXIII (May 7, 1979), 43.

1517. Tophoven, Rolf. "The Palestinians and the Network of International Terrorism." In: Marjorie Kravitz, ed. *International Summaries: A Collection of Selected Translations in Law Enforcement and Criminal Justice,* v. 3. Rockville, Md.: National Criminal Justice Reference Service, Law Enforcement Assistance Administration, Department of Justice, 1979. pp. 37–44.

1518. Willenson, Kenneth. "Terror International." *Newsweek,* XCI (May 22, 1978), 36–37.

3. Documents, Papers, and Reports

1519. Hutchinson, Martha C. "Implications of the Pattern of Transnational Terrorism." Unpublished paper, Convention of the International Studies Association, 1975.

B. *Europe*

1. General Works

a. Articles

1520. Bell, J. Bowyer. "The Gun in Europe." *New Republic,* CLXXIII (November 22, 1975), 10–12.

1521. Corrado, Raymond R. "Ethnic and Student Terrorism in Western Europe." In: Michael Stohl, ed. *The Politics of Terrorism.* New York: Marcel Dekker, 1979. pp. 191–250.

1522. Davies, Joan. "Violence and Political Impotence: Europe in the Seventies." *Canadian Forum,* LVIII (August 1978), 12–15.

1523. "Europe's Cold Civil War." *Time,* XCIX (June 19, 1972), 19–20.

1524. Grenard, Pierre. "Terrorism: Decline in the Fall." *Macleans,* XCI (October 9, 1978), 40+.

1525. Kopkind, Andrew. "Euro-Terror: Fear Eats the Soul." *New Times,* X (June 12, 1978), 28–30+.

1526. Levy, Bernard H. "War against All." *New Republic,* CLXXVIII (February 11, 1978), 14–18.

1527. Lewis, Pierre. "Old Soldiers Never Die: Alexander Haig Assassination Attempt." *Macleans,* XCII (July 9, 1979), 18–19.

1528. McCormick, Robert W. "Industrial Security in Europe: A Multinational Concept." *Security Management,* XVIII (July 1974), 8–10, 13.

1529. "Missile Alert: Preventing Arab Attacks at Airports All across Western Europe." *Newsweek,* LXXXIII (January 21, 1974), 45.

1530. Pfaff, William. "Reflections: Western European Terrorists." *New Yorker,* LIV (September 18, 1978), 135–140+.

1531. Sterling, Claire. "The Terrorist War for Europe." *Reader's Digest,* CXIII (December 1978), 92–96.

b. Documents, Papers, and Reports

1532.   Goodman, Raymond W., *et al. A Compendium of European Theater Terrorist Groups.* Research Report. Maxwell AFB, Ala.: Air War College, Air University, 1976. 218p.

2. Austria

a. Articles

1533.   Carroll, Robert. "Year of Terror: Kidnapping of OPEC Ministers in Vienna." *Newsweek,* LXXXVII (Janaury 5, 1976), 24–26.

b. Documents, Papers, and Reports

1534.   Austria. Federal Chancellery. *The Events of September 28th and 29th, 1973* [Arab Terrorist Train Hijacking]: *A Docmentary Report.* Vienna, 1973. 92p.

3. Great Britain and Northern Ireland

a. The Irish Republican Army (IRA)

(1) Books

1535.   Bell, J. Bowyer. *The Secret Army: A History of the I.R.A.* Cambridge, Mass.: MIT Press, 1974. 434p.

1536.   Coogan, Tim Pat. *The I.R.A.* New York: Praeger, 1970. 373p.

1537.   McGuire, Maria. *To Take Arms: My Year in the Provisional I.R.A.* New York: Viking, 1973. 185p.

MacStiofan, Sean, pseud. *See* Stephenson, John E. D.

1538.   O'Neill, Terence. *The Autobiography of Terence O'Neill.* London: Hart-Davis, 1972. 160p.

1539.   Stephenson, John E. D. *Revolutionary in Ireland.* By Sean MacStiofan, pseud. Farnborough, Eng.: Gordon Cremouesi, 1975. 372p.

(2) Articles

1540.   Barnes, J. "War of the Provos." *Newsweek,* LXXXI (February 19, 1973), 51–52.

1541.   Bell, J. Bowyer. "The Escalation of Insurgency: The Experiences of the Provisional I.R.A., 1969–1971." *Review of Politics,* XXXV (July 1973), 398–411.

1542. _____ . "Strategy, Tactics, and Terror: An Irish Perspective." In: Yonah Alexander, ed. *International Terrorism: National, Regional, and Global Perspectives.* New York: Praeger, 1976. pp. 65–89.

1543. Bowden, Tom. "The I.R.A. and the Changing Tactics of Terrorism." *Political Quarterly,* XLVII (October-December 1976), 425–437.

1544. Burnett, H. B., Jr. "Interview with Sean McBride." *Skeptic,* no. 11 (January-February 1976), 8–11, 54–57.

1545. Carthew, Anthony. "The Red and the Green: The Divided I.R.A." *New York Times Magazine* (March 28, 1971), 22–23+.

1546. Clark, Dennis. "Which Way the I.R.A.?" *Commonweal,* XCVII (January 5, 1973), 294–297.

1547. "Down the Road to Hell." *Time,* CVII (January 19, 1976), 40–41.

1548. George, David. "These Are the Provisionals." *New Statesman and Nation,* LXXXII (November 19, 1971), 680–681.

1549. Goulding, Cathal. "Interview." *New Left Review,* X (November-December 1970), 50–61.

1550. "The I.R.A.'s Lethal New Look." *Newsweek,* XCIII (April 16, 1979), 63.

1551. "The I.R.A.'s Money Crisis." *Newsweek,* XCII (September 31, 1978), 33.

1552. "The I.R.A.'s Young Turks." *Newsweek,* LXXXIX (February 21, 1977), 30–31.

1553. "In the Shadow of the Gunmen." *Time,* XCIX (January 10, 1972), 30–34+.

1554. "Ireland's Odd Men Out." *Newsweek,* LXXVIII (October 18, 1971), 56–58.

1555. "Keepers of the Flame: Women of the I.R.A." *Newsweek,* LXXVIII (November 29, 1971), 33–34.

1556. Kupfer, M. "The Boys of the I.R.A." *Newsweek,* LXXIV (September 1, 1969), 31.

1557. Leinster, Charles. "The Gunmen Are Here, Mister!" *Life,* LXXII (April 7, 1972), 32–39.

1558. [McMullen, Peter.] "Tantelizing Tales from the I.R.A." *Time,* CXIV (September 17, 1979), 39.

1559. Mayer, A. J. "The I.R.A. Reborn." *Newsweek*, XCI (February 27, 1978), 40.

1560. Middleton, Richard. "Urban Guerrilla Warfare and the I.R.A." *Journal of the Royal United Service Institute for Defence Studies*, CXVI (December 1971), 72–75.

1561. O'Riordan, Michael, and Betty Sinclair. "Irish Communists and Terrorism." *World Marxist Review*, XIX (October 1976), 87–97.

1562. "Outrage over the I.R.A." *Time*, XCIX (June 5, 1972), 30+.

1563. "Portrait Gallery of Provisionals: Sean Macstiofan, Ruari O. Bradaigh, and Joe Cahill." *Time*, XCIX (January 10, 1972), 39+.

1564. "Provos on the Run." *Time*, C (August 7, 1972), 25–26.

1565. "Provos' Problems." *Time*, CII (September 24, 1973), 50+.

1566. Sheed, Wilfred. "Dublin Conversation: 'Do You Support the I.R.A.?'" *New York Times Magazine*, (October 24, 1971), 32–33+.

Sinclair, Betty, jt. author. *See* O'Riordan, Michael.

1567. Stetler, Russell. "I.R.A.: Beyond the Barricades." *Ramparts*, X (March 1972), 9–12+.

1568. Van Voris, W. H. "The Provisional I.R.A. and the Limits of Terrorism." *Massachusetts Review*, XVI (Summer 1975), 413–428.

1569. 46+.

1570. Webb, Peter. "The I.R.A.'s New Look." *Newsweek*, XCIV (September 17, 1979), 64.

1571. Welles, Benjamin. "I.R.A. Terrorism." *New Republic*, CLXXI (December 17–28, 1974), 17, 33.

(3) Documents, Papers, and Reports

1572. Provisional Irish Republican Army. *Freedom Struggle*. Belfast: Irish Republican Publicity Bureau, 1973. 101p.

1573. ———. *Handbook for the Irish Republican Army*. Boulder, Colo.: Paladin Press, 1979. 40p.

b. Terrorism in Britain

(1) Books

1574. Borrell, Clive. *Crime in Britain Today*. London: Routledge, 1975. 212p.

1575.   Bunyan, Tom. *The Police State in Britain.* London: Friedman, 1971. 129p.

1576.   Clutterbuck, Richard. *Britain in Agony: The Growth of Political Violence.* London and Boston: Faber & Faber, 1978. 320p.

(2) ARTICLES

1577.   "At War with the I.R.A. [Bombers]." *Newsweek,* LXXXIV (December 9, 1974), 46+.

1578.   Barton, R. W. "Terrorist Activities in the United Kingdom." *Police College Magazine,* XIII (1975), 12–20.

1579.   Bishop, J. W. "Can Democracy Defend Itself against Terrorism?" *Commentary,* LXV (May 1978), 55–62.

1580.   Bowden, Tom. "Men in the Middle: The U.K. Police." *Conflict Studies,* no. 68 (February 1976), 1–20.

1581.   Buck, J. J. "Londoners Fight Bombs: Cheery Bravery or Steel Shutters?" *Vogue,* CLXVI (March 1976), 80+.

1582.   Campbell, Duncan. "Scotland Yard and the Return of the Bombers." *New Statesman and Nation,* XCVI (December 22–29, 1978), 843+.

1583.   Carroll, Robert. "To Catch a Terrorist: Police Tactics." *Newsweek,* LXXXVI (December 22, 1975), 36–37.

1584.   Chilton, Anthony. "Urban Guerrilla Tactics: Are They Likely to Be Employed in Britain?" *Police College Magazine,* XIV (1976), 9–18.

1585.   Clutterbuck, Richard. "Bombs in Britain." *Army Quarterly,* CV (January 1975), 15–21.

1586.   _____ . "Threats to Public Order in Britain." *Army Quarterly,* CVII (July 1977), 279–290.

1587.   Hachey, Thomas E. "Political Terrorism: The British Experience." In: Yonah Alexander, ed. *International Terrorism: National, Regional, and Global Perspectives.* New York: Praeger, 1976. pp. 90–114.

1588.   "I.R.A. Blitz." *Newsweek,* LXXXII (September 3, 1973), 51–52.

1589.   "I.R.A. Blitz, London." *Newsweek,* LXXXI (March 19, 1973), 40–41.

1590.   "The I.R.A.'s Summer Offensive." *Newsweek,* LXXXIV (July 1, 1974), 30–31.

1591. "Irish Terror Strikes Abroad: Last Gasp in the Fight for Ulster?" *U.S. News and World Report,* LXXV (September 10, 1973), 20+.

1592. Pavlov, Vladimir. "Bomb Blasts in London." *New Times* (Moscow), no. 38 (September 1975), 10–11.

1593. Robinson, B. M. U. "Social Unrest in the United Kingdom: Present Causes and Future Effects." *Royal Air Forces Quarterly,* XVII (Spring 1977), 83–88.

1594. Schellenberg, James A. "The Bombings: Four Views." *New Review,* II (March 1976), 3–10.

1595. "Smashing London's Face: I.R.A. Bombings." *Time,* CI (March 19, 1973), 22+.

1596. Stafford, David. "Anarchists in Britain Today." *Government and Opposition,* VI (March 1971), 345+.

1597. Steele, Raymond. "The I.R.A.'s Siege of London." *Newsweek,* LXXXVI (December 1, 1975), 51–52.

1598. Tereshchuk, David. "Bombing in Britain." *New Statesman and Nation,* XCI (January 9, 1976), 32–33.

1599. "Troubles Spill Over: The Letter-Bomb Campaign." *Time,* CII (September 10, 1973), 30–31.

1600. "What War on the Terrorists Is Doing to Life in London." *U.S. News and World Report,* LXXVII (December 23, 1974), 71–72.

1601. Wolf, John B. "Police Intelligence: Focus for Counter-Terrorists Operations." *Police Journal,* XLIX (January-March 1976), 19–27.

c. Terrorism in Ulster

(1) Books

1602. Barker, A. J. *Bloody Ulster.* Ballantine's Illustrated History of the Violence Century: Human Conflict, no. 5. New York: Ballantine Books, 1973. 159p.

1603. Barritt, Denis P., and Charles F. Carter. *The Northern Ireland Problem: A Study in Group Relations.* 2nd ed. London and New York: Oxford University Press, 1972. 176p.

1604. Biggs-Davison, John A. *The Hand Is Red.* London: Johnson, 1973. 202p.

1605. Boyd, Andrew. *Holy War in Belfast: A History of the Troubles in Northern Ireland.* New York: Grove Press, 1972. 220p.

1606. Busteed, Mervyn A. *Northern Ireland.* London and New York: Oxford University Press, 1974. 47p.

Carter, Charles F., jt. author *See* Barritt, Denis P.

1607. DePaoi, Liam. *Divided Ulster.* 2nd ed. H   ,dsworth, Eng.: Penguin Books, 1971. 251p.

1608. Deutsch, Richard, and Vivien Magowan. *Northern Ireland, 1968–: A Chronology of Events.* Belfast: Flackstaff Press, 1973–. v. 1–.

1609. Devlin, Bernadette. *The Price of My Soul.* New York: Knopf, 1969. 224p.

1610. Dillon, Martin, and Denis Lehane. *Political Murder in Northern Ireland.* Harmondsworth, Eng.: Penguin Books, 1973. 317p.

1611. Edmonds, Sean. *The Gun, the Law, and the Irish People.* Tralee, Ire.: Anvil Books, 1971. 279p.

1612. Elliot, R. S. P. *Ulster: A Case Study in Conflict Theory.* New York: St. Martin's Press, 1972. 180p.

1613. Farrell, Michael. *Northern Ireland: The Orange State.* London: Pluto Press, 1976. 406p.

1614. Fields, Rona M. *Society under Seige: A Psychology of Northern Ireland.* Philadelphia: Temple University Press, 1977. 267p.

1615. FitzGibbon, Constantine. *Red Hand: The Ulster Colony.* Garden City, N.Y.: Doubleday, 1972. 367p.

1616. Greaves, C. Desmond. *The Irish Crisis.* London: Lawrence & Wishart, 1972. 222p.

1617. Hastings, Max. *Barricades in Belfast: The Fight for Civil Rights in Northern Ireland.* New York: Taplinger, 1970. 211p.

1618. Hull, Roger H. *The Irish Triangle: Conflict in Northern Ireland.* Princeton: Princeton University Press, 1976. 312p.

Johnson, Don, jt. author. *See* O'Sullivan, P. Michael.

1619. Kennally, Danny. *Belfast, August 1971.* London: Independent Labour Party, 1971. 124p.

Lehane, Denis, jt. author. *See* Dillon, Martin.

1620. McCann, Eamonn. *War and an Irish Town.* Harmondsworth, Eng.: Penguin Books, 1974. 256p.

1621. McCann, Sean. *The Fighting Irish.* London: Frewin, 1972. 259p.

1622.   McCreary, Alf. *Survivors: A Documentary Account of the Victims of Northern Ireland.* New York: Beekman Books, 1977. 280p.

1623.   MacEdin, Gary. *Northern Ireland: Captive of History.* New York: Holt, Rinehart & Winston, 1971. 260p.

1624.   McKeown, Michael. *The First Two Hundred.* Belfast: Irish News, 1972. 96p.

1625.   Magee, John. *Northern Ireland: Crisis and Conflict.* London: Routledge, 1974. 196p.

Magowan, Vivien, jt. author. *See* Deutsch, Richard.

1626.   Manhattan, Avro. *Religious Terror in Ireland.* 4th ed. London: Paravision Books, 1971. 246p.

1627.   Mansback, Richard W. *Northern Ireland: A Half Century of Partition.* New York: Facts on File, 1978. 221p.

1628.   Monday, Mark. *Summer of Sunshine.* Boulder, Colo.: Paladin Press, 1979. 63p.

1629.   O'Connor, Ulick, ed. *Irish Liberation: An Anthology.* New York: Grove Press, 1974. 255p.

1630.   O'Neill, Terence. *Ulster at the Crossroads.* London: Faber & Faber, 1969. 201p.

1631.   O'Sullivan, P. Michael, and Don Johnson. *Patriot Graves: Resistance in Ireland.* Chicago: Follett, 1972. 255p.

1632.   Rose, Richard. *Governing without Consensus: An Irish Perspective.* Boston: Beacon Press, 1971. 567p.

1633.   Stetler, Russell. *The Battle of Bogside: The Politics of Violence in Northern Ireland.* London: Sheed & Ward, 1970. 212p.

1634.   Styles, S. G. *Bombs Have No Pity: My War against Terrorism.* London: W. Luscombe, 1975. 187p.

1635.   *Sunday Times.* Insight Team. *Ulster.* London: Deutsch, 1972. 315p.

1636.   Target, George W. *Unholy Smoke.* London: Hodder & Stoughton, 1969. 127p.

1637.   Van Voris, W. H. *Violence in Ulster: An Oral Documentary.* Amherst: University of Massachusetts Press, 1975. 326p.

(2) ARTICLES

1638. "Acceptable Violence?" *Time*, XCVIII (December 27, 1971), 32+.

1639. "Appalling Crime: Slaying of British Soldiers." *Time*, XCVII (March 22, 1971), 32–33.

1640. "As Open War Rages in Northern Ireland." *U.S. News and World Report*, LXXI (August 23, 1971), 36–37.

1641. "Backlash in Belfast." *Newsweek*, LXXIV (October 27, 1969), 54+.

1642. Beckett, J. C. "Northern Ireland." *Journal of Contemporary History*, VI (Winter 1971), 121–134.

1643. Beer, Colin. "Impressions from Ulster." *Army Quarterly*, CII (April 1972), 365–369.

1644. Bell, J. Bowyer. "Northern Ireland." *New Republic*, CLXXIV (June 19, 1976), 17–19.

1645. Benjamin, M. R., *et al.* "Assassination in Dublin: The Killing of British Ambassador C. T. E. Ewart-Biggs." *Newsweek*, LXXXVIII (August 2, 1976), 32+.

1646. Biggs-Davison, John. "Thoughts on the Ulster Discontents." *Contemporary Review*, CCXXXIII (August 1978), 67–74.

1647. "Bloody Spiral of Unyielding Fury." *Life*, LXXIII (December 29, 1972), 32–33.

1648. Boal, F. W. "Conflict in Northern Ireland." *Geographic Magazine*, XLI (February 1969), 331+.

Bray, Frank T. J., jt. author. *See* Moodie, Michael.

1649. Breslin, Jimmy. "Ireland: The Killing Sickness." *Nation*, CCXIV (March 27, 1972), 390–393.

1650. Buckley, C. M. "Letter from Belfast." *America*, CXXXIII (November 26, 1975), 378–379.

1651. Butler, David. "Ireland's Bloody Monday." *Newsweek*, XCIV (September 10, 1979), 28–31.

1652. Byron, C. "Armagh: This is I.R.A. Territory." *Time*, CVII (January 12, 1976), 28+.

1653. Cockburn, Alexander. "What It's Like in Belfast." *Ramparts*, IX (October 1970), 8+.

1654.   Crozier, Brian. "Ulster: Politics and Terrorism." *Conflict Studies,* no. 36 (June 1973), 1–20.

1655.   Deming, Angus. "Ulster: The End of Hope." *Newsweek,* LXXX (July 24, 1974), 43–44.

1656.   Douglas, J. N. H. "The Intransigent Quest for Peace: The Divided Island." *Geographic Magazine,* XLIX (May 1977), 510–515.

1657.   Freeman, T. W. "The Man-Made Walls of Ulster." *Geographic Magazine,* XLVI (August 1974), 594–597+.

1658.   Fromm, Joseph. "The Civil War Nobody Is Winning." *U.S. News and World Report,* LXXII (March 20, 1972), 24–26.

1659.   Gale, Richard. "Old Problem, New Setting." *Journal of the Royal United Service Institution for Defence Studies,* CXVII (March 1972), 43–46.

1660.   Garvin, Stephen. "Northern Ireland: A Question of Identity." *Journal of the Royal United Service Institution for Defence Studies,* CXVII (March 1972), 40–42.

1661.   "Going Crazy." *Time,* CI (February 12, 1973), 29–30.

1662.   Grigg, John. "Ireland Again." *Encounter,* XXXVII (December 1971), 32–37.

1663.   Hamilton, Ian. "The Irish Tangle." *Conflict Studies,* no. 6 (May 1970), 7–18.

1664.   _____. "The Spreading Irish Conflict." *Conflict Studies,* no. 17 (November 1971), 5–12.

1665.   Harris, Henry. "The Ulster Question." *Army Quarterly,* C (April 1970), 74–87.

1666.   Holden, David. "The Bad Case of Troubles Called Londonderry." *New York Times Magazine,* (August 3, 1969), 10–11+.

1667.   Holland, Jack. "Ulster, Bloody Ulster." *New York Times Magazine,* (July 15, 1979), 26–36+.

1668.   Howard, A. J. "Urban Guerrilla Warfare in a Democratic Society." *Medicine, Science, and Law,* XII (October 1972), 231–243.

1669.   Huck, S. L. M. "Bloody Ireland." *American Opinion,* XVIII (October 1975), 9–16+.

1670.   Hughes, C. R. "Ulster Revisited." *America,* CXXII (April 18, 1970), 413–415.

1671. "Indiscriminate Terror." *Time,* C (August 28, 1972), 27–28.

1672. "Ireland: The Bombs Come Home." *Newsweek,* LXXX (December 11, 1972), 45–46.

1673. "Irish vs. Irish: Why They Keep Fighting." *U.S. News and World Report,* LXIX (October 26, 1970), 80–81.

1674. Izakov, Boris. "Republic behind Barricades, Belfast." *New Times* (Moscow), (November 7–26, 1969), 20–23, 21–24, 19–21.

1675. Janke, Peter, and D. L. Price. "Ulster: Consensus and Coercion." *Conflict Studies,* no. 50 (August 1974), 1–20.

1676. Johnson, Peter. "Into the Ulster Quagmire." *New Statesman and Nation,* LXXXII (September 3, 1971), 287–288.

1677. Kingston, William. "Northern Ireland—If Reason Fails." *Political Quarterly,* XLIV (January-March 1973), 22–32.

1678. Knight, Robin. "Bombs, Bullets, and Fear: Ulster's Agony Anew." *U.S. News and World Report,* LXXVI (April 22, 1974), 61–62.

1679. ———. "Close-up of a Savage War That Knows No End." *U.S. News and World Report,* LXXXI (July 26, 1976), 58–59.

1680. ———. "For Northern Ireland: A Bloody Christmas." *U.S. News and World Report,* LXXIX (December 29, 1975), 17–18.

1681. Krumpach, Robert. "Terrorism in Northern Ireland: An Overview." In: Marjorie Kravitz, ed. *International Summaries: A Collection of Selected Translations in Law Enforcement and Criminal Justice,* v. 3. Rockville, Md.: National Criminal Justice Reference Service, Law Enforcement Assistance Administration, Department of Justice, 1979. pp. 27–36.

1682. Kupfer, M. "Ulster: In the Green Hell." *Newsweek,* LXXVII (April 5, 1971), 42+.

1683. Latey, Maurice. "Violence as a Political Weapon." *NATO's Fifteen Nations,* XVI (December 1971–January 1972), 65–71.

1684. Lavin, Deborah. "Politics in Ulster, 1968." *World Today,* XXIV (December 1968), 530–536.

1685. Lebow, Richard N. "The Origins of Sectarian Assassination: The Case of Belfast." *Journal of International Affairs,* VII (Spring-Summer 1978), 43–62.

1686. Leyton, Elliott. "Return to Northern Ireland." *Canadian Forum,* LVII (March 1978), 18–20.

1687. Lijphart, Arend. "The Northern Ireland Problem." *British Journal of Political Science*, V (January 1975), 83–106.

1688. Lynch, John. "The Anglo-Irish Problem." *Foreign Affairs*, L (July 1972), 601–617.

1689. Lyons, H. A. "Legacy of Violence in Northern Ireland." *International Journal of Offender Therapy and Comparative Criminology*, XIX (Fall 1975), 292–298.

1690. Mander, John. "Facing Reality in Ulster." *New Leader*, LV (March 6, 1972), 5–7.

1691. Marriott, John. "Britain's Mini-War in Northern Ireland." *Armed Forces Journal International*, CIX (February 1972), 23–24.

1692. Moodie, Michael. "The Patriot Game: The Politics of Violence in Northern Ireland." In: Marius H. Livingston, ed. *International Terrorism in the Contemporary World*. Westport, Conn.: Greenwood Press, 1978. pp. 94–110.

1693. _____ , and Frank T. J. Bray. "British Policy Options in Northern Ireland: 'Alternative Routes to the Cemetery.'" *Fletcher Forum*, I (Fall 1976), 3–14.

1694. Moore, Brian. "Bloody Ulster: An Irishman's Lament." *Atlantic*, CCXXVI (September 1970), 58–62.

1695. "A Nation Mourns Its Loss: The 'Troubles' in Ulster Take a Terrible Toll." *Time*, CXIV (September 10, 1979), 30–33.

1696. "Northern Ireland: Britain's Vietnam?" *U.S. News and World Report*, LXXI (September 20, 1971), 52+.

1697. "Northern Ireland: The Powder Keg." *Time*, XCVII (April 5, 1971), 26–32.

1698. "Northern Ireland: Violent Jubilee." *Time*, XCVIII (August 23, 1971), 18–21.

1699. O'Brien, Connor Cruise. "Ireland Will Not Have Peace." *Harpers*, CCLIII (December 1976), 33–42.

1700. O'Brien, Darcy. "Irish Paradox." *New York Times Magazine*, (September 11, 1977), 96–98+.

1701. O'Day, Alan. "Northern Ireland, Terrorism, and the British State." In: Yonah Alexander, David Carlton, and Paul Wilkinson, eds. *Terrorism: Theory and Practice*. Boulder, Colo.: Westview Press, 1979. Chpt. 6.

1702.   O'Leary, Cornelius. "The Northern Ireland Crisis and Its Observers." *Political Quarterly,* XLII (July 1971), 255–268.

1703.   _____. "Northern Ireland: The Politics of Illusion." *Political Quarterly,* XL (July-September 1969), 307–315.

1704.   O'Mahoney, T. P. "The Green, the Orange, and the Blood Red." *America,* CXXX (May 11, 1974), 363–367.

1705.   Power, Jonathan. "Can the Peace People Bring an Irish Peace?" *Encounter,* XLVIII (March 1977), 9–17.

Price, D. L., jt. author. *See* Janke, Peter.

1707.   Reed, David. "Northern Ireland: The Endless War." *Reader's Digest,* CVII (July 1975), 84–93.

1708.   _____. "Northern Ireland's Bloody Impasse." *Reader's Digest,* C (January 1972), 43–48.

1709.   "Renewal of a Vicious War." *Time,* CI (February 19, 1973), 39–40.

1710.   Rose, Richard. "The Northern Ireland Problem." *Contemporary Review,* CCXIX (November-December 1971), 230–233, 284–288.

1711.   Sayers, J. E. "Eruption in Londonderry." *Round Table,* LIX (January 1969), 99–104.

1712.   Schellenberg, James A. "Area Variations of Violence in Northern Ireland." *Sociological Focus,* X (January 1977), 67–78.

1713.   Shearman, H. "Conflict in Northern Ireland." In: George W. Keeton and Georg Schwarzenberg, eds. *Year Book of World Affairs, 1970.* New York: Praeger, 1970. pp. 40–53.

1714.   "'Shoot Them Down before Tea.'" *Time,* XCVI (July 13, 1970), 17+.

1715.   Shuster, Alvin. "Torment in Ulster." *New York Times Magazine,* (February 2, 1975), 8–9+.

1716.   Sinclair, Betty. "Behind the Scenes in Ulster." *World Marxist Review,* XVII (August 1974), 123–128.

1717.   _____. "Northern Ireland." *Labour Monthly,* LI (June, October 1969), 267–270, 458–462; LIII (September 1971), 402–407; LV (April 1973), 163–167; LVII (January, November 1975), 21–23+, 492–499.

1718.   "State of Siege." *Newsweek,* LXXIV (September 8, 1969), 42–43.

1719.   Stetler, Russell. "Northern Ireland: From Civil Rights to Armed Conflict." *Monthly Review,* XXII (November 1970), 12–28.

1720.   Stewart, James. "Northern Ireland: The Crisis Drags On." *World Marxist Review,* XVI (September 1973), 80–89.

1721.   "Ten Years Later: Coping and Hoping." *Time,* CXII (July 17, 1978), 36–37.

1722.   Terchek, Ronald J. "Conflict and Cleavage in Northern Ireland." *Annals of the American Academy of Political and Social Science,* CDXXXIII (September 1977), 47–60.

1723.   "Terrible Days in Northern Ireland." *Newsweek,* LXXVIII (August 23, 1971), 28–30.

1724.   Thompson, David J. "Ulster: Rebellion and Realignment." *Progressive,* XXXVII (November 1973), 43–46.

1725.   "Toward a Grim Millenary." *Time,* CIII (April 15, 1974), 44+.

1726.   "Trial by Fire in Dublin: The Killing of C. T. E. Ewart-Biggs." *Time,* CVIII (August 2, 1976), 26+.

1727.   Turner, A. C. "Britain and Ireland: Dilemmas in the British Balkans." *Current History,* LXVI (March 1974), 116–120+.

1728.   Turner, Mary. "Social Democrats and Northern Ireland, 1964–1970: The Origins of the Present Struggle." *Monthly Review,* XXX (June 1978), 30–45.

1729.   "Ulster: Bloody Dodge City." *Time,* XCVIII (November 22, 1971), 46+.

1730.   "Ulster: The Testing Time." *Newsweek,* LXXIX (April 10, 1972), 29–31.

1731.   "Ulster's Bloody Sunday." *Newsweek,* LXXIX (February 14, 1972), 30–32+.

1732.   "Ulster's Civil War: Agony without End." *U.S. News and World Report,* LXXXVII (September 10, 1979), 21–22.

1733.   Ungeheuer, F. "War of the Flea." *Time,* C (July 31, 1972), 20+.

1734.   Utley, T. E. "The Politico-Military Campaign in Northern Ireland, 1975." In: Royal United Service Institution for Defence Studies, eds. *R.U.S.I. and Brassey's Defence Yearbook, 1976–77.* Boulder, Colo.: Westview Press, 1976. pp. 210–224.

1735. Willenson, Kenneth. "Slaughterhouse." *Newsweek,* LXXXVII (January 19, 1976), 39–40.

(3) DOCUMENTS, PAPERS, AND REPORTS

1736. Atlantic Information Centre for Teachers. *Ulster at War.* Crisis Paper, no. 8. London, 1971. 20p.

1737. Carlton, Charles. *Bigotry and Blood: Documents on the Ulster Crisis.* London and Chicago: Nelson-Hall, 1977. 160p.

1738. Great Britain. Office of Information. Reference Division. *Northern Ireland.* London: H.M. Stationery Office, 1975. 19p.

1739. _____ . Parliament. Tribunal Appointed to Inquire into the Events of Sunday, 30th January 1972, Which Led to the Loss of Life in Connection with the Procession in Londonderry on That Day. *Report.* London: H.M. Stationery Office, 1972. 45p.

1740. Institute for the Study of Conflict. *The Ulster Debate: Report of a Study Group.* London: Bodley Head, 1972. 160p.

1741. Northern Ireland. Government Information Service. *Ulster: A Programme of Action.* Belfast: H.M. Stationery Office, 1969. 16p.

1742. Rose, Richard. *Northern Ireland: Time of Choice.* Foreign Affairs Study, no. 33. Washington, D.C.: American Enterprise Institute for Public Policy Research, 1976. 175p.

1743. United States. Congress. House. Committee on Foreign Affairs. Subcommittee on Europe. *Northern Ireland: Hearings.* 92nd Cong., 2nd sess. Washington, D.C.: U.S. Government Printing Office, 1972. 639p.

1744. _____ . _____ . _____ . _____ . _____ . *Report of Congressman [Lester L.] Wolff on Trip to Northern Ireland.* 92nd Cong., 2nd sess. Washington, D.C.: U.S. Government Printing Office, 1972. 23p.

1745. _____ . _____ . _____ . Committee on the Judiciary. *Northern Ireland—A Role for the United States?: Report.* 95th Cong., 2nd sess. Washington, D.C.: U.S. Government Printing Office, 1979. 675p.

d. Role of British Security and Ulster Defence Forces

(1) BOOKS

1746. Boulton, David. *U.V.F.* [Ulster Volunteer Force], *1966–1973: An Anatomy of Loyalist Rebellion.* Dublin: Gill and Macmillan, 1973. 188p.

1747. Haswell, Chetwynd J. D. *British Military Intelligence.* London: Weidenfeld & Nicolson, 1973. 262p.

1748. Hezlet, Arthur P. *"The B Specials": A History of the Ulster Special Constabulary.* London: Tom Stacey, 1972. 246p.

1749. Mark, Robert. *Policing a Perplexed Society.* London: Allen & Unwin, 1977. 132p.

1750. Miller, David W. *Queen's Rebels: Ulster Loyalism in Historical Perspective.* New York: Harper & Row, 1979. 194p.

(2) ARTICLES

1751. Archer, David. "Smelling Out the Enemy in Belfast." *Esquire,* LXXVII (February 1972), 47+.

1752. Banks, Michael. "The Army in Northern Ireland." In: James L. Moulton, ed. *Brassey's Annual, 1972.* London: Clowes, 1972. pp. 148–160.

1753. Barnes, J. "Terror in Provoland." *Newsweek,* LXXXVI (October 20, 1975), 54.

1754. Boyle, Selwyn. "Army out of Step in Ulster." *New Statesman and Nation,* XCII (August 27, 1976), 260–261.

1755. Chalfont, Alun. "The Army and the I.R.A." *New Statesman and Nation,* LXXXI (April 2, 1971), 447–448.

1756. Charters, David A. "Intelligence and Psychological Warfare Operations in Northern Ireland." *Journal of the Royal United Service Institution for Defence Studies,* CXXII (September 1977), 22–27.

1757. Deerin, James B. "Northern Ireland's 'Twilight War': Frustrating Duty for British Troops." *Army,* XXVI (December 1976), 14–21.

1758. Deming, Angus. "Men on the Spot." *Newsweek,* LXXVIII (September 6, 1971), 29–30.

1759. "Dial-a-Spy." *Newsweek,* LXXXII (August 13, 1972), 38+.

1760. Dodd, Norman L. "The Corporal's War: Internal Security Operations in Northern Ireland." *Military Review,* LVI (July 1976), 58–68.

1761. Enloe, C.H. "Police and Military in Ulster: Peacekeeping or Peace-Subverting Forces?" *Journal of Peace Research,* XV (March 1978), 243–258.

1762. Fisk, Robert. "The Effect of Social and Political Crime on the Police and British Army in Northern Ireland." In: Marius H. Livingston, ed. *International Terrorism in the Contemporary World.* Westport, Conn.: Greenwood Press, 1978. pp. 84–93.

1763.   Gonzales, A. "Open Season on the [I.R.A.] Hitmen." *Macleans,* XCII (February 19, 1979), 29–30.

1764.   Holland, Jack. "Northern Ireland since '68: Bloodshed and the Bobby Myth." *Nation,* CCXXVII (October 28, 1978), 431–434.

1765.   Lee, Alfred M. "Insurgent and 'Peacekeeping' Violence in Northern Ireland." *Social Problems,* XX (Spring 1973), 532–546.

1766.   Lunt, J. D. "Soldiers Are Not Policemen." *Army Quarterly,* CIV (July 1974), 409–411.

1767.   McWhirter, W. A. "Corporal Bell, Target of the I.R.A." *Life,* LXXII (February 18, 1972), 3, 30–36.

1768.   "'Operation Huntsman [in Belfast].'" *Journal of the Royal United Service Institution for Defence Studies,* CXVII (September 1972), 25–30.

1769.   Pengelley, R. B. "Ulster: The Name of the Internal Security Game." *International Defense Review,* XI (August 1978), 1297–1301.

1770.   Reynolds, Oliver. "Blind Man's Bluff: Tactics in Anti-Terrorist Operations." *Army Quarterly,* XCVIII (October 1968), 95–101.

1771.   Styles, S. G. "Bombs and Bomb-Beaters." *International Defense Review,* IX (October 1976), 817–819.

1772.   "The Tan Berets [Special Air Service] in Ulster." *Newsweek,* LXXXVII (May 24, 1976), 47.

1773.   "Ulster: Britain Takes Over." *Newsweek,* LXXIX (April 3, 1972), 32–34+.

1774.   "'Ulster: The Counter-Terror [Statement by a Protestant Extremist Group].'" In: Walter Laquerer, ed. *The Terrorist Reader: A Historical Anthology.* Philadelphia: Temple University Press, 1978. pp. 134–137.

1775.   Webb, Peter. "Gloucesters." *Newsweek,* LXXXI (May 14, 1973), 55+.

1776.   Wright, Frank. "Protestant Ideology and Politics in Ulster." *European Journal of Sociology,* XIV (Spring 1973), 213–280.

1777.   "Yesterday's Heroes." *Newsweek,* LXXVI (July 20, 1970), 30.

(3) Documents, Papers, and Reports

1778.   *The Campaign for Social Justice in Northern Ireland—the Mailed Fist: A Record of Army and Police Brutality from August 9–November 9, 1971.* Dungannon, 1972. 71p.

1779.   Smyth, Clifford. *Ulster Assailed.* Belfast, 1971. 36p.

1780.   _____ . *Ulster Must Fight.* Belfast, 1972. 8p.

e. Civil Rights and Detention

(1) Books

1781.   Boyle, Kevin. *Law and State: The Case of Northern Ireland.* London: Martin Robertsen, 1975. 103p.

(2) Articles

1782.   Boyd, Andrew. "Defending the Indefensible: Britain Stoops to Torture." *Nation,* CCXXIII (October 2, 1976), 299–302.

1783.   Clutterbuck, Richard. "Intimidation of Witnesses and Juries [by the I.R.A.]." *Army Quarterly,* CIV (April 1974), 285–294.

1784.   "Draconian Measures: The Anti-I.R.A. Measures in Great Britian." *Time,* CIV (December 9, 1974), 57–58.

1785.   Fox, Kenneth O. "Capital Punishment and Terrorist Murders: The Continuing Debate." *Army Quarterly,* CVI (April 1976), 189–193.

1786.   "Interrogation Procedures: Lord Gardiner's Report." *International Commission of Jurists Report,* III (June 1972), 17–22.

1787.   Kane, J. J. "Civil Rights in Northern Ireland." *Review of Politics,* XXXII (January 1971), 54–77.

1788.   Lowry, D. R. "Draconian Powers: The New British Approach to Pretrial Detention of Suspected Terrorists." *Columbia Human Rights Law Review,* IX (Spring-Summer 1977), 185–222.

1789.   O'Boyle, Michael. "Torture and Emergency Powers under the European Convention on Human Rights: Ireland vs. the United Kingdom." *American Journal of International Law,* LXXI (October 1977), 674–706.

1790.   "A Prisoner's View of a British Internment Camp." *Life,* LXXI (November 12, 1971), 36–37.

1791.   Rauck, Elmar. "The Compatability of the Detention of Terrorist Order (Northern Ireland) with the European Convention for the Protection of Human Rights." *New York University Journal of International Law and Politics,* VI (1973), 1+.

1792.   Street, Henry. "The Prevention of Terrorism (Temporary Provisions) Act." *Criminal Law Review,* XXI (April 1975), 142–149.

1793. "Ulster, Torture, and the Police." *New Statesman and Nation,* LXXXVI (July 13, 1973), 44–46.

1794.   Wilkinson, Paul. "Pros and Cons of Hanging Terrorists." *Police,* VIII (February 1976), 24–25.

(3) DOCUMENTS, PAPERS, AND REPORTS

Adams, John, jt. author. *See* Young, Rochfort.

1795.   Amnesty International. "Report on Human Rights Violations in Northern Ireland." In: U.S. Congress. House. Committee on the Judiciary. *Northern Ireland—A Role for the United States?: Hearings.* 95th Cong., 2nd sess. Washington, D.C.: U.S. Government Printing Office, 1979. pp. 457–469.

1796.   Berry, Steve. *The Prevention of Terrorism Act: Legalized Terror.* London: Socialist Worker Printers and Publishers, 1977. 15p.

1797.   European Commission of Human Rights. *Ireland against the United Kingdom of Great Britain and Northern Ireland: Annexes I and II to the Report of the Commission* [on] *Application 5310.71.* London: Council on Europe, 1976. 123p.

1798.   _____ . _____ : *Report of the Commission* [on] *Application 5310.71.* London: Council on Europe, 1976. 564p.

1799.   Great Britain. Committee of Privy Counsellors Appointed to Consider Authorized Procedures for the Interrogation of Persons Suspected of Terrorism. *Report.* London: H.M. Stationery Office, 1972. 24p.

1800.   _____ . Parliament. *Northern Ireland (Emergency Provisions) Act 1973.* London: H.M. Stationery Office, 1973. 33p.

1801.   _____ . _____ . *Northern Ireland (Emergency Provisions) (Amendment) Act 1975.* London: H.M. Stationery Office, 1975. 17p.

1802.   _____ . _____ . *Northern Ireland (Emergency Provisions) Act 1978.* London: H.M. Stationery Office, 1978. 35p.

1803.   _____ . _____ . Committee of Inquiry into Police Interrogation Procedures in Northern Ireland. *Report.* London: H.M. Stationery Office, 1979. 144p.

1804.   _____ . _____ . Committee to Consider, in the Context of Civil Liberties and Human Rights, Measures to Deal with Terrorism in Northern Ireland. *Report.* London: H.M. Stationery Office, 1975. 78p.

1805.   _____ . _____ . Commission to Consider Legal Procedures to Deal with Terrorist Activities in Northern Ireland. *Report.* London: H.M. Stationery Office, 1972. 42p.

1806. Jenkins, Reginald. *England: Prevention of Terrorism (Temporary Measures)*. London: H.M. Stationery Office, 1974. 14p.

1807. Scorer, Catherine. *The Prevention of Terrorism Acts of 1974 and 1976: A Report on the Operation of the Law.* London: National Council for Civil Liberties, 1976. 39p.

1808. Young, Rochfort, and John Adams. *The Case for Detention.* London: Bow Publications, 1974. 18p.

4. Cyprus: Articles

1809. "Debacle in Cyprus." *Newsweek,* XCI (March 6, 1978), 33–34.

1810. "Egypt's Entebbe: Freeing Hostages of Hijacked Egyptian Airliner in Luxor." *Newsweek,* LXXXVIII (September 6, 1976), 28.

1811. "'I Knew That You'd Make It': Palestinian Hijacking of Cyprus Airways Plane." *Time,* CXI (March 6, 1978), 45.

1812. "Murder and Massacre on Cyprus: Actions of Palestine Terrorists and Retaliation by Egyptian Commandos." *Time,* CXI (March 6, 1978), 40–45.

1813. "Revenge in Cyprus." *Newsweek,* XCI (February 27, 1978), 35.

5. France

a. Books

1814. Murray, Simon. *Legionnaire: My Five Years in the French Foreign Legion.* New York: Times Books, 1978. 314p.

b. Articles

1815. "Abu Daoud—Terror's Advanceman." *Time,* CIX (January 24, 1977), 30.

1816. "Atom Thriller: Bombing of Nuclear Reactors Due for Shipment to Iraq." *Time,* CXIII (May 7, 1979), 40.

1817. Carroll, Robert. "All Roads Lead to Paris." *Newsweek,* LXXXVI (July 21, 1975), 23–24.

1818. _____ . "Terror Incorporated: Latin Quarter Massacre." *Newsweek,* LXXXVI (July 14, 1975), 40+.

1819. "Crime and the Punishment: Capture of the Saudi Arabian Embassy in Paris by the Fedayeen." *Time,* CII (September 17, 1973), 39–40.

1820. "Death on Departure: Lebanese Terrorist Attack on Orly Airport." *Newsweek,* XCI (May 29, 1978), 45.

1821. Deming, Angus. "Terrorist Cross Fire: Releasing Abu Daoud." *Newsweek,* LXXXIX (January 24, 1977), 43+.

1822. "French Recipe for Cowardice: The Release of Abu Daoud." *Nation,* CCXXIV (January 29, 1977), 98–99.

1823. "L'Affair Daoud: Too Hot to Handle." *Time,* CIX (January 24, 1977), 29–31.

1824. "L'Affaire Nogrette." *Time,* XCIX (March 20, 1972), 21–22.

1825. "Maoists at Work: Political Kidnapping of Robert Nogrette in France." *Newsweek,* LXXIX (March 20, 1972), 45+.

1826. Rapoport, Sandra E. "Abu Daoud and the Law." *Commentary,* LXIII (March and May 1977), 70–72, 10–11+.

1827. Reed, David. "The Arch-Terrorist Who Went Scot-Free: Abu Daoud." *Reader's Digest,* CXI (September 1977), 114–118.

1828. Riggle, Robert. "Affaire Abou Daoud: Some Problems of Extraditing an International Terrorist." *International Lawyer,* XII (Spring 1978), 333–350.

1829. Smith, Jack. "The French Foreign Legion Rides Again [as an Anti-Terrorist Unit]." *Today, the* [Philadelphia] *Inquirer Magazine,* (January 7, 1979), 12–22, 24.

1830. ———. "Return of the Legion." *Enquirer Magazine,* (March 25, 1979), 32–48.

6. Germany

a. Urban Terrorism and the Government's Response

(1) Books

1831. Andices, Hellmut. *Rule of Terror.* Translated from the German. New York: Holt, Rinehart & Winston, 1969.

1832. Baumann, Michael C. *Terror or Love: Michael Baumann's Own Story of His Life as a West German Urban Guerrilla.* Translated from the German. New York: Grove Press, 1979. 127p.

1833. Becker, Jullian. *Hitler's Children: The Story of the Baader-Meinhof Terrorist Gang.* Translated from the German. Philadelphia: Lippincott, 1977. 322p.

Bouchey, L. F., jt. author. *See* Possony, Stefan T.

1834.   Brandt, Willy. *People and Politics: The Years 1960–1975.* Translated from the German. Boston: Little, Brown, 1978. 524p.

1835.   Possony, Stefan T., and L. F. Bouchey. *International Terrorism— The Communist Connection, with a Case Study of West German Terrorist Ulrike Meinhoff.* Washington, D.C.: American Council for World Freedom, 1978. 180p.

(2) Articles

1836.   Acherson, Neal. "The Urban Guerrillas of West Germany." *New Society,* XIII (April 10, 1975), 68+.

1837.   Allemann, Fritz R. "How Effective is Terrorism [in West Germany]?" In: Marjorie Kravitz, ed. *International Summaries: A Collection of Selected Translations in Law Enforcement and Criminal Justice,* v. 3. Rockville, Md.: National Criminal Justice Reference Service, Law Enforcement Assistance Administration, Department of Justice, 1979. pp. 73–80.

1838.   "Ambush in a Civil War: Hans-Martin Schleyer Kidnapping by Baader-Meinhof Gang." *Time,* CX (September 9, 1977), 37–38.

1839.   Baumann, Michael C. "Mind of a German Terrorist: Interview." *Encounter,* LI (September 1978), 81–88.

1840.   Beck, Barbara. "Dr. Marcuse's Children?" *Encounter,* L (February 1978), 74–77.

1841.   Bezymesky, Lev. "Sinister Front." *New Times* (Moscow), no. 5 (February 1972), 24–27.

1842.   Blum, J. "Protection of Persons and Installations at Risk: The German Way." *Police Studies,* I (December 1978), 53–61.

1843.   "Bonnie und Clyde." *Time,* XCIX (February 7, 1972), 37–38.

1844.   Botstein, Leon. "German Terrorism from Afar." *Partisan Review,* no. 46 (Summer 1979), 188–204.

1845.   Bradshaw, Jon. "Dream of Terror: The Baader-Meinhof Gang." *Esquire,* XC (July 18, 1978), 24–45+.

1846.   Carroll, Robert. "Germany's Finger Squads." *Newsweek,* XC (November 21, 1977), 64+.

1847.   _____. "The Stuttgart Four." *Newsweek,* LXXXV (June 16, 1975), 34–35.

1848.   "Criminal Law Reform: Bonn Hits at Urban Terrorists." *German International,* XIX (January 1975), 16–17.

1849. "Deadly Dinner." *Newsweek,* XCII (September 18, 1978), 43.

1850. Dische, Irene. "Germany's Terrorist Lexicon." *Nation,* CCXXV (November 19, 1977), 524–526.

1851. "Disciple of Despair: Suicide of Ulrike Meinhoff Triggers Terrorist Attacks." *Time,* CVII (May 24, 1976), 33.

1852. Dornberg, John. "West Germany's Embattled Democracy: The Anti-Terrorist Menace from the Right." *Saturday Review,* V (June 10, 1978), 18–21.

1853. Eckstein, George. "Coping with Terrorism." *Dissent,* XXV (Winter 1978), 82–84.

1854. Edinger, L. J. "West Germany: Problems and Prospects." *Atlantic Community Quarterly,* XVI (Summer 1978), 167–174.

1855. Elliott, John D. "Action and Reaction: West Germany and the Baader-Meinhof Guerrillas." *Strategic Review,* IV (Winter 1976), 60–67.

1856. Fabricius-Brand, Margarete. "Women [Terrorists] in Isolation." In: Marjorie Kravitz, ed. *International Summaries: A Collection of Selected Translations in Law Enforcement and Criminal Justice,* v. 3. Rockville, Md.: National Criminal Justice Reference Service, Law Enforcement Assistance Administration, Department of Justice, 1979. pp. 55–62.

1857. Fetscher, Iring. "Terrorism and Reaction [in West Germany]." In: Marjorie Kravitz, ed. *International Summaries: A Collection of Selected Translations in Law Enforcement and Criminal Justice,* v. 3. Rockville, Md.: National Criminal Justice Reference Service, Law Enforcement Assistance Administration, Department of Justice, 1979. pp. 45–54.

1858. "Germany: The Terror Kidnapping of Hans-Martin Schleyer by the Baader-Meinhof Gang." *Newsweek,* XC (September 19, 1977), 55–56.

1859. "Guerrillas on Trial: The Baader-Meinhof Gang." *Time,* CIV (December 9, 1974), 65–66.

1860. "Guilty as Charged." *Time,* CIX (May 9, 1977), 43.

1861. Horchem, Hans-Josef. "West Germany's Red Army Anarchists." *Conflict Studies,* no. 46 (April 1976), 1–20.

1862. "Is Germany Burning?" *Macleans,* XCI (February 20, 1978), 26–27+.

1863. Jacobs, Monica. "Civil Rights and Women's Rights in the Federal Republic of Germany Today." *New German Critique,* XIII (Winter 1978), 165–174.

1864.   Kopkind, Andrew. "Racial Revisionist: Horst Mahler." *New Times,* X (June 12, 1978), 35+.

1865.   Kramer, Jane. "Reporter in Europe: Red Army Faction of the Baader-Meinhof Gang." *New Yorker,* LIV (March 20, 1978), 44–46+.

1866.   Lasky, Melvin J. "Journey among the Ugly Germans." *Encounter,* XLIX (November 1977), 35–45.

1867.   _____. "Ulrike and Andreas: The Bonnie and Clyde of West Germany's Radical Subculture May Have Failed to Make a Revolution, but They Have Bruised the Body Politic." *New York Times Magazine,* (May 11, 1975), 14+.

1868.   _____. "Ulrike Meinhof and the Baader-Meinhof Gang." *Encounter,* XLIII (July 1974), 60–62; XLIV (June 1975), 9–23.

1869.   Ledeen, Michael A. "Visions of Hobnails: European Criticism of West Germany's Anti-Terrorist Measures." *New Republic,* CLXXVII (November 19, 1977), 17–19.

1870.   "Life in a State of Siege." *Time,* CX (September 26, 1977), 34–35.

1871.   "Link to Carlos?: Swiss Capture of West German Terrorist Gabriele Kroecher-Tiedemann." *Newsweek,* XCI (January 2, 1978), 25.

1872.   "Living Dangerously in Berlin: The Political Kidnapping of [Mayoral Candidate] Peter Lorenz." *Time,* CV (March 10, 1975), 51–52.

1873.   Mahler, Horst. "Terrorism in West Germany: An Interview." *Socialist Review,* XXXIX (May-June 1978), 118–123.

1874.   Mairowitz, David Z. "Scissors in the Head." *Harpers,* CCLVI (May 1978), 28–31.

1875.   Mayer, Margit. "The German October of 1977." *New German Critique,* XIII (Winter 1978), 155–163.

1876.   Moons, Eric J. H. "The Political and Judicial Approach to Terrorism and Anarchistic Criminality in the Federal Republic of Germany." In: Marjorie Kravitz, ed. *International Summaries: A Collection of Selected Translations in Law Enforcement and Criminal Justice,* v. 3. Rockville, Md.: National Criminal Justice Reference Service, Law Enforcement Assistance Administration, Department of Justice, 1979. pp. 123–130.

1877.   Morrow, Lance. "Terrorism—Why West Germany?: A *Time* Essay." *Time,* CX (December 19, 1977), 37–38.

1878.   Negt, Oskar. "Terrorism and the German State's Absorption of Conflicts." *New German Critique,* XII (Fall 1977), 15–27.

1879. "No More Extensions [for Schleyer]." *Time,* CX (October 24, 1977), 53.

1880. "No Refuge." *Newsweek,* XCII (July 3, 1978), 42.

1881. Oestreicher, Paul. "Roots of Terrorism: West Germany—A Special Case?" *Round Table,* no. 269 (January 1978), 75–80.

1882. Powers, Thomas. "Peacetime: The Baader-Meinhof Gang." *Commonweal,* CIV (November 11, 1977), 723–725.

1883. "Reign of Terror." *Newsweek,* LXXXVIII (December 27, 1976), 35.

1884. Schmidt, Helmut. "Schmidt on Terrorism: Interview." *Newsweek,* XC (November 28, 1977), 77.

1885. "Shoot-out in Frankfurt." *Newsweek,* LXXIX (June 12, 1972), 59–60.

1886. "Standing up to the Gang: Takeover of the West German Embassy in Stockholm by Supporters of the Baader-Meinhof Gang." *Time,* CV (May 5, 1975), 42+.

1887. "Terrorism against the Constitutional State." In: National Criminal Justice Reference Service. *International Summaries: A Collection of Selected Translations in Law Enforcement and Criminal Justice,* v. 1. Rockville, Md.: NCJRS, Law Enforcement Assistance Administration, Department of Justice, 1978. pp. 1–14.

1888. "Terrorism in Germany: Groping for Answers." *U.S. News and World Report,* LXXXIII (November 7, 1977), 56+.

1889. Tinnin, David. "Like Father [Andreas Baader]." *Time,* CX (August 8, 1977), 71.

1890. "The Trapping of a Terrorist [Christian Klar]." *Time,* CXII (September 18, 1978), 52.

1891. "The Urban Guerrilla in the Federal Republic of Germany—Origin and Prospects." In: National Criminal Justice Reference Service. *International Summaries: A Collection of Selected Translations in Law Enforcement and Criminal Justice,* v. 1. Rockville, Md.: NCJRS, Law Enforcement Assistance Administration, Department of Justice, 1978. pp. 15–22.

1892. Urquhart, Ian. "The Case of the Treacherous Tourist [Kristina Berster]." *Macleans,* XCI (August 7, 1978), 18–19.

1893. "War without Boundaries: West Germany Takes the Offensive against Skyjackers and Kidnappers." *Time,* CX (October 31, 1977), 28–34, 41.

1894. Weiss, Peter. "Joe McCarthy is Alive and Well and Living in West Germany: Terror and Counter-terror in the Federal Republic." *New York University Journal of International Law and Politics,* IX (Spring 1976), 61–88.

1895. Whitney, Craig R. "Germany in Thrall." In: William P. Lineberry, ed. *The Struggle against Terrorism.* Reference Shelf, v. 49, no. 3. New York: H. W. Wilson, 1977. pp. 72–75.

(3) DOCUMENTS, PAPERS, AND REPORTS

1896. Middendorff, Wolfgang. *New Developments in the Taking of Hostages and Kidnapping: Summary.* Translated from the German. Rockville, Md.: National Criminal Justice Reference Service, Law Enforcement Assistance Administration, Department of Justice, 1975. 9p.

1897. United States. Congress. Senate. Committee on the Judiciary. Subcommittee on Criminal Laws and Procedures. *West Germany's Political Response to Terrorism: Hearings.* 95th Cong., 2nd sess. Washington, D.C.: U.S. Government Printing Office, 1978. 23p.

1898. West Germany. Press and Information Office. *Documentation of the Events and Decisions Connected with the Kidnapping of Hans-Martin Schleyer and the Hijacking of the Lufthansa Jet "Landshut."* Translated from the German. Bonn, 1977. 209p.

b. The Munich Massacre

(1) BOOKS

1899. Groussard, Serge. *The Blood of Israel: The Massacre of the Israeli Athletes, the Olympics, 1972.* Translated from the German. New York: William Morrow, 1975. 464p.

(2) ARTICLES

1900. "A.B.C.'s Grim T.V. First: Coverage of Terrorist Raid on the Munich Olympics." *Newsweek,* LXXX (September 18, 1972), 67–68.

1901. Adam, Corinna. "Another Name for Munich." *New Statesman and Nation,* LXXXIV (September 15, 1972), 343–344.

1902. "Arab Terrorism: Outraged World Seeks an Answer." *U.S. News and World Report,* LXXIII (September 18, 1972), 16–18+.

1903. "Black September's Ruthless Few." *Time,* C (September 18, 1972), 33.

1904. Copeland, Miles. "Arabs and Terrorists." *National Review,* XXIV (September 29, 1972), 1060–1061+.

1905. "Death at the Olympics." *Reader's Digest,* CI (December 1972), 70–74.

1906. "Europe's Black September." *Time,* C (September 25, 1972), 23–24.

1907. Graham, R. "The Effect of Munich on the Palestinian Dilemma." *Middle East International* (November 1972), 8–10.

1908. "Horror and Death at the Olympics." *Time,* C (September 18, 1972), 22–25+.

1909. Kahn, Ely J., Jr. "Letter from Munich." *New Yorker,* XLVIII (September 16, 1972), 100+.

1910. Kirshenbaum, Jerry. "Sanctuary Violated." *Sports Illustrated,* XXXVII (September 18, 1972), 24–27.

1911. "The Return of Black September: Skyjackers Secure Release of Arab Olympic Terrorists." *Time,* C (November 13, 1972), 29–30.

1912. "Shadow of Death at Munich." *Life,* LXXIII (September 15, 1972), 4–11.

1913. "Terror at the Olympics: Members of Black September Group Assassinate Jewish Atheletes." *Newsweek,* LXXX (September 18, 1972), 24–32.

(3) DOCUMENTS, PAPERS, AND REPORTS

1914. Fulton, Arthur B. *Countermeasures to Combat Terrorism at Major Events: A Case Study.* Washington, D.C.: Department of State, 1976. 66p.

7. Holland: Articles

1915. Benjamin, M. R. "Dutch Entebbe: Rescue of South Moluccan Captives." *Newsweek,* LXXXIX (June 20, 1977), 40+.

1916. "Children of Terror: Hostages Seized by South Moluccans." *Newsweek,* LXXXIX (June 6, 1977), 42–43.

1917. "Commandos Strike at Dawn: Raid on South Moluccan Terrorists." *Time,* CIX (June 20, 1977), 32–34.

1918. "Death through the Rear Window: Murder of British Ambassador Sir Richard Sykes." *Newsweek,* XCIII (April 2, 1979), 53.

1919. Hofman, Peter. "Dutch [Kidnap] Victim [Maurits Caransa]: Self-Made Man." *New York Times Biographical Service,* VIII (October 1977), 1365.

1920. Hughes, Edward. "Terror on Train 734: Hostages Taken by South Moluccan Guerrillas." *Reader's Digest,* CIX (August 1976), 64–69.

1921. Mathevson, William. "Incident in Holland: Reprinted from the *Wall Street Journal*, January 6, 1977." In: William P. Lineberry, ed. *The Struggle against Terrorism*. Reference Shelf, v. 49, no. 3. New York: H. W. Wilson, 1977. pp. 62–71.

1922. "Murder in the Hague: Death of British Ambassador Richard Sykes." *Time*, CXIII (April 2, 1979), 38.

1923. "The Red Army Returns." *Time*, CIV (September 30, 1974), 44+.

1924. "Security Tightens in Wake of Hijack: The Hijack of Japan Air Lines Boeing 747." *Aviation Week and Space Technology*, XCIX (July 30, 1973), 25–26.

1925. "Skyjackers Strike Again: Palestinian Capture of Japan Air Lines Plane." *Time*, CII (July 30, 1973), 30–31.

1926. Stevens, Mack. "Strangers on a Train: Hostages Held by South Moluccan Guerrillas." *Newsweek*, LXXXVI (December 15, 1975), 59–60.

8. Italy

a. Urban Terrorism

(1) Books

1927. Acquaviva, Sabino, and Mario Santuccio. *Social Structure in Italy: Crisis of a System*. Boulder, Colo.: Westview Press, 1976. 236p.

1928. Earle, John. *Italy in the 1970's*. London: David & Charles, 1975. 208p.

1929. Pepper, Curtis B. *Kidnapped: 17 Days of Terror*. New York: Harmony Books, 1978. 150p.

1930. *The Red Brigades*. New York: Manor Books, 1978. 110p.

Santuccio, Mario, jt. author. *See* Acquaviva, Sabino.

1931. Silz, Alexxandro. *Never Again without a Rifle: The Origins of Italian Communism*. Translated from the Italian. New York: Karz Publishers, 1979. 233p.

(2) Articles

1932. "Aldo Moro's Ordeal." *Newsweek*, XCI (May 1, 1978), 34–35.

1933. Allum, Percy. "Political Terrorism in Italy." *Contemporary Review*, CCXXXIII (August 1978), 75–84.

1934. Barzini, Luigi. "Italian Notebook." *Encounter,* LII (February 1979), 87–93.

1935. Bell, J. Bowyer. "Violence and Italian Politics." *Conflict,* I (Summer 1978), *passim.*

1936. Bentley, L. "Disillusioned Italian Kidnap Victim [Giovanni Amati]." *People,* IX (July 19, 1978), 36–37.

1937. "The Blood-Hungry Red Brigades." *Time,* CXI (March 27, 1978), 43.

1938. Bondy, Francoise. "Italian Notebook." *Encounter,* L (February 1978), 42–45.

1939. Carli, Guido. "Italy's Malaise." *Foreign Affairs,* LIV (July 1976), 708–718.

1940. "Death before Lunch: Murder of Genoa Chief Prosecuter Francesco Coco." *Time,* CVII (June 21, 1976), 39.

1941. "'Don't Let Her Suffer': Italian Kidnapping Cases." *Time,* CX (October 17, 1977), 46–47.

1942. "Dossier of Terror." *Police,* X (June 1978), 24–30.

1943. Feustel, Sandy. "Terrorism: Not Just an Italian Problem." *European Community,* XXIV (May-June 1978), 19–22.

1944. "Further Plea [for Moro]." *Time,* CXI (April 17, 1978), 32+.

1945. "Holy War." *Newsweek,* LXXXVII (June 21, 1976), 47.

1946. "In Search of the Red Brigades." *Time,* CXI (April 3, 1978), 38+.

1947. "Inside the Red Brigades." *Newsweek,* XCI (May 15, 1978), 43–44+.

1948. "Italy in Torment." *Atlas,* XXV (May 1978), 23–24+.

1949. "Italy: State of Siege." *Newsweek,* XCI (April 3, 1978), 49+.

1950. "Italy under the Gun." *Newsweek,* XC (August 1, 1977), 32–33.

1951. "Italy's Agony: Assassination of Aldo Moro by the Red Brigades." *Newsweek,* XCI (May 22, 1978), 30–32+.

1952. Keerdoza, E. "Golden Hippie [Eugene Getty]." *Newsweek,* XC (November 28, 1977), 24+.

1953. Kelly, Robert. "World Record: One Outrage Every 4 Hours, 6 Minutes." *Far Eastern Economic Review,* C (April 21, 1978), 52–53.

1954. "Kidnap Epidemic." *Newsweek,* XC (October 17, 1977), 61.

1955. Lurie, Ted. "Running Hard to Stand Still." *Macleans,* XCII (June 4, 1979), 38–39.

1956. Luzzi, Aldo. "Terrorist Criminality [in Italy]." In: Marjorie Kravitz, ed. *International Summaries: A Collection of Selected Translations in Law Enforcement and Criminal Justice,* v. 3. Rockville, Md.: National Criminal Justice Reference Service, Law Enforcement Assistance Administration, Department of Justice, 1979. pp. 131–138.

1957. Mannin, Michael. "Consensus through Violence: Italy's Controlled Crises." *Contemporary Review,* CCXXXII (June 1978), 281–291.

1958. "Minus One Ear: The Release of Paul Getty." *Time,* CII (December 24, 1973), 39–40.

1959. "Most Barbarous Assassins: The Red Brigades' Murder of Aldo Moro." *Time,* CXI (May 22, 1978), 30–32+.

1960. Murray, William. "Letter from Rome." *New Yorker,* LIII (January 16, 1978), 72–82.

1961. "Nation in Torment." *Time,* CXI (May 1, 1978), 26–31.

1962. "Now Italy Is Shaken by Terrorist Siege." *U.S. News and World Report,* LXXXIV (March 27, 1978), 92.

1963. Pepper, Curtis B. "Kidnapped." *New York Times Magazine,* (November 20, 1977), 42–46+.

1964. _____ . "Possessed: The Murder of Antonio Esposito by the Red Brigade." *New York Times Magazine,* (February 18, 1979), 29–32+.

1965. Possony, Stefan T. "Hostage Negotiation: Could Moro Have Been Saved?" *Defense and Foreign Affairs Digest,* VI (June 1978), 38.

1966. "Roman Outrage: Violence by the Red Brigades." *Time,* CXIII (May 14, 1979), 50.

1967. Ronchey, Alberto. "Guns and Gray Matter: Terrorism in Italy." *Foreign Affairs,* LVII (Spring 1979), 921–940.

1968. _____ . "Terror in Italy: After Moro's Murder." *Dissent,* XXV (Fall 1978), 383–385.

1969. _____ . "Terror in Italy: Between Red and Black." *Dissent,* XXV (Spring 1978), 150–156.

1970. Sheehan, Thomas. "Italy behind the Ski Mask: The Red Brigades." *New York Review of Books*, XXVI (August 16, 1979), 20–26.

1971. "State of Siege." *Macleans*, XCI (April 3, 1978), 61–62.

1972. Sterling, Claire. "Italy: The [Gianglacomo] Feltrinelli Case." *Atlantic*, CCXXX (July 1972), 10+.

1973. "Striking at Italy's Heart." *Newsweek*, XCI (March 27, 1978), 65–66+.

1974. "Terrorism in Italy: A New Dimension." *Security Management*, XXII (November 1978), 42–45.

1975. "Terrorist Roundup." *Time*, CXII (October 16, 1978), 72.

1976. "Terrorists Declare War." *Time*, CXI (March 27, 1978), 40+.

1977. "Verdicts against Anarchy." *Time*, CXII (July 3, 1978), 26.

1978. Whetton, Lawrence L. "Italian Terrorism: Record Figures and Political Dilemmas." *Terrorism*, I (1978), 377–396.

1979. Wiley, F. "Gorilla Theater: Kidnapping of the Wealthy in Italy." *Newsweek*, LXXXV (May 12, 1975), 68+.

(3) Documents, Papers, and Reports

1980. Ledeen, Michael A. *Italy in Crisis*. Washington Papers, v. 5, no. 43. Beverly Hills, Calif.: Sage, 1977. 76p.

b. Rome Airport Massacre: Articles

1981. "Death in Rome Aboard Flight 110." *Time*, CII (December 31, 1973), 28+.

1982. "'Operation Helton': Murder, Firebombing, and Hijacking in Rome." *Newsweek*, LXXXII (December 31, 1973), 17–18.

1983. "The Story of the Bloodiest Skyjacking: Terrorism in the Rome Airport." *U.S. News and World Report*, LXXV (December 31, 1973), 16–17.

9. Russia

a. Books

1984. Gross, Feliks. *Violence in Politics: Terror and Political Assassination in Eastern Europe and Russia*. The Hague: Mouton, 1972. 139p.

b. Articles

1985.   Hendel, Samuel. "The Price of Terrorism in the U.S.S.R." In: Marius H. Livingston, ed. *International Terrorism in the Contemporary World.* Westport, Conn.: Greenwood Press, 1978. pp. 122–130.

10. Spain

a. Books

1986.   Agirre, Julen. *"Operation Ogro": The Execution of Admiral Luis Carrero Blanco* [in 1973]. New York: Quadrangle Books, 1975. 196p.

1987.   Preston, Paul, ed. *Spain in Crisis.* New York: Barnes & Noble, 1976. 341p.

b. Articles

1988.   Baird, D. "Open Season on Tourists: Basque Terrorism." *Macleans,* XCII (July 16, 1979), 28+.

1989.   "Basques: Business and Bombs." *Time,* CIII (January 7, 1974), 48–49.

1990.   "Basques Wage a Vacation War." *Newsweek,* XCIV (July 16, 1979), 48.

1991.   Brennan, Peter. "New Basque Terror." *New Statesman and Nation,* LXXXIX (June 27, 1975), 818–819.

1992.   Heiberg, Marianne. "Insiders/Outsiders: Basque Nationalism." *European Journal of Sociology,* XVI (Spring 1975), 169–193.

1993.   Medvedenko, Anatoly. "The Ultras Turn to Terror: Spain." *New Times* (Moscow), no. 6 (February 1977), 8–9.

1994.   "New Visit from the Old Demons." *Time,* CIX (February 7, 1977), 42–43.

1995.   "Political Crime [in Spain]." In: National Criminal Justice Reference Service. *International Summaries: A Collection of Selected Translations in Law Enforcement and Criminal Justice,* v. 1. Rockville, Md.: NCJRS, Law Enforcement Assistance Administration, Department of Justice, 1978. pp. 39–50.

1996.   Preston, Paul. "The Basque Problem." *Nation,* CCXXI (July 19, 1975), 45–46+.

1997.   "Target of Basque Attacks: Spain's Tourists." *U.S. News and World Report,* LXXXVII (July 16, 1979), 9.

1998. "Wave of Basque Terror." *Time,* CXIII (January 22, 1979), 51.

1999. "Week of the Long Knives." *Newsweek,* LXXXIX (February 7, 1977), 45–46.

c. Documents, Papers, and Reports

2000. Menges, Constantine C. *Spain: The Struggle for Democracy Today.* Washington Papers, no. 58. Beverly Hills, Calif.: Sage, 1978. 80p.

11. Sweden

a. Articles

2001. Elwin, Goran. "Swedish Anti-Terrorist Legislation." *Contemporary Crises,* I (July 1977), 289–301.

2002. Sundberg, Jacob. "The Anti-Terrorist Legislation in Sweden." In: Marius H. Livingston, ed. *International Terrorism in the Contemporary World.* Westport, Conn.: Greenwood Press, 1978. pp. 111–112.

b. Documents, Papers, and Reports

2003. Haggman, Bertil. *Sweden's Maoist 'Subversives': A Case Study.* London: Institute for the Study of Conflict, 1975. 20p.

12. Turkey

a. Articles

2004. Butler, David. "Arab Siege in Turkey." *Newsweek,* XCIV (July 23, 1979), 42.

2005. Feroz, Ahmad. "The Turkish Guerrillas: Symptom of a Deeper Malaise." *New Middle East,* VI (April 1973), 13–16.

2006. Fleming, J. "Established Pattern of Terror: Palestinian Attack on the Egyptian Embassy in Ankara." *Macleans,* XCII (July 23, 1979), 26–27.

2007. Stevens, Mack. "Entebbe II: Attack by the Popular Front for the Liberation of Palestine on El Al Passengers in Istanbul Airport." *Newsweek,* LXXXVIII (August 23, 1976), 50–51.

2008. Tomlinson, Kenneth Y. "Turkey in Trouble." *Reader's Digest,* CXV (July 1979), 130–134.

b. Documents, Papers, and Reports

2009. Reilly, Donald E. *Urban Guerrillas in Turkey: Causes and Consequences.* Carlisle Barracks, Pa.: U.S. Army War College, 1972. 62p.

2010. United States. Congress. Senate. Committee on Foreign Relations. *Terrorist Attack at Istanbul Airport: Report.* 94th Cong., 2nd sess. Washington, D.C.: U.S. Government Printing Office, 1976. 5p.

13. Yugoslavia: Articles

2011. Alpern, David M. "Skyjacking for Croatia." *Newsweek,* LXXXVIII (September 20, 1976), 25+.

2012. "Big Catch in Zagreb: Arrest of West German Terrorists." *Time,* CXI (June 12, 1978), 43–44.

2013. "Bombs for Croatia." *Time,* CVIII (September 20, 1976), 25+.

2014. Brockman, Richard. "Notes while Being Hijacked: Croatian Terrorists." *Atlantic,* CCXXXVIII (December 1976), 68–75.

2015. "Closing Down a Hideout: Arrest of Four German Terrorists by Yugoslav Police." *Newsweek,* XCI (June 12, 1978), 63.

2016. Frey, C. W. "Yugoslav Nationalisms and the Question of Limited Sovereignty." *East European Quarterly,* X (Winter 1977), 79–108.

2017. Lendvai, Paul. "Yugoslavia in Crisis." *Encounter,* XXXIX (August 1972), 68–75.

C. The Middle East

1. General Works

a. Books

2018. Bell, J. Bowyer. *The Long War: Israel and the Arabs since 1946.* Englewood Cliffs, N.J.: Prentice-Hall, 1969. 467p.

Creech, James, jt. author. *See* El-Ad, Avri.

2019. Curtis, Michael, ed. *People and Politics in the Middle East: Proceedings of the Annual Conference of the American Academic Association for Peace in the Middle East.* New Brunswick, N.J.: Transaction Books, 1971. 325p.

Dan, Uri, jt. author. *See* Eisenberg, Dennis.

Deacon, Richard, pseud. *See* McCormick, Donald.

2020. Dortzbach, Karl, and Debbie. *Kidnapped.* New York: Harper & Row, 1975. 179p.

2021. Dupuy, Trevor N. *Elusive Victory: The Arab-Israeli Wars, 1947–1974.* New York: Harper & Row, 1978. 672p.

2022. Eisenberg, Dennis, Uri Dan, and Eli Landau. *The Mossad—Inside Stories: Israel's Secret Intelligence Service.* New York: Paddington Press, 1978. 272p.

2023. El-Ad, Avri, and James Creech. *Decline of Honor: An Autobiography.* Chicago: Contemporary Books, 1976. 364p.

2024. Geyer, Georgie A. *The New Hundred Years War.* Garden City, N.Y.: Doubleday, 1972. 318p.

2025. Heikal, Mohamed. *The Road to Ramadan.* London: Collins, 1975.

Landau, Eli, jt. author. *See* Eisenberg, Dennis.

2026. Laqueur, Walter Z. *The Struggle for the Middle East.* New York: Macmillan, 1969. 360p.

2027. McCormick, Donald. *The Israeli Secret Service.* By Richard Deacon, pseud. New York: Taplinger, 1978. 318p.

McNicol, John, jt. author. *See* Tatford, Frederick A.

2028. Moore, John N., ed. *Arab-Israeli Conflict: Readings and Documents.* Rev. ed. Princeton: Princeton University Press, 1977. 1,285p.

2029. O'Neill, Bard E. *Revolutionary Warfare in the Middle East: The Israelis* [vs. the PLO]. Boulder, Colo.: Paladin Press, 1974. 140p.

2030. Oren, Uri. *Ninety-Nine Days in Damascus: The Story of Professor Shlomo Samueloff and the Hijack of TWA Flight 840 to Damascus.* London: Weidenfeld & Nicolson, 1970. 194p.

2031. Sobel, Lester A., ed. *Israel and the Arabs: The October 1973 War.* New York: Facts on File, 1974. 185p.

2032. Tatford, Frederick A., and John McNicol. *Middle East Cauldron.* Eastbourne, Eng.: P.W. Publishing House, 1971. 104p.

2033. Tinnin, David B. *Hit Team.* Boston: Little, Brown, 1976. 240p.

b. Articles

2034. Anabtawi, Samir N. "The Palestinians and the 1973 Middle East War." *Middle East Information Series,* XXV (Winter 1973–1974), 38–41.

2035. Ashhab, Maim. "The Palestinian Aspect of the Middle East Crisis." *World Marxist Review,* XVII (April 1974), 88–95.

2036. Ben Porathy, Y. "The Secret Warriors." *Israel Magazine,* III (January 1973), 37–42.

2037. Beres, Louis R. "The Ever-Violent Middle East." In: William P. Lineberry, ed. *The Struggle against Terrorism.* Reference Shelf, v. 49, no. 3. New York: H. W. Wilson, 1977. pp. 76–82.

2038. Blechman, Barry M. "The Impact of Israel's Reprisals on Behavior of the Bordering Arab Nations Directed at Israel." *Journal of Conflict Resolution,* XVI (March 1972), 155–181.

2039. "Boosting the P.L.O.: Arafat's Visit to Iran." *Newsweek,* XCIII (March 5, 1979), 65.

2040. Broder, Jonathan D. "The War of the Innocents." *Oui,* IV (August 1975), 54+.

2041. Calvert, Peter. "The Diminishing Returns of Political Violence." *New Middle East,* LVI (May 1973), 25–27.

2042. "Can Oil Be Guarded?" *Newsweek,* XCI (June 12, 1978), 79–80.

Dan, Uri, jt. author. *See* Zion, Sidney.

2043. Dinstein, Yoram. "Terrorism and the War of Liberation: An Israeli Perspective on the Arab-Israeli Conflict." In: M. Cherif Bassiouni, ed. *International Terrorism and Political Crimes: Proceedings of the Third Conference on Terrorism and Political Crimes, Syracuse, Sicily, 1973.* Springfield, Ill.: C. C. Thomas, 1974. pp. 155–172.

2044. _____. "Terrorism and Wars of Liberation Applied to the Arab-Israeli Conflict: An Israeli Perspective." *Israel Yearbook of Human Rights,* III (1973), 78–96.

2045. El Ayouty, Yassim. "The Palestinians and the Fourth Arab-Israeli War." *Current History,* LXVI (February 1974), 74–78.

2046. "Fatal Error: The Murder of Ahmed by Israeli Killers." *Time,* CII (August 6, 1973), 31–32.

2047. Flapan, Simha. "The P.L.O., Israel, and Jordan." *New Outlook,* XX (January-February 1977), 5–10+.

2048. "Flight of 006 and Other Terrorism and Anti-Terrorism Tactics." *Newsweek,* LXXXII (August 20, 1973), 37–38.

2049. Geist, Benjamin. "Israel's Options in the Middle East Conflict." *World Today,* XXXII (November 1976), 407–412.

2050. Gendzier, I. "Reflections on an Assassination [Said Hammami]." *Nation,* CCXXVI (January 21, 1978), 36–37.

2051. Heradstveit, Daniel. "The Role of International Terrorism in the Middle East Conflict and Its Implication for Conflict Resolution." In: David Carlton and Carlo Schaef, eds. *International Terrorism and World Security*. New York: Wiley, 1975. pp. 93–103.

2052. Horowitz, Irving. "The Delicate Balance of Middle East Terror: A Global Estimate." *New Outlook*, XVII (February 1974), 7–14.

2053. Hughes, Edward. "Guerrilla Threat in the Middle East." *Time*, XCII (December 13, 1968), 29–32+.

2054. "The Institute Strikes Again: The Work of the Mossad." *Time*, CVI (July 14, 1975), 31–32.

2055. "Israel's Counter-Terror." *Israel and Palestine*, XIX (March 1973), 1–9.

2056. "Israel's Fierce Reprisals for Munich." *Newsweek*, LXXX (September 25, 1972), 49–50+.

2057. Jacobs, Paul. "Israel's Early Warning System in the Arab World." *New York Times Magazine* (February 8, 1970), 23–25+.

2058. Jones, David L. "Reprisal: Israeli Style." *Military Review*, L (August 1970), 91–96.

2059. Klein, Joe. "Journal from the Middle East." *Rolling Stone*, XI (June 15, 1978), 78–86.

2060. "The Middle East: Capital of World Terrorism." *U.S. News and World Report*, LXXXIV (May 22, 1978), 32.

2061. "The Middle East: The Military Dimension." *Journal of Palestine Studies*, IV (Summer 1975), 3–25.

2062. O'Ballance, Edgar. "Israeli Counter-Guerrilla Operations." *Journal of the Royal United Service Institution for Defence Studies*, CXVII (March 1972), 47–52.

2063. _____. "Terrorism in the Middle East." In: Marius H. Livingston, ed. *International Terrorism in the Contemporary World*. Westport, Conn.: Greenwood Press, 1978. pp. 160–164.

2064. O'Neill, Bard E. "Israel and the Fedayeen: Persistance or Transformation?" *Strategic Review*, IV (Spring 1976), 89–101.

2065. Paust, Jordan J. "Selected Terroristic Claims Arising from the Arab-Israeli Conflict." *Akron Law Review*, VII (Spring 1978), 404–421.

2066. "Real-Life Thriller: Palestinian Guerrilla Hijacking." *Time*, XCIX (March 6, 1972), 32+.

2067. "Resistance Operations during August 1971." *Arab Palestine Resistance,* III (September 1971), 54–58.

2068. Rothstein, Raphael. "Undercover Terror: The Other Mid-East War." *World,* II (January 30, 1973), 21–22.

2069. Scali, John A. "U.S. Opposes Middle East Violence and Terrorism." *Department of State Bulletin,* LXVIII (May 21, 1973), 656–660.

2070. Silverburg, Sol. "The Israeli Reaction to Terrorism." *New Outlook,* XII (January 1969), 41–43.

2071. Smith, Terence. "Israel Takes a Hard Line." In: William P. Lineberry, ed. *The Struggle against Terrorism.* Reference Shelf, v. 49, no. 3. New York: H. W. Wilson, 1977. pp. 157–160.

2072. Tinnin, David B. "The Wrath of God." *Playboy,* XXIII (August 1976), 70–180.

2073. "War among the Terrorists: Iraqui-P.L.O. Struggle." *Newsweek,* XCII (August 14, 1978), 25+.

2074. Willoughby, John. "Problems of Counterinsurgency in the Middle East." *Journal of the Royal United Service Institution for Defence Studies,* CXIII (May 1968), 104–112.

2075. Wolf, John B. "A Mideast Profile: The Cycle of Terror and Counterterror." *International Perspectives,* II (November-December 1973), 27–32.

2076. Zion, Sidney, and Uri Dan. "The Untold Story of the Mideast Talks." *New York Times Magazine,* (January 21, 1979), 20–22, 46–53.

c. Documents, Papers, and Reports

2077. Blechman, Barry. "The Consequences of Israeli Reprisals: An Assessment." Unpublished Ph.D. dissertation, Georgetown University, 1971.

2078. Harkabi, Yehoshafat. *The Bomb in the Middle East.* New York: Friendship Press, 1969. 69p.

2079. Israel. Ministry of Foreign Affairs. Research Division. *Arab Thinking on: Solving the Problem of Israel, Terrorism, International Relations, Human Rights, Domestic Problems.* Jerusalem, 1969. 221p.

2080. United States. Congress. House. Committee on Foreign Affairs. Subcommittee on the Near East. *The Continuing Near East Crisis: Background Information.* Washington, D.C.: U.S. Government Printing Office, 1969. 40p.

2081. _____ . _____ . _____ . _____ . _____ . *The Middle East in Crisis—Problems and Prospects: Report.* 92nd Cong., 1st sess. Washington, D.C.: U.S. Government Printing Office, 1971. 28p.

2082. _____ . _____ . _____ . Committee on International Relations. Subcommittee on Investigations. *The Palestinian Issue in the Middle East Peace Effort: Hearings.* 94th Cong., 1st sess. Washington, D.C.: U.S. Government Printing Office, 1975. 293p.

2. The Palestine Liberation Organization (PLO)

a. Books

2083. Alon, Dafna. *Arab Radicalism.* Jerusalem: Israel Economist, 1969. 100p.

2084. Codley, John K. *Green March, Black September: The Story of the Palestinian Arabs.* London: Cass, 1973. 159p.

2085. Dobson, Christopher. *Black September: Its Short, Violent History.* New York: Macmillan, 1974. 179p.

2086. Hussain, Mehmood. *The Palestine Liberation Organization: A Study in Ideology, Strategy, and Tactics.* New Delhi: University Publishers, 1975. 156p.

2087. Ismael, Tareq Y. *The Arab Left.* Syracuse: Syracuse University Press, 1976. 300p.

2088. Jureidini, Paul A. *The Palestinian Movement in Politics.* Boston: Lexington-Heath, 1976. 139p.

2089. Kaufmann, Myron S. *The Coming Destruction of Israel.* Signet Broadside, N-4431. New York: New American Library, 1970. 128p.

2090. Kazziha, Walid W. *Revolutionary Transformation in the Arab World:* [George] *Habash and His Comrades from Nationalism to Marxism.* New York: St. Martin's Press, 1975. 118p.

2091. Khaled, Leila. *My People Shall Live: The Autobiography of a Revolutionary.* London: Hodder & Stoughton, 1973. 223p.

2092. Kiernan, Thomas. *Arafat: The Man and the Myth.* New York: W. W. Norton, 1976. 281p.

2093. Laffin, John. *Fedayeen: The Arab-Israeli Dilemma.* New York: Macmillan, 1973. 160p.

2094. Ma'oz, Moshe, ed. *Palestinian Arab Politics.* Jerusalem: Jerusalem Academic Press for the Harry S Truman Research Institute of the Hebrew University of Jerusalem, 1975. 146p.

2095. O'Ballance, Edgar. *Arab Guerrilla Power, 1967–1972.* Hamden, Conn.: Archon Books, 1974. 246p.

2096. Pryce-Jones, David. *The Face of Defeat: Palestine Refugees and Guerrillas.* New York: Holt, Rinehart & Winston, 1972. 179p.

2097. Quandt, William B., *et al. The Politics of Palestinian Nationalism.* Berkeley: University of California Press, 1973. 234p.

Rothstein, Raphael, jt. author. *See* Schiff, Ze'ev.

2098. Schiff, Ze'ev, and Raphael Rothstein. *Fedayeen: Guerrillas against Israel.* New York: McKay, 1972. 246p.

2099. Yaari, Ehud. *Strike Terror: The Story of Fatah.* Translated from the Hebrew. New York: Sabra Books, 1970. 387p.

2100. Yahalom, Dan. *File on Arab Terrorism.* Jerusalem: Carta, 1973. 129p.

2101. Yahalom, Yivtah. *Arab Terror.* Vol. II of *Attitudes.* 11 vols. Tel Aviv: World Labour Zionist Movement, 1969–1970. Unpaged.

b. Articles

2102. "The ABC's of Arafat's P.L.O." *U.S. News and World Report,* LXXXVII (September 3, 1979), 16.

2103. "ABC's of the Palestine Question." *Arab Palestinian Resistance,* III (September 1971), 48–54.

2104. Abu-Lughod, Ibrahim. "Altered Realities: The Palestinians since 1967." *International Journal,* XXVIII (Autumn 1973), 648–669.

2105. Alexander, Yonah. "The Legacy of Palestinian Terrorism." *International Problems,* XV (Fall 1976), 56–64.

2106. Al-Fattal, R. K. "The Palestine Liberation Organization." *Islamic Review,* LVII (June 1969), 33–36.

2107. Al-Kaddoumi, F. "P.L.O. Still Hangs Tough: Excerpt from an Interview." *Newsweek,* LXXXIX (March 14, 1977), 37.

2108. Allman, T. D. "Palestinian Dilemma." *Harpers,* CCLVI (March 1978), 18–20+.

2109. An-Nahar. Arab Report Research Staff. "The Palestine Liberation Organization: A Promise Unfulfilled." In: its *Politics in Uniform: A Study of the Military in the Arab World and Israel.* Beirut: Cooperative Printing, S.A.L., 1972. pp. 75–88.

2110.   Arafat, Yassir. "Arafat—A New Dawn: Excerpts from an Interview." *Newsweek,* XCI (March 27, 1978), 42.

2111.   ———. "Interview: Excerpts." *Time,* CXIII (April 9, 1979), 46.

2112.   ———. "A Militant's Viewpoint—Mideast Pact Won't Work: Interview." *U.S. News and World Report,* LXXIX (October 13, 1975), 25.

2113.   ———. "Solutions, Not Theatrics: Excerpts from an Interview." *Time,* CIX (March 21, 1977), 33.

2114.   ———, and William Khoury. "The Palestinian Terrorists: Statements." In: Jay Mallin, ed. *Terror and Urban Guerrillas: A Study of Tactics and Documents.* Coral Gables, Fla.: University of Miami Press, 1971. pp. 45–50.

2115.   Bar-Moshe, I. "Palestinian Terrorists." *Atlas,* XVII (April 1969), 22–23.

2116.   Bassiouni, M. Cherif. "Self-Determination and the Palestinians." *American Journal of International Law,* LXV (September 1971), 31–40.

2117.   Bell, J. Bowyer. "Arafat's Man in the Mirror: The Myth of the Fedayeen." *New Middle East,* XIX (April 1970), 19–24.

2118.   Benjamin, M. R. "P.L.O. Center Stage." *Newsweek,* LXXXVII (January 19, 1976), 38–39.

2119.   ———. "P.L.O. Coming on Strong." *Newsweek,* LXXXVI (December 15, 1975), 55–56.

2120.   Bishop, Vaughn F. "The Role of Political Terrorism in the Palestinian Resistance Movement: June 1967–October 1973." In: Michael Stohl, ed. *The Politics of Terrorism.* New York: Marcel Dekker, 1979. pp. 323–350.

2121.   "Black September's Assassins." *Newsweek,* LXXXI (March 19, 1973), 42+.

2122.   "Boasting Their Way to Oblivion." *Atlas,* XX (March 1971), 44–45.

2123.   "Browne, Donald R. "The Voices of Palestine: A Broadcasting House Divided." *Middle East Journal,* XXIX (Spring 1975), 133–150.

2124.   Carroll, Robert. "Will Arafat Say Uncle?" *Newsweek,* LXXXVIII (October 11, 1976), 41+.

2125.   "Children of the Storm: The Arab Commandos." *Newsweek,* LXXIV (December 22, 1969), 37–38+.

2126. "Commandos: Peace Is Their Greatest Fear." *Newsweek,* LXXVI (September 21, 1970), 27–28.

2127. Copeland, Miles. "Arabs and Terrorists." *National Review,* XXIV (September 29, 1972), 1060–1061+.

2128. DeBorchgrave, Andre. "The P.L.O.'s Ebb Tide." *Newsweek,* LXXXV (June 23, 1975), 34–35.

2129. Deming, Angus. "The P.L.O.: A New Image?" *Newsweek,* XCIV (September 3, 1979), 24–25.

2130. "Dr. [George] Habash's Strong Medicine." *Newsweek,* LXXVI (September 21, 1970), 28.

2131. Dorsey, W. H. "Arab Commandos." *New Republic,* CLXI (November 22, 1969), 19–21.

2132. Ellenberg, Edward S. "The P.L.O. and Its Place in Violence and Terror." In: Marius H. Livingston, ed. *International Terrorism in the Contemporary World.* Westport, Conn.: Greenwood Press, 1978. pp. 165–176.

2133. "Exporting Violence: Bomb and Skyjack Plots by Arab Terrorists." *Time,* XCV (January 5, 1970), 27–28.

2134. "The Evolution of the P.L.O." *Imprecor* (February 13, 1975), 16–24.

2135. Fishman, Gideon. "Criminological Aspects of International Terrorism: The Dynamics of the Palestinian Movement." In: Marc Riedel and Terence P. Thornberry, eds. *Crime and Delinquency: Dimensions of Deviance.* New York: Praeger, 1974. pp. 103–113.

2136. Franzieh, Samir. "How Revolutionary Is the Palestinian Resistance?: A Marxist Intrepretation." *Journal of Palestine Studies,* I (Winter 1972), 32–60.

2137. Friendly, Alfred. "Fedayeen." *Atlantic,* CCXXIV (September 1969), 12+.

2138. Gaspard, J. "Palestine: Who's Who among the Guerrillas." *New Middle East,* XVIII (March 1970), 12–16.

2139. Gendzier, I. "The Palestinian Revolution, Palestine, Fatah, the Jews, and Other Matters." *New Middle East,* XIX (January 1971), 38–41.

2140. "Genius [Arafat] for Survival." *Time,* CIX (February 28, 1977), 28.

2141.   Gershman, Carl. "The Failure of the Fedayeen." In: Irving Howe and Carl Gershman, eds. *Israel, the Arabs, and the Middle East.* New York: Bantam Books, 1972. pp. 224–248.

2142.   Gimlin, Hoyt. "Arab Guerrillas." *Editorial Research Reports,* XLVI (April 25, 1969), 309–328.

2143.   Habash, George. "Israel Will Fall: Excerpt from an Interview." *Time,* CX (December 19, 1977), 33.

2144.   _____. "Palestinian Leader Comments on Israeli War: Translated from *Paris Match,* December 23, 1977." *Translations on the Near East and North Africa* (JPRS), no. 1750 (January 17, 1978), 1–3.

2145.   Halliday, F. "An Interview with Ghassan Kannafani on the Popular Front for the Liberation of Palestine and the September Attack." *New Left Review,* no. 67 (May-July 1971), 47–57.

2146.   Hamid, Rashid. "What Is the P.L.O.?" *Journal of Palestine Studies,* IV (Summer 1975), 90–109.

2147.   Harkabi, Yehoshaphat. "Fedayeen Action and Arab Strategy." *Midstream,* XV (May 1969), 14–22.

2148.   _____. "Scope and Limit of the Fedayeen Consensus." *Wiener Library Bulletin,* XXIV (1970–1971), 1–7.

2149.   "Headline Hunters." *Newsweek,* LXXIV (September 22, 1969), 45–46.

2150.   Heradstveit, Daniel. "A Profile of the Palestine Guerrillas." *Cooperation and Conflict,* VII (Winter 1972), 13–36.

2151.   Hermann, Karl. "Reason from the Barrel of a Gun." *Atlas,* XIX (May 1970), 23–25.

2152.   Hirst, D. "Force, the Faith of al Fatah." *Middle East Forum,* XLV (January-February 1968), 113–116.

2153.   Holden, David. "Which Arafat?" *New York Times Magazine,* (March 23, 1975), 11+.

2154.   Hollinger, A. "Black September." *Swiss Review of World Affairs,* XXII (August 1972), 3–8.

2155.   Hudson, Michael C. "Developments and Setbacks in the Palestinian Resistance Movement." *Journal of Palestine Studies,* I (Spring 1972), 64–84.

2156.   _____. "The Palestinian Arab Resistance Movement: Its Significance in the Middle East Crisis." *Middle East Journal,* XXIII (Summer 1969), 291–307.

2157. _____. "The Palestinian Resistance Movement since 1972." In: Willard A Beling, ed. *The Middle East: Quest for an American Policy.* Albany: State University of New York Press, 1973. pp. 101–125.

2158. Hughes, Edward. "Yassir Arafat's Fight for the Palestinians." *Reader's Digest,* CVIII (April 1976), 116–120.

2159. Jiryis, Sabri. "A P.L.O. Moderate Speaks Out: An Interview." *New Outlook,* XVIII (September 1975), 11–17.

2160. Kamleh, T. "The Palestine Liberation Army: Ten Years of Challenge." *Arab Palestinian Resistance,* VII (March 1975), 17–42.

2161. Karnow, Stanley. "Would-be Liberators of Palestine: Fragmented and in Flux." *New Republic,* CLXXII (March 1, 1975), 19–21.

2162. Kearney, V. S. "The Tiger Nassar Can't Ride: The Palestine Liberation Movement." *America,* CXXII (February 28, 1970), 208–211.

2163. Kelidar, Abbas. "The Palestine Guerrilla Movement." *World Today,* XXIX (October 1973), 412–420.

Khoury, William, jt. author. *See* Arafat, Yassir.

2164. Kuroda, Yasumasa. "Young Palestinian Commandos in Political-Socialization Perspective." *Middle East Journal,* XXVI (Summer 1972), 253–270.

2165. Law, John. "Arab Commandos Growing Power in the Mideast." *U.S. News and World Report,* LXVII (November 24, 1969), 82–83.

2166. _____. "With the Arab Commandos: No Peace for Israel—A Campaign of Terror." *U.S. News and World Report,* LXVI (February 24, 1969), 60–62.

2167. Lewis, Bernard. "Palestinians and the P.L.O." *Commentary,* LIX (January 1975), 32–48.

2168. Little, Tom. "Fedayeen: Palestinian Commandos." *Military Review,* L (November 1970), 49–55.

2169. _____. "The Nature of the Palestinian Resistance Movement." *Asian Affairs,* LVII (June 1970), 157–169.

2170. _____. "New Arab Extremists: A View from the Arab World." *Conflict Studies,* no. 4 (May 1970), 5–22.

2171. Lotuf, Abu. "Hidden Leader of the Arab Guerrillas: An Interview." *Look,* XXXIV (June 30, 1970), 24–26.

2172. Louvish, Misha. "The Meaning of Black September." *Jewish Frontier,* XXXIX (October 1972), 6–8.

2173. Macintyre, Ronald R. "The Palestine Liberation Organization: Tactics, Strategies, and Options toward the Geneva Peace Conference." *Journal of Palestine Studies,* IV (Summer 1975), 65–89.

2174. "Maoist Paper Interviews Secret P.L.O. Representative 'Abu Mohammed': Translated from *Arbejderavisen,* November 24–30, 1977." *Translations on the Near East and North Africa,* Joint Publications Research Service (JPRS), no. 1744 (January 3, 1978), 1–3.

2175. Mertz, Robert A. "Why George Habash Turned Marxist." *Mid East,* X (August 1970), 31–36.

2176. "Middle East: The Fedayeen Revisited." *Time,* XCIII (June 13, 1969), 42+.

2177. Moreau, R. "P.L.O. Game Plan." *Newsweek,* XCIII (May 21, 1979), 55.

2178. Morgan, John. "Arab Guerrillas." *New Statesman and Nation,* LXXX (September 25, 1970), 357–358.

2179. Mroue, Karim. "The Arab National Liberation Movement." *World Marxist Review,* XV (October 1972), 44+.

2180. Muslik, Muhammad Y. "Moderates and Rejectionists within the Palestine Liberation Organization." *Middle East Journal,* XXX (Spring 1976), 127–140.

2181. Nakhleh, Emile A. "The Anatomy of Violence: Theoretical Reflections on Palestinian Resistance." *Middle East Journal,* XXV (Spring 1971), 429–443.

2182. O'Ballance, Edgar. "Some Arab Guerrilla Problems." *Military Review,* LII (October 1972), 27–34.

2183. O'Neill, Bard E. "Towards a Typology of Political Terrorism: The Palestine Resistance Movement." *Journal of International Affairs,* VII (Spring-Summer 1978), 17–42.

2184. "The P.L.O. 15-Point Resolution." *New Outlook,* XX (April-May 1977), 9–11.

2185. "P.L.O. Strategy: Fight and Talk." *Time,* CV (January 27, 1976), 41–42.

2186. "Palestine Arab Commandos." *Life,* LXVIII (June 12, 1970), 26D–34.

2187. "Palestinians: A New Unity." *Time,* CX (August 29, 1977), 41–42.

2188. "Palestinians Becoming a Power." *Time*, CIV (November 11, 1974), 27–32+.

2189. "Palestinian Tug-of-War: Palestine Liberation Organizations." *Newsweek*, LXXXIV (November 4, 1974), 36–38.

2190. Plascov, Avi. "The Palestinian [P.L.O.] Predicament after Camp David." *World Today*, XXXIV (December 1978), 467–471.

2191. Popular Front for the Liberation of Palestine. "Platform of the Popular Front for the Liberation of Palestine." In: Walter Laqueur, ed. *The Terrorism Reader: A Historical Anthology.* Philadelphia: Temple University Press, 1978. pp. 145–149.

2192. "The Position of the Palestinian Organization." *Middle East Review*, VII (Fall 1974), 8–27.

2193. Powers, Thomas. "Chance for the P.L.O." *Commonweal*, CVI (April 27, 1979), 232–233.

2194. "Pro and Con: Should the U.S. Deal with the P.L.O.?" *U.S. News and World Report*, LXXXVII (September 3, 1979), 17–18.

2195. Pryce-Jones, David. "P.L.O. Debris: Dead or Divided." *New Republic*, CLXXV (August 21, 1976), 9–11.

2196. "Real Block to Mideast Peace." *U.S. News and World Report*, LXXIII (September 25, 1972), 32–34.

2197. Reed, David. "Fedayeen: Israel's Fanatic Foe." *Reader's Digest*, XCVII (October 1970), 168–173.

2198. "Resistance Issue." *Arab World*, XV (May 1969), 3–55.

2199. Rouleau, Eric. "The Wandering Palestinians: Conflict, Terror, Disarray." *New Outlook*, XVI (February 1973), 2–8.

2200. Schleifer, Abdullah. "The Emergence of Fatah." *Arab World*, XV (May 1969), 16–20.

2201. Sharabi, Hisham. "Liberation or Settlement: The Dialectics of the Palestinian Struggle." *Journal of Palestine Studies*, II (Winter 1973), 33–48.

2202. _____ . "Next Phase for Palestinian Guerrillas: Peoples' War." *Mid East*, X (June 1970), 15–17.

2203. _____ . "Palestine Guerrillas: Their Credibility and Effectiveness." *Middle East Forum*, XLVI (1970), 19–64.

2204. _____ . "Palestine Resistance: Crisis and Reassessment." *Middle East Newsletter,* V (January 1971), 11–14.

2205. Sheehan, E. R. F. "Why Sadat and Faisal Chose Arafat." *New York Times Magazine* (December 8, 1974), 31+.

2206. Sherman, Alfred. "The Palestinians: A Case of Mistaken National Identity?" *World Today,* XXVII (March 1971), 104–114.

2207. "Since Jordan: The Palestinian Fedayeen." *Conflict Studies,* no. 38 (September 1973), 3–18.

2208. Singh, K. R. "The Commandos: Violence in Palestine." *United Service Institution* [of India] *Journal,* CXCIX (October-December 1969), 371–386.

2209. Stanley, Bruce. "Fragmentation and National Liberation Movements: The P.L.O." *Orbis,* XXII (Winter 1979), 1033–1055.

2210. Stern, Sol. "My Jewish Problem, and Ours." *Ramparts,* X (August 1971), 30–40.

2211. Strasser, Steven. "Collision Course over the P.L.O." *Newsweek,* XCIV (September 3, 1979), 18–24.

2212. Sumbatyan, Yuri. "In the Forefront: The Arab Liberation Movement." *Soviet Military Review,* no. 9 (September 1972), 53–55.

2213. Terzi, Z. L. "Face to Face with a Palestinian Leader: An Interview." *Senior Scholastic,* CXI (February 8, 1979), 14–15.

2214. Weisband, Edward. "Palestinian Terrorism: Violence, Verbal Strategy, and Legitimacy." In: Yonah Alexander, ed. *International Terrorism: National, Regional, and Global Perspectives.* New York: Praeger, 1976. pp. 258–319.

2215. "Well-Heeled Guerrillas." *Time,* CX (July 18, 1977), 34+.

2216. Wolf, John B. "Black September: Militant Palestinians." *Current History,* LXIV (January 1973), 5–8+.

2217. _____ . "The Palestinian Resistance Movement." *Current History,* LX (January 1971), 26–31+.

2218. Wren, Christopher. "Confronting the P.L.O." *New York Times Magazine,* (September 9, 1979), 32–42+.

2219. Yaari, Ehud. "Al-Fath's Political Thinking." *New Outlook,* XI (November-December 1968), 20–33.

2220. _____ . "The Decline of al-Fatah." *Midstream,* XVII (May 1971), 3–12.

2221.   Yalin-Mar, N. "A Letter to a Black September Fighter." *Middle East International,* no. 22 (April 1973), 14–16.

2222.   "Yassir Arafat." *Current Biography,* XXXII (March 1971), 3–5.

2223.   _____ . In: Orina Fallaci. *Interview with History.* New York: Liveright, 1976. pp. 123–139.

c. Documents, Papers, and Reports

2224.   Chaliand, Gerald. *The Palestine Resistance Movement.* Beirut: Fifth of June Society, 1969. 45p.

2225.   *A Dialogue with Fatah.* [Cairo?] Palestine National Liberation Movement [1969?]. 104p.

2226.   Fifth of June Society. *Aims of the Palestinian Resistance Movement with Regard to the Jews.* Beirut: Palestine Research Center, 1970. 14p.

2227.   *The Futility of Terror: A Summing Up of Palestinian Terrorist Activity.* Tel Aviv: Israeli Reply, 1971. 33p.

2228.   Ganahl, John. *Time, Trial, and Terror: An Analysis of the Palestinian Guerrilla Movement.* Maxwell AFB, Ala.: Air War College, Air University, 1975. 85p.

2229.   Harkabi, Yehoshafat. *Fedayeen Action and Arab Strategy.* Adelphi Papers, no. 53. London: International Institute for Strategic Studies, 1968. 23p.

2230.   Horton, Alan W. *Several Faces of Arab-Israeli Peace.* Report, no. 4. Hanover, N.H.: American University Field Staff, 1979. 10p.

2231.   Israel. Ministry for Foreign Affairs. Division of Information. *Accessories to Terror: The Responsibility of Arab Governments for the Organization of Terrorist Activities.* Jerusalem: Israel Information Center, 1973.

2232.   Jabber, Frank. *The Palestinian Resistance and Inter-Arab Politics.* RAND Paper P-4653. Santa Monica, Calif.: RAND Corp., 1971. 34p.

2233.   Kadi, Leila S., comp. *Basic Political Documents of the Armed Palestinian Resistance Movement.* Palestine Books, no. 27. Beirut: P.L.O. Research Center, 1969. 254p.

2234.   Moughrabi, Fouad. "The Refusal Front: A Study of the High-Risk Politics in the Palestinian Resistance Movement." Unpublished paper, 17th Annual Convention of the International Studies Association, 1976.

2235.   O'Neill, Bard E. "Revolutionary Warfare in the Middle East: An Analysis of the Palestinian Guerrilla Movement, 1967–1972." Unpublished Ph.D. dissertation, University of Denver, 1972.

2236.   Palestine National Liberation Movement. *Political Armed Struggle*. Beirut: Fifth of June Society, 1970. 47p.

2237.   _____. *Revolution: United Victory*. Beirut: Fifth of June Society, 1970. 30p.

2238.   Quandt, William B. *Palestinian Nationalism: Its Political and Military Dimensions*. RAND Report R-782-ISA. Santa Monica, Calif.: RAND Corp., 1971. 132p.

2239.   Saleiby, Samir S. *The Palestine Problem*. London: Institute of International Studies, 1970. 92p.

2240.   Sharabi, Hisham. *Palestine Guerrillas: Their Credibility and Effectiveness*. Washington, D.C.: Center for Strategic and International Studies, Georgetown University, 1970. 35p.

2241.   Weigert, Gideon. *Whoso Killeth a Believer*. Jerusalem: Israel Communications, 1971. 48p.

2242.   Woods, Stephen R., Jr. *The Palestinian Guerrilla Organization: Revolution or Terror as an End*. Carlisle Barracks, Pa.: U.S. Army War College, 1973. 80p.

2243.   Yaniv, A. *P.L.O.: A Profile*. Jerusalem: Israel Universities Study Group for Middle East Affairs, 1974. 39p.

3. Terrorism in Israel

a. Books

2244.   Allon, Yigal. *Shield of David*. New York: Random House, 1970. 272p.

2245.   Aruri, Naseer, ed. *The Palestinian Resistance to Israeli Occupation: Essays Presented at the Second Annual Convention of the Association of Arab-American University Graduates, Detroit, 1969*. Wilmette, Ill.: Medina University Press, 1970. 171p.

2246.   Avineri, Shlomo, ed. *Israel and the Palestinians: Reflections on the Clash of Two National Movements*. New York: St. Martin's Press, 1971. 168p.

2247.   Curtis, Michael. *The Palestinians: People, History, Politics*. New Brunswick, N.J.: Transaction Books, 1975. 277p.

2248.   Fabin, Larry L., and Ze'ev Schiff, eds. *Israelis Speak: About Themselves and the Palestinians*. Washington, D.C.: Carnegie Endowment for International Peace, 1977. 258p.

2249.   Forrest, Alfred C. *The Unholy Land.* Old Greenwich, Conn.: Devin-Adair, 1972. 178p.

2250.   Harkabi, Yehoshafat. *Palestinians and Israel.* New York: Wiley, 1974. 285p.

2251.   Horowitz, Irving L. *Israeli Ecstasies/Jewish Agonies.* New York and London: Oxford University Press, 1974. 272p.

2252.   Katz, Shmuel. *Battleground: Fact and Fantasy in Palestine.* London and New York: W. H. Allen, 1973. 271p.

2253.   O'Neill, Bard E. *Armed Struggle in Palestine: A Political-Military Analysis.* Boulder, Colo.: Westview Press, 1979. 320p.

2254.   Rabin, Yitzhak. *The Memoirs of Yitzhak Rabin.* Boston: Little, Brown, 1979. 310p.

2255.   Said, Edward. *The Question of Palestine.* New York: Times Books, 1979. 256p.

Schiff, Ze'ev, jt. editor. *See* Fabin, Larry L.

2256.   Sharabi, Hisham. *Palestine and Israel: The Lethal Dilemma.* New York: Pegasus, 1969. 224p.

2257.   Stetler, Russell, comp. *Palestine, the Arab-Israeli Conflict: A Ramparts Reader.* San Francisco: Ramparts Press, 1972. 297p.

b. Articles

2258.   "Again the Palestinians: Fatah Raid on Nahariya and Israeli Retaliation." *Time,* CIV (July 8, 1974), 18+.

2259.   "Anti-Terror Units on Alert during Sadat's Visit: Translated from *Ha'arez,* November 24, 1977." *Translations on the Near East and North Africa* (JPRS), no. 1744 (Janaury 3, 1978), 63–67.

2260.   "Arab Terrorism." *Jewish Frontier,* XXXVI (January 1969), 13–16.

2261.   "Attacks on Palestinians." *Middle East International,* no. 20 (February 1973), 20–23.

2262.   Benjamin, M. R. "Night Raid on the Savoy." *Newsweek,* LXXXV (March 17, 1975), 37–38.

2263.   Bruzousky, M. A. "The P.L.O. and Israel." *Contemporary Review,* CCXXIX (August 1976), 64–71.

2264. "Bullets, Bombs, and a Sign of Hope: Maalot Attack by the P.L.O. and Israeli Retaliation in Lebanon." *Time,* CIII (May 27, 1974), 24–26+.

2265. "Chronology of Zionist and Israeli Terrorism." *Palestine Digest,* II (January 1973), 3–8.

2266. Colebrook, Joan. "Israel—With Terrorists." *Commentary,* LVIII (July 1974), 30–39.

2267. Dershowitz, A. M. "Terrorism and Preventive Detention: The Case of Israel." *Commentary,* L (December 1970), 67–78.

2268. Dowty, Alan. "Israel's Palestinian Policy." *Midstream,* XXI (April 1975), 7–18.

2269. Fraker, S. "Israel Hangs Tough." *Newsweek,* XC (August 22, 1977), 36–37.

2270. Goldberg, J. J. "The West Bank: Policies and Alternatives." *Jewish Frontier,* XLII (January 1975), 14–19.

2271. Goldstein, Michael. "Israeli Security Measures in the Occupied Territories: Administrative Detention." *Middle East Journal,* XXXII (Winter 1978), 35–44.

2272. Gray, Colin S. "The Security of Israel." *Military Review,* LIII (October 1973), 22–35.

2273. Hitchens, Christopher. "West Bank Autonomy: The P.L.O. and the Palestinians." *Nation,* CCXXVIII (February 17, 1979), 161+.

2274. "How to Foil a Hijacking: Israelis Defeat Arabs at Lydda Airport." *Newsweek,* LXXIX (May 22, 1972), 42+.

2275. "Israeli Policy towards the Palestinians: 25 Years of Terrorism." *Arab Palestinian Resistance,* VIII (January 1975), 23–32.

2276. "Israel's Night of Carnage: Massacre at Tel Aviv's Lod Airport." *Time,* XCIX (June 12, 1972), 23–25.

2277. "Israel's Wagons in a Circle." *Newsweek,* LXXXIV (December 2, 1974), 44–45+.

2278. Kimche, J. "Can Israel Contain the Palestine Revolution?" *Conflict Studies,* no. 13 (June 1971), 1–11.

2279. Krosney, Herbert. "Israel: Terror and Promise." *Nation,* CCXVIII (June 8, 1974), 717–719.

2280. Kuriyama, Yoshikiro. "Terrorism at Tel Aviv Airport and a 'New Left' Group in Japan."*Asian Survey*, XIII (March 1973), 336–346.

2281. "Lydda Massacre—Murder by Proxy: Japanese Gunmen Recruited by the Popular Front for the Liberation of Palestine."*Newsweek*, LXXIX (June 12, 1972), 57+.

2282. McPeak, Merrill A. "Israel: Borders and Security." *Foreign Affairs*, LIV (April 1976), 426–443.

2283. Mecklin, John M. "Fire and Steel for Palestine." *Fortune*, LXXXII (July 1970), 84–89+.

2284. "Mideast—Blood and Hope: The Maalot Massacre."*Newsweek*, LXXXIII (May 27, 1974), 36–40.

2285. "Mideast Cross Fire: Fatah Attack on Nahariya." *Newsweek*, LXXXIV (July 8, 1974), 36–37.

2286. "Nation Sorely Besieged: Bet She'an Raid by the P.L.O." *Time*, CIV (December 2, 1974), 43–44+.

2287. Okamoto, Kozo. "Portrait of a [Lod Airport] Terrorist: An Interview." *Asian Survey*, XVI (September 1976), 830–845.

2288. Peretz, Don. "Arab Palestine: Phoenix or Phantom?" *Foreign Affairs*, XLVIII (January 1970), 322–333.

2289. "Sabbath of Terror: Al-Fatah Attack." *Time*, CXI (March 20, 1978), 25–27.

2290. Salpeter, Eliahu. "Israel's View of the Palestinian Question." *New Outlook*, LIX (March 1, 1976), 8–10.

2291. Schiff, Z. "Arab Terror."*Israel Magazine*, VI (June 1974), 44–50.

2292. "Shock, Terror, and Slender Hopes: Arab Raid on the Village of Qiryat Shemona." *Time*, CIII (April 22, 1974), 36–37.

2293. "Slaughter in Israel: Al Fatah Assault." *Newsweek*, XCI (March 20, 1978), 24+.

2294. Steele, Raymond. "Massacre at Zion Square." *Newsweek*, LXXXVI (July 14, 1975), 34–35.

2295. "Terrorism Complicates a Mission of Peace: Al Fatah Attack on Tel Aviv Hotel [the Savoy]." *Time*, CV (March 17, 1975), 31–33.

2296. "Torturing the Truth: Allegations of Israeli Torture of Palestinians Reported in *Washington Post.*" *New Republic*, CLXXX (February 24, 1979), 5–6+.

2297. "Unpromising Start for Peace: P.L.O. Attack on Nahariya, Israel, and the Israeli Retaliation." *Time,* CXIII (May 7, 1979), 35.

2298. "War of Attrition." *Newsweek,* LXXXIV (July 1, 1974), 31–32.

c. Documents, Papers, and Reports

2299. Bavly, Dan, and David Farhi. *Israel and the Palestinians.* Pamphlet, no. 29. London: Anglo-Israel Association, 1971. 48p.

2300. *Palestine: Crisis and Liberation.* Havanna: Tricontinental, 1970. 223p.

4. Terrorism in Jordan

a. Books

2301. Powers, Thomas. *Diana: The Making of a Terrorist.* Boston: Houghton Mifflin, 1971. 225p.

2302. Snow, Peter, and David Phillips. *The Arab Hijack War.* New York: Ballantine Books, 1970. 176p.

b. Articles

2303. "Act of Patriotism: Hijacking of Olympic Airways Plane by Arab Terrorists." *Time,* XCVI (August 3, 1970), 19–20.

2304. Brandon, Henry. "Jordan: The Forgotten Crisis." *Foreign Policy,* X (Spring 1973), 158–170.

2305. Brown, Neville. "Jordanian Civil War." *Military Review,* LI (September 1971), 38–48.

2306. _____ . "Palestinian Nationalism and the Jordanian State." *World Today,* XXVI (September 1970), 370–378.

2307. "Chaos in the Skies: Palestinian Guerrillas Strike at the Big Jets." *Life,* LXIX (September 18, 1970), 30–37.

2308. "Civil War Explodes in Jordan." *Newsweek,* LXXVI (September 28, 1970) 35–38+.

2309. "Drama on the Desert: The Week of the Hostages." *Time,* XCVI (September 21, 1970), 18–20+.

2310. Grant, Z. B. "Commando Revolution: A Hundred Years War in the Middle East?" *New Republic,* CLXII (January 24, 1970), 9–11.

2311. Guldescu, Slanko. "Behind the Scenes of the Jordanian Civil Strife." *Queen's Quarterly,* LXXVIII (Summer 1971), 250–260.

2312.   Held, Jean-Francis. "Lost Illusions: A Report from Jordan on the Setback of the Palestinian Guerrilla Organization." *New Outlook,* XIV (March 1971), 31–36.

2313.   "Hijack War: Palestinian Terrorists Hijack Four Airliners." *Newsweek,* LXXVI (September 21, 1970), 20–28.

2314.   Howard, H. N. "Jordan in Turmoil." *Current History,* LXII (January 1972), 14–19.

2315.   "Jordan's Nine-Day War." *Newsweek,* LXXVI (October 5, 1970), 36–37.

2316.   "Ordeal for the Innocent: Story of Hijack Victims and Arab Hijackers." *U.S. News and World Report,* LXIX (September 21, 1970), 20–21.

2317.   Pace, Eric. "The Violent Men of Amman." *New York Times Magazine,* (July 19, 1970), 8–9+.

2318.   Price, D. L. "Jordan and the Palestinians: The P.L.O.'s Prospects." *Conflict Studies,* no. 66 (December 1975), 1–20.

2319.   Staieh, E. "The Jordanian-Palestinian Civil War of 1970." *India Quarterly,* XXX (January-March 1974), 42–59.

2320.   Stork, John. "The Battle of Amman." *Ramparts,* IX (December 1970), 14+.

2321.   "Tangled Aftermath: Destruction of Planes by Arab Guerrillas, September 1970." *Newsweek,* LXXVII (February 8, 1971), 39–40.

2322.   "War on the Long Breath." *Time,* XCV (March 30, 1970), 32–37.

5. Terrorism in Lebanon

a. Books

2323.   Deeb, Marius. *The Lebanese Civil War.* New York: Praeger, 1979. 150p.

2324.   Gabriel, Philip L. *In the Ashes: The Story of Lebanon.* Ardmore, Pa.: Whitmore Publishing, 1978. 249p.

2325.   Vocke, Harald. *The Lebanese War: Its Origins and Political Dimensions.* Translated from the German. New York: St. Martin's Press, 1978. 81p.

b. Articles

2326.   "At War with the P.L.O.: Retaliatory Raid on Lebanon for P.L.O. Attack on Nahariya." *Newsweek,* XCIII (May 7, 1979), 53+.

2327. "The Beirut Retaliation: A Case Study of the Use of Force in Time of Peace." *New York University Journal of International Law and Politics*, II (Spring 1969), 105–131.

2328. "Beirut's Dr. Death [Bassom Muhammad al Farkh]." *Newsweek*, XCIII (January 1, 1979), 32.

2329. Black, Ian. "Begin's War and the Revival of the P.L.O." *New Statesman and Nation*, XCV (April 21, 1978), 518+.

Blum, Yehuda Z., jt. author. *See* Falk, Richard A.

2330. Carroll, Robert. "Case of Arab against Arab: Fighting between Lebanon's Phalangists and the Fedayeen." *Newsweek*, LXXXV (April 28, 1975), 39–40.

2331. _____. "Death of a Terrorist: The Murder of Abu Hassan Is Charged to the Mossad." *Newsweek*, XCIII (February 5, 1979), 61.

2332. Chamie, Joseph. "The Lebanese Civil War: An Investigation into the Causes." *World Affairs*, CXXXIX (Winter 1976–1977), 171–188.

2333. "Death of a Terrorist: The Murder of Abu Hassan in Beirut." *Time*, CXIII (February 5, 1979), 111–112.

2334. Falk, Richard A., and Yehuda Z. Blum. "The Beirut Raid and the International Law of Retaliation." *American Journal of International Law*, LXIII (July 1969), 415–443; LXIV (January 1970), 73–105.

2335. Gendzier, I. "Lebanon and the Palestinians." *New Outlook*, XII (February 1969), 2–27.

2336. Hudson, Michael C. "Fedayeen Are Forcing Lebanon's Hand." *Mid East*, X (February 1970), 7–14.

2337. _____. "The Palestinian Factor in the Lebanese Civil War." *Middle East Journal*, XXXII (Summer 1978), 261–278.

2338. Hussein, Mahmoud. "Reflections on the Lebanese Impasse." *Monthly Review*, XXXVIII (November 1976), 14–27.

2339. "Israel Strikes Back." *Newsweek*, XCI (March 27, 1978), 26–29.

2340. Johnson, Leigh. "Lebanon: A Search for Peace." *Defense and Foreign Affairs Digest*, VI (December 1978), 36–37.

2341. Kapeliuk, Annon. "Lebanon's Hour of Trial." *New Outlook* XII (November-December 1969), 7–16.

2342. "Mideast's Latest Hot Spot: The Squeeze on Lebanon." *U.S. News and World Report*, LXVII (August 25, 1969), 30–31.

2343. "Morning after a Night of Terror: Attacks in Beirut." *Newsweek,* LXXXI (April 23, 1973), 35–36.

2344. Muftic, M. "A Background Study of the Recent Lebanese Tussle with the Fatah Organization." *Islamic Review,* LVII (October 1969), 14–17.

2345. "Nowhere to Go: Palestinian Guerrillas in Lebanon." *Newsweek,* LXXIX (March 13, 1972), 38+.

2346. O'Ballance, Edgar. "Goliath's War: Israeli Operation 'Litani,' 15–17 March 1978." *Marine Corps Gazette,* LXII (December 1978), 34–40.

2347. Pryce-Jones, David. "War of the Arabs: The P.L.O. in Lebanon." *New Republic,* CLXXIV (June 19, 1976), 11–14.

2348. Rejwan, Nissim. "Lebanon and the Guerrillas." *Midstream,* XV (December 1969), 15–21.

2349. Rubin, Barry. "The Situation in Lebanon." *Contemporary Review,* CCXXVII (November 1975), 235–239.

2350. Stoakes, Frank. "Civil War in Lebanon . . *World Today,* XXXII (January 1976), 8–17.

2351. "Strange Turn in Lebanon's Agonizing War: The Palestine Liberation Organization." *U.S. News and World Report,* LXXXI (August 9, 1976), 49–50.

2352. "Terror to End Terror?: Israel's Raid on Beirut." *Time,* CI (April 23, 1973), 19–20+.

2353. Waterman, Charles. "Lebanon's Continuing Crisis." *Current History,* LV (January 1978), 19–24.

2354. Wolf, John B. "Lebanon: The Politics of Survival." *Current History,* LXII (January 1977), 20–24+.

2355. _____. "Shadow on Lebanon." *Current History,* LVIII (January 1970), 21–26.

c. Documents, Papers, and Reports

2356. Chalouhi, Robert G. "The Crisis in Lebanon: A Test of Consociational Theory." Unpublished Ph.D. dissertation, University of Florida, 1978.

D. Asia

1. Afghanistan: Articles

2357. "Death behind a Key Hole: Murder of U.S. Ambassador Adolph Dubs." *Time*, CXIII (February 26, 1979), 34.

2358. "Death of an Envoy: The Killing of Adolph Dubs." *Newsweek*, XCIII (February 26, 1979), 26–27.

2359. "Time of Terror for U.S. Diplomats." *U.S. News and World Report*, LXXXVI (February 26, 1979), 13+.

2. India: Articles

2360. Burki, S. J. "Social and Economic Detriments of Political Violence: A Case Study of the Punjab." *Middle East Journal*, XXV (August 1971), 465–480.

2361. Hula, Richard C. "Political Violence and Terrorism in Bengal." In: Michael Stohl, ed. *The Politics of Terrorism*. New York: Marcel Dekker, 1979. pp. 351–372.

2362. Qureshi, Saleem. "Political Violence in the South Asian Subcontinent." In: Yonah Alexander, ed. *International Terrorism: National, Regional, and Global Perspectives*. New York: Praeger, 1976. pp. 151–193.

3. Japan: Articles

2363. Deming, Angus. "Red Army's Coup: Japanese Hijacking." *Newsweek*, XC (October 10, 1977), 48.

2364. "Fly Me to Pyongyang: Japan Air Lines 727." *Newsweek*, LXXV (April 13, 1970), 40+.

2365. "Hijackings by Japan's Red Army." *Japan Quarterly*, XXIV (January-March 1978), 8–11.

2366. Iwahawa, Takashi. "The Making of a Terrorist: The Suicidal Fanaticism of the Japanese Red Army." *Atlas*, XXIII (January 1976), 33+.

2367. "Japan Cowers before the Red Army: Guerrillas Who Breed Disgust." *Far Eastern Economic Review*, XCVIII (October 14, 1977), 15–16.

2368. "Japan: Violence for Hire." *U.S. News and World Report*, LXXXIV (May 22, 1978), 32–33.

2369. "Japan's United Red Army." *Newsweek*, LXXIX (June 12, 1972), 59+.

2370. Ringwald, George B. "Terrorists in the Safest City [Toyko]." *Worldview,* XIX (May 1976), 21–24.

2371. "Samurai Skyjackers." *Time,* XCV (April 13, 1970), 30+.

2372. Stockwin, Herbert. "Deadly Pattern from the Past." *Far Eastern Economic Review,* LXXXIV (June 17, 1974), 14–16.

2373. Thornton, R. Y. "Mobile Task Forces of Japan: The Kidotai [Riot Police]." *Police Chief,* XXXVIII (July 1971), 65–73.

4. Singapore-Malaysia: Articles

2374. "Again the Red Army: Kuala Lumpur Attack." *Time,* CVI (August 18, 1975), 27–28.

2375. Das, K. "Hi—Shut Up." *Far Eastern Economic Review,* CI (September 1, 1978), 64.

2376. _____ . "Last Word on Flight MH-653." *Far Eastern Economic Review,* CI (September 22, 1978), 20–22.

2377. _____ . "Terrorists Go to Town." *Far Eastern Economic Review,* LXXXIX (September 12, 1975), 10–12.

2378. Morrow, M. "Singapore's Week of the Jackals." *Far Eastern Economic Review,* LXXXIII (February 11, 1974), 10–12.

5. Thailand: Articles

2379. "Backdown in Bangkok: Black September Group Captures Israeli Embassy in Thailand." *Time,* CI (January 8, 1973), 29–30.

2380. Tandrup, A. "Thai Terrorists' Hidden Strength." *Far Eastern Economic Review,* XCI (February 27, 1976), 31+.

2381. "The Thais and the Terrorists." *Newsweek,* LXXI (January 8, 1973), 26+.

E. Africa

1. General Works

a. Books

2382. Gibson, Richard. *African Liberation Movements: Contemporary Struggles against White Minority Rule.* New York: Published for the Institute of Race Relations by Oxford University Press, 1972. 350p.

2383. Venter, Al J. *Portugal's Guerrilla War: The Campaign for Africa.* Capetown, South Africa: John Malherbe, 1973. 220p.

b. Articles

2384. Mojekwu, Christopher C. "From Protest to Terror-Violence: The African Experience." In: Marius H. Livingston, ed. *International Terrorism in the Contemporary World.* Westport, Conn.: Greenwood Press, 1978. pp. 177–181.

2385. Morrison, Donald, and Hugh M. Stevenson. "Integration and Instability: Patterns of African Political Development." *American Political Science Review,* LXVI (September 1972), 902–927.

Stevenson, Hugh M., jt. author. *See* Morrison, Donald.

2386. Sundiata, I. K. "Integrative and Disintegrative Terror: The Case of Equatorial Guinea." In: Marius H. Livingston, ed. *International Terrorism in the Contemporary World.* Westport, Conn.: Greenwood Press, 1978. pp. 182–194.

2387. Welfling, Mary. "Terrorism in Sub-Sahara Africa." In: Michael Stohl, ed. *The Politics of Terrorism.* New York: Marcel Dekker, 1979. pp. 259–300.

c. Documents, Papers, and Reports

2388. Jacobs, W. D. *Terrorism in Southern Africa: Portents and Prospects.* New York: American-African Affairs, 1973. 35p.

2389. Metrowich, F. R. *Terrorism in Southern Africa.* Pretoria, South Africa: Africa Institute of South Africa, 1973. 79p.

2. Zimbabwe

a. Books

2390. Hills, Denis C. *Rebel People.* New York: Holmes & Meier, 1978. 248p.

2391. Raeburn, Michael. *Black Fire: Accounts of the Guerrilla War in Rhodesia.* London: J. Friedmann, 1978. 243p.

2392. *Rhodesia/Zimbabwe, 1971–1977.* New York: Facts on File, 1977. 166p.

2393. Shay, Reg. *The Silent War.* Salisbury, Rhodesia: Galaxie Press, 1971. 267p.

b. Articles

2394. "Again, Death Flight SAM-7: Patriotic Front Guerrilla Attack on Rhodesian Plane." *Time,* CXIII (February 26, 1979), 40.

2395. Nkomo, Joshua. "'We Shot It Down': Airliner Attack, Excerpt from Interview." *Newsweek,* XCII (September 18, 1978), 47.

2396.   Norman, Geoffrey. "Rhodesia: The Storm before the Storm." *Esquire,* XC (November 21, 1978), 98–100+.

2397.   "'Please, Don't Kill Us': Attack on Airliner and Massacre of Crash Survivors." *Newsweek,* XCII (September 18, 1978), 45+.

2398.   "Rhodesia: Anti-Terrorist Measures and Human Rights." *International Commission of Jurists Review, 1975.* Geneva: International Commission of Jurists, 1975. pp. 20–25.

c. Documents, Papers, and Reports

2399.   Catholic Commission for Justice and Peace in Rhodesia. *Civil War in Rhodesia: Abduction, Torture, and Death in the Counterinsurgency Campaign—A Report.* Salisbury, Rhodesia, 1976. 102p.

3. Somalia: Articles

2400.   Benjamin, M. R. "Detour to Dubai: Lufthansa 737." *Newsweek,* XC (October 24, 1977), 62.

2401.   Brelis, Dean. "The Thin Blue Line." *Time,* CXI (May 29, 1978), 38+.

2402.   Brockman, Richard. "Notes while Being Hijacked." *Reader's Digest,* CX (June 1977), 15–18+.

2403.   Deming, Angus. "New War on Terrorism: Rescue of Hostages by German Commandos in Mogadishu, Somalia." *Newsweek,* XC (October 31, 1977), 48–50+.

2404.   "The German Entebbe: Mogadishu." *National Review,* XXIX (November 11, 1977), 1285–1286.

2405.   "Hostage Syndrome: Mogadishu Aftermath." *Newsweek,* XCI (May 8, 1978), 17–18.

2406.   "Is the Tide Turning against Terrorists?: West German Rescue of Hostages at Mogadishu, Somalia." *U.S. News and World Report,* LXXXIII (October 31, 1977), 22–24.

2407.   Ropelewski, Robert R. "Commandos Thwart Hijackers: The Rescue of 85 Hostages of Lufthansa 737 in Somalia." *Aviation Week and Space Technology,* CVII (October 24, 1977), 14–16.

2408.   "Terror and Triumph at Mogadishu: The New Breed of Commando." *Time,* CX (October 31, 1977), 42–44.

2409.   "The Triumph at Mogadishu." *Reader's Digest,* CXII (March 1978), 120–126.

4. South Africa

a. Books

2410. Morris, Michael. *Terrorism: The First Full Account in Detail of Terrorism and Insurgency in South Africa.* Cape Town, South Africa: H. Timmins, 1971. 249p.

b. Articles

2411. Efrat, E. S. "Terrorism in South Africa." In: Yonah Alexander, ed. *International Terrorism: National, Regional, and Global Perspectives.* New York: Praeger, 1976. pp. 194–208.

2412. International Commission of Jurists. "The Terrorism Act of South Africa." *Current History,* LVI (May 1969), 298–299+.

2413. "The View from BOSS." *Newsweek,* LXXXVIII (October 25, 1976), 53–54.

c. Documents, Papers, and Reports

2414. *Administration of Security Legislation in South Africa, January 1976–March 1977.* Johannesburg: South African Institute of Race Relations, 1977. 82p.

2415. Brigham, Daniel T. *Blueprint for Conflict.* New York: American-African Affairs, 1969. 34p.

2416. *Security and Related Trials in South Africa, July 1976–May 1977.* Johannesburg: South African Institute of Race Relations, 1977. 81p.

2417. South Africa. Department of Foreign Affairs. *South West Africa: Measures Taken to Combat Terrorism.* Cape Town, 1968. 28p.

5. Sudan

a. Articles

2418. "Black September, Somber March: Executions in the Saudi Arabian Embassy, Khartoum." *Newsweek,* LXXXI (March 12, 1973), 18–20.

2419. "Blacker September: Reactions to the Massacre in Khartoum." *Time,* CI (March 19, 1973), 26–27.

2420. "Fallout from Khartoum." *Newsweek,* LXXXI (March 19, 1973), 41–42.

2421. "The Killers of Khartoum." *Time,* CI (March 12, 1973), 22+.

b. Documents, Papers, and Reports

2422.   United States. Department of State. Bureau of Public Affairs. *Background Documentation relating to the Assassination of Amb. Cleo A. Noel and George Curtis Moore.* Washington, D.C., 1973. Unpaged.

6. Uganda: The Entebbe Rescue

a. Books

2423.   Ben-Porat, Yeshayahu, Eitan Haber, and Ze'ev Schiff. *Entebbe Rescue.* New York: Dial Press, 1977. 346p.

Haber, Eitan, jt. author. *See* Ben-Porat, Yeshayahu.

2424.   Hastings, Max. *"Yuri"* [Col. Jonathan Netanyahu]: *Hero of Entebbe.* New York: Dial Press, 1979. 384p.

Schiff, Ze'ev, jt. author. *See* Ben-Porat, Yeshayahu.

2425.   Stevenson, William. *90 Minutes at Entebbe, with Material by Uri Dan.* New York: Bantam Books, 1976. 216p.

b. Articles

2426.   Day, Samuel H., Jr. "Some Questions about Entebbe." *Bulletin of the Atomic Scientists,* XXXII (September, November 1976), 7, 5–7.

2427.   Deming, Angus. "Countdown in Uganda: Freeing the Hostages of Palestinian Hijacked Plane in Israeli Raid." *Newsweek,* LXXXVIII (July 12, 1976), 28–29.

2428.   Eaker, Ira C. "Israel Solves a Hijacking." *Air Force Times,* XXXVI (July 26, 1976), 13–14.

2429.   Fisher, Adrian. "Will 'Hot Pursuit' Stop Terrorism—Israeli Raiders in Uganda Left a Clear Message: An Interview." *U.S. News and World Report,* LXXXI (July 19, 1976), 30–31.

2430.   Foxley-Norris, Christopher. "Entebbe and After." *Army Quarterly,* CVI (October 1976), 397–401.

2431.   Hotz, Robert. "Israel Points the Way: Ugandan Rescue." *Aviation Week and Space Technology,* CV (July 12, 1976), 7+.

2432.   "Israeli Commando C-130 Raid Frees 115." *Aviation Week and Space Technology,* CV (July 12, 1976), 15–16.

2433.   Johnson, Paul. "The Long Arm of Justice." *New Statesman and Nation,* XCII (July 9, 1976), 35–36.

2434. Kolcum, E. H. "Israeli Defense Minister Explains Tactics." *Aviation Week and Space Technology,* CV (August 2, 1976), 25+.

2435. Kubie, M. J. "How the Israelis Pulled It Off: Rescuing the Hostages at Entebbe Airport, Uganda." *Newsweek,* LXXXVIII (July 19, 1976), 42–44+.

2436. Medwed, Howard. "Third Thoughts on Entebbe." *Bulletin of the Atomic Scientists,* XXXII (November 1976), 8–9.

2437. "Rescue at Entebbe: How the Israelis Did It." *Reader's Digest,* CIX (October 1976), 122–128.

2438. "Rescue—We Do the Impossible: Freeing of Hijacked Hostages by Israeli Commandos." *Time,* CVIII (July 12, 1976), 21–23.

2439. "Thirty-Six Minutes: Freeing of Hijacked Hostages by Israeli Commandos." *New Republic,* CLXXV (July 17, 1976), 7–9.

F. Latin America

1. General Works

a. Books

2440. Agee, Philip. *Inside the Company: CIA Diary.* New York: Stonehill, 1975. 640p.

2441. Debray, Regis. *Revolution in the Revolution?: Armed Struggle and Political Struggle in Latin America.* Translated from the French. New York: Monthly Review Press, 1967. 126p.

2442. Duff, Ernest A., and John F. McCamant. *Violence and Repression in Latin America: A Quantitative and Historical Analysis.* New York: Macmillan, 1976. 322p.

2443. Gott, Richard. *Guerrilla Movements in Latin America.* Garden City, N.Y.: Doubleday, 1971. 626p.

2444. Horowitz, Irving L., *et al.*, eds. *Latin American Radicalism, 1969.* London: Cape, 1969. 656p.

2445. Huberman, Leo, and Paul M. Sweezy, eds. *Regis Debray and the Latin American Revolution: A Collection of Essays.* New York: Monthly Review Press, 1968. 138p.

2446. Kohl, James, and John Litt, eds. *Urban Guerrilla Warfare in Latin America.* Cambridge, Mass.: MIT Press, 1974. 425p.

2447. Larteguy, Jean. *The Guerrillas: New Patterns of Revolution in Latin America*. New York: Signet Books, 1972. 237p.

Litt, John, jt. editor. *See* Kohl, James.

McCamant, John F., jt. author. *See* Duff, Ernest A.

2448. Mercier-Vega, Luis. *Guerrillas in Latin America: The Technique of the Counter-State*. Translated from the Spanish. New York: Praeger, 1969. 246p.

Mitrani, Barbara, jt. editor. *See* Moreno, Francisco J.

2449. Moreno, Francisco J., and Barbara Mitrani, eds. *Conflict and Violence in Latin American Politics*. Ithaca, N.Y.: Cornell University Press, 1971. 452p.

Sweezy, Paul M., jt. editor. *See* Huberman, Leo.

2450. Wiarda, Howard J., ed. *Latin American Politics and Development*. Boston: Houghton Mifflin, 1979. 525p.

b. Articles

2451. Aguilar, L. E. "Regis Debray: Where Logic Failed." *Reporter,* XXXVII (December 28, 1967), 31–32.

2452. Allemann, Fritz R. "Terrorism in Latin America: Motives and Forms." In: Marjorie Kravitz, ed. *International Summaries: A Collection of Selected Translations in Law Enforcement and Criminal Justice,* v. 3. Rockville, Md.: National Criminal Justice Reference Service, Law Enforcement Assistance Administration, Department of Justice, 1979. pp. 19–26.

2453. Anderson, Thomas P. "Political Violence and Cultural Patterns in Central America." In: Marius H. Livingston, ed. *International Terrorism in the Contemporary World*. Westport, Conn.: Greenwood Press, 1978. pp. 153–159.

2454. "Business Digs in against Terrorists: American Companies in Brazil and Argentina." *Business Week,* (November 29, 1969), 34+.

2455. Butler, Robert E. "Terrorism in Latin America." In: Yonah Alexander, ed. *International Terrorism: National, Regional, and Global Perspectives*. New York: Praeger, 1976. pp. 46–61.

2456. Cobo, Juan. "The Roots of 'Violencia.'" *New Times* (Moscow), no. 8 (August 5, 1970), 25–27.

2457. Craig, Alexander. "The Urban Guerrilla in Latin America." *Survey,* XVII (Summer 1971), 112–128.

2458.   Deas, Malcolm. "Guerrillas in Latin America: A Perspective." *World Today,* XXIV (February 1968), 72–78.

2459.   "Diplomacy by Terror: Is It Getting Out of Control?" *U.S. News and World Report,* LXIX (August 24, 1970), 22–23.

2460.   Glick, Edward B. "Isolating the Guerrilla: Some Latin American Examples." *Orbis,* XII (Fall 1968), 873–886.

2461.   Goodsell, James N. "Urban Guerrillas in Latin America." *Commentator,* XIV (November 1970), 7–8.

2462.   Gott, Richard. "The Future of Guerrilla Warfare: What Lessons from Latin America?" *Current,* CXXX (1971), 55–59.

2463.   ———. "Latin American Guerrillas." *Listner,* LXXXIV (1970), 437–440.

2464.   Green, Nan. "Revolutionary Upsurge in Latin America." *Marxism Today,* XII (February 1968), 38–45.

2465.   Hennessy, A. "The New Radicalism in Latin America." *Journal of Contemporary History,* VII (January-April 1972), 1–26.

Hildner, Robert A., jt. author. *See* Russell, Charles A.

2466.   Hobsbawm, Eric J. "Guerrillas in Latin America." In: Ralph Miliband and John Saville, eds. *Socialist Register, 1970.* London: Merlin Press, 1970. pp. 51–61.

2467.   International Commission of Jurists. "Latin America: Integration, the Guerrilla Movement, and Human Rights." *International Commission of Jurists Review,* I (December 1969), 34–42.

2468.   Jaquett, J. S. "Women in Revolutionary Movements in Latin America." *Journal of Marriage and the Family,* XXXV (May 1973), 344–354.

2469.   Jarrin, Edgardo M. "Insurgency in Latin America: Its Impact on Political and Military Strategy." *Military Review,* XLIX (March 1969), 10–20.

2470.   Lamberg, Robert F. "Latin America's Urban Guerrillas." *Swiss Review of World Affairs,* XX (Fall 1970), 18–19.

2471.   Lawrence, William. "The Status under International Law of Recent Guerrilla Movements in Latin America." *International Lawyer,* VII (1973), 405+.

2472.   Martinez-Codo, Enrique. "Guerrilla Warfare after Guevera." *Military Review,* XLIX (July 1969), 24–30.

2473. _____ . "Insurgency: Latin American Style." *Military Review,* XLVII (November 1967), 3–12.

2474. Martz, John D. "Guerrilla Warfare and Violence in Contemporary Latin America." *Southeastern Conference of Latin American Studies Annual,* I (March 1970), 141–165.

2475. Mieres, Francisco. "Lessons of October and Contemporary Revolutionary Movements in Latin America." *World Marxist Review,* X (November 1967), 77–81.

2476. "Nervous in the Service: Diplomats in Latin America." *Newsweek,* LXXV (April 6, 1970), 40–41.

2477. "New Terror Tactic: Diplomatic Kidnapping in Latin America." *Time,* XCV (April 6, 1970), 37–38.

2478. Petras, James. "Guerrilla Movements in Latin America." *New Politics,* VI (Spring 1967), 80–94.

2479. _____ . "New Forms of Struggle in Latin America." *New Politics,* VIII (Spring 1969), 58–61.

2480. Russell, Charles A., and Robert A. Hildner. "Urban Insurgency in Latin America: Its Implications for the Future." *Air University Review,* XXII (September-October 1971), 54–64.

2481. Sloan, John W. "Political Terrorism in Latin America: A Critical Analysis." In: Michael Stohl, ed. *The Politics of Terrorism.* New York: Marcel Dekker, 1979. pp. 301–322.

2482. "Spreading Political Terrorism in the Americas." *U.S. News and World Report,* LXXVIII (January 13, 1975), 19–20.

2483. "Terrorism in Latin America." *Atlas,* XX (November 1971), 18–21.

2484. "Urban Guerrillas in Latin America." *Conflict Studies,* no. 8 (October 1970), 4–15.

c. Documents, Papers, and Reports

2485. Einaudi, Luigi R. *Latin American Student Radicalism: A Different Type of Struggle.* RAND Paper P-3897. Santa Monica, Calif.: Rand Corp., 1968. 16p.

_____ , jt. author. *See* Ronfeldt, D. F.

2486. Estep, Raymond. *Guerrilla Warfare in Latin America, 1963– 1975.* AU-202-75-IPD. Maxwell AFB, Ala.: Air University Institute, 1975. 96p.

2487. Halperin, Ernst. *Terrorism in Latin America.* Washington Papers, v. 4, no. 33. Beverly Hills, Calif.: Sage, 1976. 90p.

2488. Ronfeldt, D. F., and Luigi R. Einaudi. *Internal Security and Military Assistance to Latin America in the 1970's.* RAND Report R-924-ISA. Santa Monica, Calif.: RAND Corp., 1971. 55p.

2489. United States. Congress. House. Committee on Foreign Affairs. Subcommittee on Inter-American Affairs. *Air Piracy in the Caribbean Area: Hearings.* 90th Cong., 2nd sess. Washington, D.C.: U.S. Government Printing Office, 1968. 27p.

2. Argentina: Articles

2490. Buckley, William F., Jr. "Argentine Terror." *National Review,* XXIX (March 4, 1977), 286–287.

2491. "Crime Does Pay: Political Kidnappings in Argentina." *Time,* CII (April 23, 1973), 32–33.

2492. "Hostage: The Case of V. Samuelson in Argentina." *Newsweek,* LXXXIII (March 25, 1974), 52+.

2493. Janke, Peter. "Guerrilla Politics in Argentina." *Military Review,* LVII (January 1977), 62–70.

2494. _____ . "Terrorism in Argentina." *Journal of the Royal United Service Institution for Defence Studies,* CXIX (September 1974), 43–44+.

2495. Johnson, Kenneth F. "Guerrilla Politics in Argentina." *Conflict Studies,* no. 63 (September 1975), 1–20.

2496. "Living in Fear: Executive Kidnappings." *Newsweek,* LXXXI (June 11, 1973), 93–94.

2497. McCrary, Edward. "Coping with Terrorism in Argentina." *Business Week* (March 9, 1974), 40+.

2498. "Trial by Terror: The Kidnapping of Foreign Executives." *Time,* CIII (January 14, 1974), 24–25.

2499. "Why Argentina Is Becoming the 'Land of Vanishing Americans.'" *U.S. News and World Report,* LXXVI (March 11, 1974), 59–60.

3. Brazil

a. Books

2500. Alves, Marcio M. *A Grain of Mustard Seed: The Awakening of the Brazilian Revolution.* Garden City, N.Y.: Doubleday, 1973. 194p.

2501. Flynn, Peter. *Brazil: A Political Analysis.* Boulder, Colo.: Westview Press, 1978. 564p.

2502. Marighella, Carlos. *For the Liberation of Brazil.* Harmondsworth, Eng.: Penguin Books, 1971. 147p.

2503. Quartim, Joao. *Dictatorship and Armed Struggle in Brazil.* Translated from the French. New York: Monthly Review Press, 1972. 250p.

b. Articles

2504. Alves, Marcio M. "Brazil: What Terror Is Like." *Nation,* CCXII (March 15, 1971), 337–341.

2505. Darragh, Shaun M. "The Urban Guerrilla of Carlos Marighella." *Infantry,* LXIII (July-August 1973), 23–26.

2506. Evands, R. D. "Brazil: The Road Back from Terrorism." *Conflict Studies,* no. 47 (July 1974), 3–20.

2507. "Guerrilla War in the Streets." *Newsweek,* LXXIV (December 8, 1969), 66–68.

2508. Truskier, Andy. "Politics of Violence—The Urban Guerrillas of Brazil: Interviews with Four Revolutionists." *Ramparts,* IX (October 1970), 30–34, 39.

c. Documents, Papers, and Reports

2509. Pearson, Neal. "Guerrilla Warfare in Brazil." Unpublished paper, Conference of the Midwest Association of Latin American Studies at Southern Illinois University, 1972.

4. Guatemala: Articles

2510. Gall, Norman. "Slaughter in Guatemala." *New York Review of Books,* IV (May 20, 1971), 12+.

2511. Johnson, Kenneth F. "Guatemala: From Terrorism to Terror." *Conflict Studies,* no. 23 (May 1972), 4–17.

2512. _____ . "On the Guatemalan Political Violence." *Politics and Society,* IV (Fall 1973), 55+.

2513. Perera, Victor. "Guatemala: Always 'La Violencia.'" *New York Times Magazine* (June 30, 1971), 57+.

5. Mexico

a. Books

2514. Hellman, Judith A. *Mexico in Crisis.* New York: Holmes & Meier, 1978. 229p.

2515. Stevens, Evelyn P. *Protest and Response in Mexico.* Cambridge, Mass.: MIT Press, 1974. 372p.

b. Articles

2516. "Another Kidnap: J. Patterson, U.S. Vice Consul in Mexico." *Newsweek,* LXXXIII (April 8, 1974), 39.

2517. Blum, Bill. "Terror in Mexico." *Progressive,* XLIII (April 1979), 11–12.

2518. "Slow Death [of Hugo M. Charles]." *Newsweek,* XCII (September 11, 1978), 49+.

6. Uruguay

a. Books

2519. Fly, Claude. *No Hope but God.* New York: Hawthorn Books, 1973. 200p.

2520. Gilio, Marie M. *The Tupamaro Guerrillas: The Structure and Strategy of the Guerrilla Movement.* Translated from the Spanish. New York: Saturday Review Press, 1972. 204p.

2521. Jackson, Geoffrey. *Surviving the Long Night: An Autobiographical Account of a Political Kidnapping.* New York: Vanguard Press, 1974. 226p.

2522. Labrousse, Alain. *The Tupamaros: Urban Guerrillas in Uruguay.* Harmondsworth, Eng.: Penguin Books, 1973. 168p.

2523. Langguth, A. J. *Hidden Terrors.* New York: Pantheon, 1978. 339p.

2524. Max, Alphonse. *Tupamaros: A Pattern for Urban Guerrilla Warfare in Latin America.* The Hague: International Documentation and Information Centre, 1970. 16p.

2525. Nunez, Carlos. *The Tupamaros: Urban Guerrillas of Uruguay.* New York: Times Change Press, 1970. 48p.

2526. Porzencanski, Arturo C. *Uruguay's Tupamaros: The Urban Guerrilla.* New York: Praeger, 1973. 80p.

2527. Wilson, Carlos. *The Tupamaros: The Unmentionables.* Boston: Branden Press, 1974. 171p.

b. Articles

2528. Alves, Marcio M. "Kidnapped Diplomats: Greek Tragedy in a Latin Style." *Commonweal,* XCII (June 26, 1970), 311–314.

2529. "Back in Action: Seizure of Geoffrey H. S. Jackson by Uruguay's Tupamaros." *Newsweek,* LXXVII (January 18, 1971), 34+.

2530. Baitx, Aristobulo, pseud. "Uruguay: An Analysis of the Current Situation." *Bank of London and South American Review,* IV (December 1970), 667–672.

2531. Begue, Carlos. "The Robin Hoods of Uruguay." *Atlas,* XVIII (July 1969), 45–47.

2532. Connolly, Stephen. "The Tupamaros: The New Focus in Latin America." *Journal of Contemporary Revolutions,* III (Summer 1971), 59–68.

2533. D'Oliveira, Sergio L. "Uruguay and the Tupamaro Myth." *Military Review,* LIII (April 1973), 25–36.

2534. Foland, Frances M. "Uruguay's Urban Guerrillas: A New Model for Revolution?" *New Leader,* LIV (October 4, 1971), 8–11.

2535. Friggens, Paul. "Claude Fly's Seven Month Nightmare." *Reader's Digest,* XCIX (September 1970), 64–70.

2536. Gerassi, Marysa N. "Uruguay: Urban Guerrillas." *New Left Review,* (July-August 1970), 22–29.

2537. _____ . "Uruguay's Urban Guerrillas: The Tupamaros." *Nation,* CCIX (September 29, 1969), 306–310.

2538. Litt, J. "The Guerrillas of Montevideo." *Nation,* CCXIV (February 28, 1972), 269–272.

2539. Malin, Jay. "The Military vs. Urban Guerrillas." *Marine Corps Gazette,* LVII (January 1973), 18–25.

2540. Miller, James A. "The Tupamaro Insurgents of Uruguay." In: Bard E. O'Neill, ed. *Political Violence and Insurgency: A Comparative Approach.* Arvada, Colo.: Phoenix Books, 1974. pp. 199–283.

2541. Moss, Robert. "Urban Guerrillas in Uruguay." *Problems of Communism,* XX (September-October 1971), 14–23.

2542. "Murder: Tupamaro-Style." *Time,* XCVI (August 24, 1970), 20+.

2543. Nenez, Carlos. "The Tupamaros: Armed Vanguard in Uruguay." *Tricontinental,* (January-February 1969), 43–66.

2544. Peter, Robert. "'It was a Terrible Scene': Kidnappings and Deaths by Tupamaros in Uruguay." *National Review,* XXII (September 22, 1970), 1001+.

2545. Porzecanski, Arturo C. "Uruguay's Continuing Dilemma." *Current History*, LXVI (January 1974), 28–30+.

2546. Reed, David. "Taps for the Tupamaros." *Reader's Digest*, CI (November 1972), 173–176+.

2547. Shapiro, Stephen. "Uruguay's Lost Paradise." *Current History*, LXII (February 1972), 98–103.

2548. Teller, Woolsey. "What's Happening in Uruguay: The National Liberation Front Known as the Tupamaros." *Saturday Evening Post*, CCXLIII (Winter 1971), 50–51+.

2549. "Tupamaros Tunnel Out [of Prison]." *Time*, XCVIII (September 20, 1971), 35–36.

2550. "Uruguay: The Tupamaros in Action." *Tricontinental*, (April-May 1970), 45–60.

7. Venezuela: Articles

2551. Callanan, Edward F. "Terror in Venezuela." *Military Review*, XLIX (February 1969), 49–56.

2552. Cross, Benedict, pseud. "Maoism in Venezuela." *Problems of Communism*, XXII (November-December 1973), 51–70.

2553. "Terror and Takeover: Kidnapping of General Manager William F. Niehouse and Government Takeover of Owens-Illinois." *Time*, CVII (April 19, 1976), 71–72.

2554. Webb, Peter. "Ordeal [of Niehouse] in the Jungle." *Newsweek*, XCIV (July 16, 1979), 41.

G. North America

1. Canada

a. Books

2555. Auf der Maur, Nick. *Quebec—A Chronicle, 1968–1972: A Last Post Special.* Toronto: James Lewis & Samuel, 1972. 166p.

2556. Butler, Rick. *Quebec: The People Speak.* Garden City, N.Y.: Doubleday, 1978. 335p.

2557. *Canada and the French.* New York: Facts on File, 1977. 226p.

2558. Daniels, Dan. *Quebec, Canada, and the October Crisis.* Montreal: Black Rose, 1973. 124p.

2559.   Gellner, John. *Bayonets in the Street: Urban Guerrillas at Home and Aboard.* Don Mills, Ont.: Collier-Macmillan Canada, 1974. 196p.

2560.   McRoberts, Kenneth, and Dale Postgate. *Quebec: Social Change and Political Crisis.* Toronto: McClelland & Stewart, 1976. 216p.

2561.   Manzer, Ronald. *Canada: A Socio-Political Report.* New York: McGraw-Hill, 1974. 349p.

2562.   Moore, Brian. *The Revolution Script.* New York: Holt, Rinehart & Winston, 1971. 261p.

2563.   Morf, Gustave. *Terror in Quebec: Case Studies of the F.L.Q.* Toronto: Clarke, Irwin, 1970. 185p.

2564.   Pelletier, Gerard. *The October Crisis.* Translated from the French. Toronto: McClelland & Stewart, 1971. 247p.

Postgate, Dale, jt. author. *See* McRoberts, Kenneth.

2565.   Radwanski, George. *Trudeau.* New York: Taplinger, 1978. 372p.

2566.   Reid, Malcolm. *The Shouting Signpainters: A Literary and Political Account of Quebec Revolutionary Nationalism.* New York: Monthly Review Press, 1972. 315p.

2567.   Saywell, John T. *Quebec '70: A Documentary Narrative.* Toronto: University of Toronto Press, 1971. 152p.

2568.   Stewart, James P. *The F.L.Q.: Seven Years of Terrorism—A Special Report of the Montreal Star.* Montreal: Montreal Star in cooperation with Simon & Schuster, Canada, 1970. 84p.

Two French-language studies should be noted: 1) Jacques Lacoursière, *Alarme Citoyens* (Ottawa: Les Éditions La Presse, Guy Lalumière & Associes, 1972. 438p.) and 2) Jean-Claude Trait, *F.L.Q. '70: Offensive d'Automne* (Ottawa: Les Éditions de l' Homme Ltée, 1970. 230p.).

b. Articles

2569.   Beaton, Leonard. "Crisis in Quebec." *Round Table,* no. 241 (January 1971), 147–152.

2570.   Beauregard, Fernand. "Who Inspired the F.L.Q. Terrorists?" *Atlas,* XIX (December 1970), 24.

2571.   "Bombs Rattle Quebec's Economy." *Business Week* (March 1, 1969), 84–85+.

2572.   Bourne, Robin. "Terrorist Incident Management and Jurisdictional Issues: A Canadian Perspective." *Terrorism,* I (1978), 307–314.

2573. Buckley, Thomas. "The Testing of Pierre Trudeau." *New York Times Magazine* (December 6, 1970), 50–51+.

2574. "Canada: The End of a Bad Dream." *Time,* XCVI (December 14, 1970), 29–30.

2575. "Canada—The Answer Was Murder: War Measures Act Invoked against the F.L.Q."*Newsweek,* LXXVI (October 26, 1970), 35–36.

2576. "Canada: This Very Sorry Moment." *Time,* XCVI (October 26, 1970), 33–34.

2577. Canadian Correspondent. "Quebec: The Challenge from Within." *Conflict Studies,* no. 20 (January 1972), 1–20.

2578. Desbarats, Peter. "In Our Weeks of Anguish: A Journal of October." *Saturday Night,* LXXXV (December 1970), 19–25.

2579. _____. "Quebec: The Revolution That Never Was." *Saturday Night,* LXXXIV (December 1969), 28+.

2580. "F.L.Q.: Blue-Collar Terrorists." *Newsweek,* LXXVI (October 26, 1970), 36.

2581. "Fertile Soil for Terror." *Canada and the World,* XXXVI (December 1970), 16–19.

2582. Fraser, Geoffrey. "Ghosts of October '70." *Macleans,* XCI (May 29, 1978), 17–18.

2583. Gagnon, Charles. "Interview." *New Left Review,* X (November-December 1970), 62–68.

2584. Godin, Gerald. "Notes on Terrorism." *Canadian Forum,* LI (November 1971), 26–27.

2585. Green, L. C. "Terrorism: The Canadian Perspective." In: Yonah Alexander, ed. *International Terrorism: National, Regional, and Global Perspectives.* New York: Praeger, 1976. pp. 3–29.

2586. Greening, W. E. "The Crisis in French Canada." *Contemporary Review,* CCXVI (March 1970), 125–128.

2587. Hutchinson, Bruce. "Canada's Time of Troubles." *Foreign Affairs,* LVI (October 1971), 175–189.

2588. Kasurak, Pierre. "Coping with Urban Guerrillas: Democracy's Challenge." *Canadian Defence Quarterly,* III (Fall 1974), 41–46.

2589. La Pierre, Lauvrier. "Quebec: October 1970." *North American Review,* VIII (Fall 1971), 23–33.

2590. Leduc, Pierre. "Quebec: Terrorism and Separatism." *Nation,* CCXI (November 2, 1970), 422–423.

2591. MacDonald, David. "Wing of Madness: Canada's Trial by Terror." *Reader's Digest,* C (March 1972), 213–216+.

2592. Mallory, J. R. "The Canadian Dilemma." *Political Quarterly,* XLI (July-September 1970), 281–297.

2593. Pious, Richard. "Canada and the Crisis of Quebec." *Journal of International Affairs,* XXVII (1973), 53–55.

2594. "Return of the Unapprehended Insurrectionists." *Macleans,* XCII (January 29, 1979), 22+.

2595. "Specialists in Terror: Quebec's F.L.Q." *U.S. News and World Report,* LXIX (November 2, 1970), 18+.

2596. "Task Force on Kidnapping." *External Affairs,* XXIII (1971), 6–11.

2597. "Terror in Quebec." *America,* CXXIII (November 7, 1970), 366–367.

2598. "Terrorism in Canada: Pierre E. Trudeau's Reaction to Violence." *U.S. News and World Report,* LXIX (November 2, 1970), 17–19.

2599. "Trapped Like Rats: The Arrest of Pierre La Porte's Suspected Kidnap-Killers." *Newsweek,* LXXVII (January 11, 1971), 44+.

c. Documents, Papers, and Reports

2600. Redlick, Amy S. "Transnational Factors Affecting Quebec Separatist Terrorism." Unpublished paper, 17th Annual Convention of the International Studies Association, 1976.

2. United States

a. General Works

(1) Books

2601. Cantor, Milton. *Divided Left: American Radicalism, 1900–1975.* New York: Hill & Wang, 1978. 248p.

2602. Fainstein, Norman I., and Susan S. *Political Movements: The Search for Power by Minority Groups in American Cities.* Englewood Cliffs, N.J.: Prentice-Hall, 1974. 271p.

2603. Lasch, Christopher. *The Agony of the American Left.* New York: Vintage, 1969. 212p.

2604.   Viorst, Milton. *Fire in the Streets: America in the 1960's.* New York: Simon & Schuster, 1980. 384p.

2605.   Young, Nigel. *An Infantile Disorder?: The Crises and Decline of the New Left.* Boulder, Colo.: Westview Press, 1978. 490p.

(2) ARTICLES

2606.   Abrahamsen, David. "Political Terror in the U.S.: What Next—An Interview." *U.S. News and World Report,* LXXVI (March 4, 1974), 15–17.

2607.   Burgess, Anthony. "Freedom, We Have Lost: *Time* Essay." *Time,* CXI (May 8, 1978), 44+.

2608.   "California's Underground." *Time,* CVI (October 6, 1975), 25+.

2609.   Cott, Laurence V. "End of the Road for California's Bomb Terrorists." *Human Events,* XXXVI (April 10, 1976), 10+.

2610.   "Cuban Exiles: Miami Haven for Terrorists." *Nation,* CCXXIV (March 19, 1977), 326–331.

2611.   "Cuban Extremists in the U.S.: A Growing Terror Threat." *U.S. News and World Report,* LXXXI (December 6, 1976), 29–32.

2612.   "Death at Cerro Maravilla [Puerto Rico]: Police Ambush of Suspected Terrorists." *Time,* CXIII (May 14, 1979), 27+.

2613.   Elliott, John D. "International Terrorism: Threat to U.S. Security?" *Armed Forces Journal International,* CXIV (September 1977), 38–39.

2614.   "Hijacking That Backfired: Serbian Nationalist Nikola Kavaja's Attempt." *Newsweek,* XCIV (July 2, 1979), 36.

2615.   Hoge, Thomas A. "Are Terrorists Staling America's Bicentennial?" *American Legion Magazine,* C (March 1976), 18–21+.

2616.   Homer, Frederic D. "Terror in the United States: Three Perspectives." In: Michael Stohl, ed. *The Politics of Terrorism.* New York: Marcel Dekker, 1979. pp. 373–406.

2617.   Howe, Irving. "Political Terrorism: Hysteria on the Left." *New York Times Magazine,* (April 12, 1970), 25–27+.

2618.   "The Infiltrating of the Underground [by Judith Bissell]." *Time,* CXI (January 9, 1978), 13–14.

2619.   "Is the U.S. Next?" *Newsweek,* XCI (May 22, 1978), 38+.

2620. Johnpoll, Bernard K. "Perspectives on Political Terrorism in the United States." In: Yonah Alexander, ed. *International Terrorism: National, Regional, and Global Perspectives.* New York: Praeger, 1976. pp. 30–45.

2621. Kroes, R. "Violence in America: Spontaneity and Strategy." In: J. Niezing, ed. *Urban Guerrilla: Studies on the Theory, Strategy, and Practice of Political Violence in Modern Societies.* Rotterdam, Holland: Rotterdam University Press, 1974. pp. 81–93.

2622. Kupperman, Robert H. "Terrorism—Why the U.S. Is Vulnerable: An Interview." *U.S. News and World Report,* LXXXIV (March 6, 1978), 66–68.

2623. "La Guardia Blast: 'My God It Was Terrible.'" *Time,* CVII (January 12, 1976), 8–11.

2624. Landes, W. M. "Economic Study of U.S. Aircraft Hijackings, 1961–1976." *Journal of Law and Economics,* XXI (April 1978), 1–31.

2625. Lerner, Max. "Anarchism and the American Counter-Culture." *Government and Opposition,* V (April 1970), 430–455.

2626. Louv, Richard. "The Terrorists Are Coming." *San Diego Magazine,* XXX (February 1978), 100+,

2627. McGuire, E. Patrick. "Terrorist Bombings Sputter Back to Normal." *Conference Board Report,* X (October 1973), 6–9.

2628. Meyer, A. H. "Foreign Terrorism Spreading to the U.S.?: An Interview." *U.S. News and World Report,* LXXV (July 16, 1973), 37–40.

2629. Mosher, T. E. "Inside the Revolutionary Left." *Reader's Digest,* XCIX (September 1971), 53–57.

2630. "1971 Worst Year for Nationwide Bombings." *Police Officers Association of Michigan Law Enforcement Journal,* (Spring 1972), 29.

2631. "Political Kidnapping: An Ugly Turn in the U.S." *U.S. News and World Report,* LXXVI (February 25, 1974), 24–25.

2632. Popov, M. I. "The American Extreme Left: A Decade of Conflict." *Conflict Studies,* no. 29 (December 1972), 1–19.

2633. Prosser, George. "Terror in the United States: 'An Introduction to Elementary Tactics' and 'Some Questions on Tactics.'" In: Jay Mallin, ed. *Terror and Urban Guerrillas: A Study of Tactics and Documents.* Coral Gables, Fla.: University of Miami Press, 1971. pp. 51–66.

2634. Rose, G. F. "The Terrorists Are Coming." *Politics Today,* V (July 1978), 22–26+.

2635. Salmons, S., *et al.* "Everything Blew: Bombing at La Guardia Airport, New York City." *Newsweek,* LXXXVII (January 12, 1976), 31+.

2636. "Terrorism in California." *Criminal Justice Digest,* II (July 1974), 1–8.

2637. "Terrorism in the United States." In: William P. Lineberry, ed. *The Struggle against Terrorism.* Reference Shelf, v. 49, no. 3. New York: H. W. Wilson, 1977. pp. 96–98.

2638. "Threat for Bicentennial Year: Terrorists Getting Ready." *U.S. News and World Report,* LXXIX (July 21, 1975), 23–25.

2639. Train, John. "It Shouldn't Happen Here." *Forbes,* CCXXIII (March 5, 1979), 160–161.

2640. Willwerth, J. "Forecast—More Bombs Ahead: Puerto Rican Terrorists." *Time,* CX (October 24, 1977), 39–40.

2641. Zmuda, Charles W. "Bombing Incidents." *Police,* XV (January–February 1977), 6–10.

(3) DOCUMENTS, PAPERS, and REPORTS

2642. California. Legislature. Senate. Subcommittee on Civil Disorder. *Report.* Sacramento, 1975. 361p.

2643. United States. Congress. House. Committee on Internal Security. *America's Maoists—The Revolutionary Union—The Venceremos Organization: Hearings.* 92nd Cong., 2nd sess. Washington, D.C.: U.S. Government Printing Office, 1972. 225p.

2644. _____ . _____ . _____ . _____ . *Revolutionary Activities Directed toward the Administration of Penal or Correctional Systems: Hearings and the Testimony of A. R. Norusis.* 93rd Cong., 1st sess. Washington, D.C.: U.S. Government Printing Office, 1973. 377p.

2645. _____ . _____ . Senate. Committee on the Judiciary. Subcommittee to Investigate the Administration of the Internal Security Act and Other Internal Security Laws. *Terroristic Activity, Part 8: Terrorism in the Miami Area—Hearings.* 94th Cong., 2nd sess. Washington, D.C.: U.S. Government Printing Office, 1976. 62p.

2646. _____ . _____ . _____ . _____ . _____ . *Trotskyite Terrorist International: Hearings.* 94th Cong., 1st sess. Washington, D.C.: U.S. Government Printing Office, 1975. 474p.

2647. _____ . Federal Aviation Administration. Civil Aviation Security Service. *Chronology of Hijackings of U.S. Registered Aircraft and Current Legal Status of Hijackers.* Washington, D.C., 1979. 54p.

2648. _____ . _____ . _____ . *Hijacking Statistics, U.S. Registered Aircraft, 1961 –Present.* Washington, D.C., 1979. 18p.

2649. _____ . Federal Bureau of Investigation. National Bomb Data Center. *Bomb Survey: A Comprehensive Report on Incidents Involving Explosive and Incendiary Devices in the Nation, 1974.* Washington, D.C., 1975. 32p.

2650. _____ . _____ . _____ . _____ : *January-June 1975.* Washington, D.C., 1975. 24p.

2651. Watson, Francis M. *Movement—The Role of U.S. Activities: Threats to Free Society.* London: Institute for the Study of Conflict, 1977. 16p.

b. Major Terror Groups

    (1) HANAFI MUSLIMS: ARTICLES

2652. "America's Menacing Misfits: The Taking of Hostages by Terrorists." *Time,* CIX (March 21, 1977), 20.

2653. "Behind the Siege of Terror in Washington." *U.S. News and World Report,* LXXXII (March 21, 1977), 19–21+.

2654. Clemons, J. T. "'Allah Was on Our Side': Washington, D.C., Siege by Hanafi Muslims." *Christian Century,* XCIV (April 6, 1977), 319–320.

2655. Fenyvesi, Charles. "From the Concrete Floor: Thoughts while Being Held Hostage [in] Washington, D.C., Siege of Hanafi Muslims." *New Republic,* CLXXVI (March 26, 1977), 16–17.

2656. _____ . "Living with a Fearful Memory: Effects of the Washington, D.C. Siege by Hanafi Muslims." *Psychology Today,* XI (October 1977), 61+.

2657. Goldman, Peter. "The Delicate Art of Handling Terrorists." *Newsweek,* LXXXIX (March 21, 1977), 25–27.

2658. Rabinowitz, Dorothy. "Hostage Mentality." *Commentary,* LXIII (June 1977), 70–72; LXIV (August 1977), 7–9.

2659. "Seizing Hostages: Scourge of the '70's." *Newsweek,* LXXXIX (March 21, 1977), 16–21+.

2660. "38 Hours—Trial by Terror: Washington, D.C., Siege by Hanafi Muslims." *Time,* CIX (March 21, 1977), 14–20.

(2) Symbionese Liberation Army (sla)

(a) **Books**

2661. Alexander, Shana. *Anyone's Daughter.* New York: Viking Press, 1979. 562p.

Avery, Paul, jt. author. *See* McLillan, Vin.

2662. Baker, Marilyn. *Exclusive!: The Inside Story of Patricia Hearst and the S.L.A.* New York: Macmillan, 1974. 246p.

2663. Beal, M. F. *Safe House: A Casebook Study of Revolutionary Feminism in the 1970's.* Eugene, Oreg.: Northwest Matrix, 1976. 954p.

Belcher, Jerry, jt. author. *See* West, Don.

2664. Boulton, David. *The Making of Tania Hearst.* London: New English Library, 1975. 224p.

Craven, C. jt. author. *See* Payne, L.

2665. Goldsmith, Gail. *Ballad of Patty Hearst.* New York: Forsyth Gallery, 1978. 108p.

2666. Hearst, Patricia. *The Trial of Patty Hearst* [Transcript]. San Francisco: Great Fidelity Press, 1976. 738p.

2667. McLillan, Vin, and Paul Avery. *The Voices of Guns: The Definitive and Dramatic Story of the 22-Month Career of the Symbionese Liberation Army.* New York: Putnam, 1976. 544p.

2668. Payne, L., and C. Craven. *Life and Death of the S.L.A.* New York: Ballantine Books, 1976. 369p.

2669. Weed, Steven. *My Search for Patty Hearst.* New York: Crown, 1976. 343p.

2670. West, Don, and Jerry Belcher. *Patty/Tania.* New York: Pyramid Books, 1975. 347p.

(b) **Articles**

2671. Adams, Nathan M. "The Rise and Fall of the S.L.A." *Reader's Digest,* CV (September 1974), 64–69.

2672. "After Hearst Arrest: Drive to Root Out Terror Gangs." *U.S. News and World Report,* LXXIX (October 6, 1975), 22+.

2673. Alpern, David M. "The Story of Patty." *Newsweek,* LXXXVI (September 29, 1975), 20–22+.

2674. Atwood, Angela. "Cheerleader for a Revolution." *New York Times Magazine,* (June 21, 1974), 10–11+.

2675. Bailey, F. Lee. "Patty Hearst: The Untold Story." *Ladies Home Journal,* XCIII (September 1976), 36+.

2676. "Battle over Patty's Mind." *Time,* CVII (March 8, 1976), 25–26+.

2677. "The Cobra Strikes." *Time,* CIII (February 18, 1974), 15–16.

2678. Davidson, S. "Notes from the Land of the Cobra." *New York Times Magazine,* (June 2, 1974), 36–38+.

2679. "Dragnet Spreads for Patty." *Newsweek,* LXXXIII (June 3, 1974), 28–30+.

2680. Farrell, Barry. "Let-Burn Situation." *Harpers,* CCXLIX (September 1974), 31–36.

2681. "Fiery End for Six of Patty's Captors." *Time,* CIII (May 27, 1974), 9–10.

2682. Geis, Gilbert. "Women and Terror: The S.L.A." *Nation,* CCXVIII (June 29, 1974), 812–813.

2683. "Hostage—A Game of Terror: Patty Hearst." *Newsweek,* LXXXIII (February 25, 1974), 18–21.

2684. Johnson, J. A. "The Real Story of Patty Hearst." *Good Housekeeping,* CLXXXIV (February-March 1977), 95–97+, 105+.

2685. Mathews, T. "Patty Tells Her Story." *Newsweek,* LXXXVII (February 23, 1976), 15–16+.

2686. _____. "The Three Faces of Patty." *Newsweek,* LXXXVII (March 8, 1976), 32+.

2687. _____. "Travels with Tania." *Newsweek,* LXXXVI (October 13, 1975), 30–32.

2688. Morris, Roger. "Patty Hearst and the New Terror." *New Republic,* CLXXIII (November 22, 1975), 8–10.

2689. "Patty's Terrifying Story." *Time,* CVII (February 23, 1976), 15–17.

2690. "Patty's Twisted Journey." *Time,* CVI (September 29, 1975), 11–14+.

2691. "The Politics of Terror: The Patty Hearst and Robert Murphy Cases." *Time,* CIII (March 4, 1975), 11–15.

2692. Popkin, Richard H. "Strange Tale of the Secret Army Organization." *Ramparts,* XII (October 1973), 36+.

2693. "Queen of the S.L.A.?" *Time,* CVII (January 22, 1975), 17–18.

2694. "The Saga of Patty Hearst." *Newsweek,* LXXXIII (April 29, 1974), 20–24+.

2695. Salmans, S. "Victim or Terrorist?" *Newsweek,* LXXXVI (October 6, 1975), 37–38.

2696. Steele, Raymond. "Three for the Road [Hearst and Harrises]: Tania's Last Comrades." *Newsweek,* LXXXVI (September 29, 1975), 22–23.

2697. "The Symbionese Liberation Army: Terrorism and the Left." *Ramparts,* XII (May 1974), 21–27.

2698. "This Is Tania." *Time,* CIII (June 3, 1974), 16–17.

2699. "The War for Patty." *Newsweek,* LXXXIII (May 27, 1974), 18–21.

(c) Documents, Papers, and Reports

2700. Pearsall, R. B., ed. *Symbionese Liberation Army: Documents and Communications.* Amsterdam, Neth.: Rodopi N. V. Keizergracht, 1974. 158p.

2701. United States. Congress. House. Committee on Internal Security. *Symbionese Liberation Army: A Staff Study.* 93rd Cong., 2nd sess. Washington, D.C.: U.S. Government Printing Office, 1974. 21p.

(3) WEATHERMEN

(a) Books

2702. Adelson, Alan. *S.D.S.: A Profile.* New York: Scribners, 1972. 276p.

2703. Goode, Stephen. *Affluent Revolutionaries: A Portrait of the New Left.* New York: New Viewpoints, 1974. 117p.

2704. Grathwohl, Larry. *Bringing Down America: An F.B.I. Informer with the Weathermen.* New Rochelle, N.Y.: Arlington House, 1976. 191p.

2705. Jacobs, Harold, ed. *Weathermen.* Berkeley, Calif.: Ramparts Press, 1970. 519p.

2706. Sale, J. K. *S.D.S.* New York: Random House, 1973. 752p.

2707. Stern, Susan. *With the Weathermen: The Personal Journal of a Revolutionary Woman.* Garden City, N.Y.: Doubleday, 1975. 374p.

(b) Articles

2708.   Bennett, Robert K. "Brotherhood of the Bomb." *Reader's Digest,* XCVII (December 1970), 102–106.

2709.   "Bombing—A Way of Protest and Death: Bombs Exploding at the Manhattan Headquarters of Mobil Oil, I.B.M., and General Telephone and Electronics." *Time,* XCV (March 23, 1970), 8–11.

2710.   "Bombs Away: Bombings by the Weather Underground." *Newsweek,* LXXXV (February 10, 1975), 20+.

2711.   "Bombs Blast a Message of Hate." *Life,* LXVIII (March 27, 1970), 28–32.

2712.   "Bombs: Indictments." *Newsweek,* LXXVI (August 3, 1970), 14–15.

2713.   Bongartz, Roy. "The Weathermen." *Esquire,* LXXIV (August 1970), 112–114+.

2714.   Daniels, S. "The Weathermen." *Government and Opposition,* IX (January 1974), 430–459.

2715.   Derber, Charles. "Terrorism and the Movement." *Monthly Review,* XXII (February 1971), 36–45.

2716.   Dotton, Thomas. "House on 11th Street." *Newsweek,* LXXV (March 23, 1970), 29.

2717.   "F.B.I.'s Toughest Foe: The Kids." *Newsweek,* LXXVI (October 26, 1970), 22–23.

2718.   Goldman, Peter. "When G-Men Break the Law: Covert Operations against the Weathermen." *Newsweek,* LXXXIX (May 30, 1977), 28+.

2719.   Greene, William. "Militants Who Play with Bombs." *New York Times Magazine,* (October 25, 1970), 38–39+.

2720.   Horowitz, David. "Revolutionary Karma vs. Revolutionary Politics." *Ramparts,* IX (March 1971), 27–33.

2721.   "House on Fourth Street: Bomb Terrorists and Explosions, New York City." *Newsweek,* LXXIV (November 24, 1969), 37–38.

2722.   Iglitzin, L. B. "Democracy and the Radical Challenge." *Midwest Quarterly,* XII (Fall 1970), 59–77.

2723.   ———. "Violence and American Democracy." *Journal of Social Issues,* XXVI (Winter 1970), 165–186.

2724. "Infiltrating the Underground: F.B.I. Capture of Weather Underground Members." *Time,* CXI (January 9, 1978), 13.

2725. Jaffa, H. V. "The Weathermen and Fort Sumter: Wrongful Use of Violence against the Government." *National Review,* XXII (December 28, 1978), 1403+.

2726. Johnson, Valerie M. "An American Tragedy [Extradition Hearing for Karleton Armstrong] in a Canadian Court." *Saturday Night,* LXXXVII (September 1972), 22–26.

2727. Kifner, John. "Vandals in the Mothern Country." *New York Times Magazine* (January 4, 1970), 14–16+.

2728. Luce, Philip A. "You Don't Need a Weatherman." In: his *The New Left Today: America's Trojan Horse.* Washington, D.C.: The Capitol Hill Press, 1971. pp. 111–121.

2729. Neary, John. "Two Girls from No. 18." *Life,* LXVIII (March 27, 1970), 27–28.

2730. "'Prairie Fire.'" *Skeptic,* no. 11 (January-February 1976), 30–33.

2731. Sale, J. K. "Ted Gold: Education for Violence." *Nation,* CCX (April 13–May 4, 1970), 423–429, 513+.

2732. "Sanctuary in Evanston." *Newsweek,* LXXIV (October 27, 1969), 73+.

2733. Spiegel, John P. "Behind the Terror Bombings." *U.S. News and World Report,* LXVIII (March 30, 1970), 15–17.

2734. "Terrorism on the Left." *Newsweek,* LXXV (March 23, 1970), 26–38.

2735. "They Bombed in New York." *Time,* XCIV (November 21, 1969), 26–27.

(c) Documents, Papers, and Reports

2736. Dohrn, Bernardine, *et al. Prairie Fire: The Politics of Revolutionary Anti-Imperialism.* [New York?] Weather Underground, 1974. 158p.

2737. United States. Congress. Senate. Committee on Public Works, Subcommittee on Public Buildings and Grounds. *Security on the Capitol Grounds relating to the Bombing of the U.S. Capitol: Hearings.* 92nd Cong., 1st sess. Washington, D.C.: U.S. Government Printing Office, 1971. 21p.

2738. _____ . _____ . _____ . Committee on the Judiciary. Subcommittee to Investigate the Administration of the Internal Security Act and Other Internal Security Laws. *Terroristic Activities, Part 2: Inside the Weatherman Movement—Hearings.* 93rd Cong., 2nd sess. Washington, D.C.: U.S. Government Printing Office, 1974. 68p.

c. Anti-Terrorism Legislation and Measures

(1) Books

2739.   Barnet, Richard J. *Intervention and Revolution: America's Confrontation with Insurgent Movements around the World.* Cleveland: World Publishing, 1968. 302p.

2740.   Evans, Ernest. *Calling a Truce to Terror: The American Response to International Terrorism.* Contributions in Political Science, no. 29. Westport, Conn.: Greenwood Press, 1979. 200p.

Gillers, Stephen, jt. editor. *See* Waters, Pat.

2741.   Schott, Joseph L. *No Left Turns: The F.B.I. in Peace and War.* New York: Praeger, 1975. 214p.

2742.   Sullivan, William C., with Bill Brown. *The Bureau: My Thirty Years in Hoover's F.B.I.* New York: W. W. Norton, 1979. 191p.

2743.   Turner, William W. *Hoover's F.B.I.: The Men and the Myth.* Los Angeles: Sherbourne Press, 1970. 352p.

2744.   Ungar, Sanford J. *F.B.I.* Boston: Little, Brown, 1975. 682p.

2745.   Waters, Pat, and Stephen Gillers, eds. *Investigating the F.B.I.* Garden City, N.Y.: Doubleday, 1973. 518p.

2746.   Wright, Richard O., ed. *Whose F.B.I.?* New York: Open Court Publishing, 1974. 405p.

(2) Articles

2747.   "Antiterror Bill Opposed by the Administration." *Aviation Week and Space Technology,* CX (February 19, 1979), 24.

2748.   "As Violence Spreads, U.S. Goes on Guard." *U.S. News and World Report,* LXIX (November 2, 1970), 15–16.

2749.   Binder, David. "Antiterrorist Policy of the U.S. Called Weak: Reprinted from the *New York Times,* April 23, 1978." In: U.S. Congress. Senate. Select Committee on Intelligence. *National Intelligence Reorganization and Reform Act of 1978: Hearings.* 95th Cong., 2nd sess. Washington, D.C.: U.S. Government Printing Office, 1978. pp. 111–113.

2750.   Civiletti, Benjamin F. "Terrorism: The Government's Response Policy." *F.B.I. Law Enforcement Bulletin,* XLVIII (January 1979), 19–22.

2751.   Clifford, George. "Diplomat Who Protects Diplomats, Anthony Quainton, Is Our Man against Terror: Office for Combatting Terrorism [Department of State]." *People,* XI (May 3, 1979), 39–40.

2752. Hoagland, John H. "Changing Patterns of Insurgency and American Response." *Journal of International Affairs,* XXV (Winter 1971), 120–141.

2753. Hoffacker, Lewis. "The U.S. Government Response to Terrorism: A Global Approach." *Department of State Bulletin,* LXX (March 18, 1974), 274–278.

2754. Hoover, J. Edgar. "Law Enforcement Faces the Revolutionary-Guerrilla Criminal." *F.B.I. Law Enforcement Bulletin,* XXXIX (December 1970), 20–22, 28.

2755. "President Nixon Establishes Cabinet Committee to Combat Terrorism: Text of Memorandum." *Department of State Bulletin,* LXVII (October 23, 1972), 475–480.

2756. Rapaport, Daniel. "The Government Is Up in the Air over Combatting Mass Terrorism." *National Journal,* II (November 26, 1977), 1853–1856.

2757. Rein, Bert. "A Government Perspective." *Journal of Air Law and Commerce,* XXXVII (1971), 183–193.

2758. Smith, Gaddis. "The U.S. and International Terrorists." *American Heritage,* XXVIII (August 1977), 36–43.

2759. Vance, Cyrus R. "Scope of the Threat and Need for Effective Legislation: Statement, January 23, 1978." *Department of State Bulletin,* LXXVIII (March 1978), 53–55.

(3) Documents, Papers, and Reports

2760. Browne, Jeffery T. *International Terrorism: The American Response.* Washington, D.C.: School of International Service, The American University, 1973.

2761. Church League of America. Research Department. *Protecting Traitors, Spies, and Terrorists—How America's Internal Security Is Being Destroyed: A Documented Report.* Washington, D.C., 1977. 78p.

2762. Hoover, J. Edgar. *Increase in Violence: Statement before the National Commission on the Causes and Prevention of Violence.* Washington, D.C.: Federal Bureau of Investigation, 1968. 12p.

2763. Jenkins, Brian. *Combatting International Terrorism: The Role of Congress.* RAND Paper P-5808. Santa Monica, Calif.: RAND Corp., 1977. 18p.

2764. _____ , et al. *U.S. Preparations for Future Low-Level Conflict.* RAND Paper P-5830. Santa Monica, Calif.: RAND Corp., 1977. 20p.

2765.   Lopez, Vincent C. *What the U.S. Army Should Do about Urban Guerrilla Warfare.* Carlisle Barracks, Pa.: Strategic Studies Institute, U.S. Army War College, 1975. 36p.

2766.   United States. Congress. House. Committee on International Relations. Subcommittee on Internal Security and Scientific Affairs. *International Terrorism: Legislative Initiatives.* 95th Cong., 2nd sess. Washington, D.C.: U.S. Government Printing Office, 1978. 201p.

2767.   _____ . _____ . _____ . Committee on the Judiciary. *Implementing International Conventions against Terrorism: Report, with Dissenting Views.* 94th Cong., 1st sess. Washington, D.C.: U.S. Government Printing Office, 1976. 16p.

2768.   _____ . _____ . _____ . _____ . Subcommittee on Civil and Constitutional Rights. *F.B.I. Oversight: Hearings.* 95th Cong., 1st and 2nd sess. Washington, D.C.: U.S. Government Printing Office, 1978. 391p.

2769.   _____ . _____ . _____ . _____ . _____ . *Federal Capabilities in Crisis Management and Terrorism: Hearings.* 95th Cong., 2nd sess. Washington, D.C.: U.S. Government Printing Office, 1978. 116p.

2770.   _____ . _____ . _____ . _____ . _____ . *Federal Capabilities in Crisis Management and Terrorism: Staff Report.* 95th Cong., 2nd sess. Washington, D.C.: U.S. Government Printing Office, 1978. 232p.

2771.   _____ . _____ . _____ . Permanent Select Committee on Intelligence. *An Act to Combat International Terrorism: Report.* 95th Cong., 2nd sess. Washington, D.C.: U.S. Government Printing Office, 1978. 27p.

2772.   _____ . _____ . Senate. Committee on Foreign Relations. *Combatting International and Domestic Terrorism: Hearings.* 95th Cong., 2nd sess. Washington, D.C.: U.S. Government Printing Office, 1978. 119p.

2773.   _____ . _____ . _____ . Committee on Governmental Affairs. *An Act to Combat International Terrorism: Hearings.* 95th Cong., 2nd sess. Washington, D.C.: U.S. Government Printing Office, 1978. 1190p.

2774.   _____ . _____ . _____ . _____ . _____ : *Report.* 95th Cong., 2nd sess. Washington, D.C.: U.S. Government Printing Office, 1978. 430p.

2775.   _____ . _____ . _____ . Committee on the Judiciary. Subcommittee on Administrative Practice and Procedures. *F.B.I. Statutory Charter: Hearings.* 95th Cong., 2nd sess. 2 pts. Washington, D.C.: U.S. Government Printing Office, 1978.

2776. _____ . _____ . _____ . Select Committee to Study Governmental Operations with Respect to Intelligence Activities. *Book 6—The Federal Bureau of Investigation: Hearings.* 94th Cong., 1st sess. Washington, D.C.: U.S. Government Printing Office, 1976. 1,000p.

2777. _____ . General Accounting Office. *F.B.I. Domestic Intelligence Operations—Their Purpose and Scope: Issues That Need to Be Resolved.* Washington, D.C.: U.S. Government Printing Office, 1976. 232p.

2778. _____ . Library of Congress. American Law Division. *Internal Security Manual, Revised to July 1973.* 2 vols. Washington, D.C.: U.S. Government Printing Office, 1974.

Appendix: Magazines and Journals Containing at Least One Article Relative to This Guide

Across the Board
Aeronautical Journal
Aerospace Medicine
Africa Quarterly
Air Force Times
Air Line Pilot
Air University Review
Akron Law Review
Albany Law Review
Alternative
America
American Aviation
American Behavioral Scientist
American Heritage
American Journal of International Law
American Journal of Orthopsychiatry
American Journal of Psychiatry
American Journal of Psychotherapy
American Legion Magazine
American Opinion
American Political Science Review
American Psychologist
American Psychology
American Sociological Review
American University Law Review
Annals of International Studies

Annals of the American Academy of Political and Social Science
Applied Psychology
Arab Palestine Resistance
Arab World
Archives of General Psychiatry
Armed Forces Journal International
Army
Army Quarterly
Asian Survey
Assets Protection
Atlantic Community Quarterly
Atlas
The Australian and New Zealand Journal of Criminology
The Australian and New Zealand Journal of Psychiatry
Australian Journal of Forensic Sciences
Australian Police Journal
Aviation, Space, and Environmental Medicine
Aviation Week and Space Technology
Bank of London and South American Review
Bankers Magazine
Barrister
British Journal of Psychiatry

Bulletin of the Atomic Scientists
Bulletin of the International Commission of Jurists
California Western International Law Journal
Canada and the World
Canadian Defence Quarterly
Canadian Dimension
Canadian Forum
Catholic Lawyer
Chitty's Law Journal
Christian Century
Christianity Today
Cincinnati Inquirer Magazine
Civil Liberties Review
Columbia Human Rights Law Review
Columbia Journal of Transnational Law
Columbia Journalism Review
Columbia Law Review
Commentary
Commonweal
Comparative Political Studies
Comparative Politics
Comparative Studies of Sociology and History
Conditional Reflex
Conference Board Record
Conflict
Conflict Studies
Congressional Record
Contemporary Review
Cooperation and Conflict
Cornell International Law Journal
Counterforce
Criminal Justice Digest
Criminal Law Bulletin
Criminology
Crossbow
Current
Current Foreign Policy
Current History
Current Legal Problems
Defense and Foreign Affairs Digest

Denver Journal of International Law and Policy
Department of State Bulletin
Department of State Newsletter
Dissent
Duke Law Journal
Duquesne Law Review
Ebony
Editorial Research Reports
Electronic Warfare/Defense
Electronics
Encore
Encounter
Esquire
European Community
European Journal of Sociology
External Affairs
Far Eastern Economic Review
FBI Law Enforcement Bulletin
Fletcher Forum
Forbes
Foreign Affairs
Fortune
Freedom at Issue
Futurist
Geographic Magazine
Georgetown Law Journal
Georgia Journal of International and Comparative Law
German International
Good Housekeeping
Government and Opposition
Harpers
Harrangue
Harvard International Law Journal
History and Theory
Howard Law Journal
Human Relations
Humanist
Illinois Bar Journal
Illustrated London News
Imprecor
India Quarterly
Indian Journal of International Law

Indiana Police Journal
Infantry
Instant Research on Peace and Violence
Intellect
Interavia
The Inter-Dependent
Internal Security
International Affairs
International and Comparative Law Quarterly
International Atomic Energy Agency Bulletin
International Conciliation
International Criminal Police Review
International Defense Review
International Journal
International Journal of Criminology and Penology
International Journal of Group Tensions
International Journal of Offender Therapy and Comparative Criminology
International Journal of Psychiatry
International Lawyer
International Legal Materials
International Perspectives
International Philosophical Quarterly
International Police Academy Review
International Problems
International Review of Criminal Policy
International Review of History and Political Science
International Security
International Studies Notes
I.R. & T. Nuclear Journal
Islamic Review
Israel and Palestine
Israel Law Review
Israel Magazine

Israeli Annals of Psychiatry
Japanese Annual of International Law
Jerusalem Journal of International Relations
Jewish Frontier
Journal of Air Law and Commerce
Journal of California Law Enforcement
Journal of Conflict Resolution
Journal of Consulting Clinical Psychology
Journal of Contemporary History
Journal of Criminal Law and Criminology
Journal of Forensic Sciences
Journal of Human Relations
Journal of International Law and Economy
Journal of Law and Economics
Journal of Marriage and the Family
Journal of Palestine Studies
Journal of Peace Research
Journal of Personal and Social Psychology
Journal of Personality and Social Psychology
Journal of Police Science and Administration
Journal of Political and Military Sociology
Journal of Politics
Journal of Psychology
Journal of Social Issues
Journal of Southeast Asia and the Far East
Journal of the British Medical Association
Journal of the Forensic Science Society
Journal of the Royal United Service Institution for Defence Studies
Kentucky Law Journal
Labour Monthly
Ladies Home Journal

Law and Order
Law and Policy in International Business
The Law Society's Gazette
Lawyer of the Americas
Life
Listener
Macleans
Magazine of Banking Administration
Manitoba Law Journal
Marine Crops Gazette
Marquette Law Review
Marxism Today
Massachusetts Review
Medical Science Law
Medicine, Science, and Law
Michigan Law Review
Mid East
Middle East Forum
Middle East International
Middle East Journal
Middle East Newsletter
Midstream
Midwest Quarterly
Military Affairs
Military Police Law Enforcement Journal
Military Review
Millenium
Monthly Review
Nation
National Journal
National Review
NATO's Fifteen Nations
Naval War College Review
New England Law Review
New German Critique
New Leader
New Left Review
New Middle East
New Outlook
New Politics
New Republic
New Statesman and Nation

New Times
New Times (Moscow)
New York Law Forum
New York Times Biographical Service
New York Times Magazine
New York University Journal of International Law and Politics
New Yorker
New Zealand University Law Review
Newsweek
North American Review
Notre Dame Lawyer
Nursing Times
Office
Ohio Northern University Law Review
Orbis
Oui
Parade Magazine
Parameters
Partisan Review
Penthouse
People
Playboy
Police
Police Chief
Police College Journal
Police Journal
Police Officers Association of Michigan Law Enforcement Journal
Police Review
Police Studies
Political Quarterly
Political Science Quarterly
Political Studies
Politics and Society
Politics Today (Skeptic)
Polity
Popular Mechanics
Popular Science
The Practitioner
Problems of Communism
Progressive

Psychiatry
Psychoanalytic Review
Psychology Today
Public Health
Queen's Quarterly
Ramparts
Reader's Digest
The Record of the Association of the Bar of the City of New York
Reporter
The Review
Review of International Affairs (Belgrade)
Review of Politics
Rolling Stone
Round Table
Royal Air Forces Quarterly
Rutgers-Camden Law Journal
Sage Professional Papers in Comparative Politics
San Diego Magazine
Saturday Evening Post
Saturday Night
Saturday Review
Saturday Review of Literature
Science
Science and Public Affairs
Science Digest
Science News
Security Gazette
Security Management
Security Register
Senior Scholastic
Sierra Club Bulletin
Signal
Skeptic (Politics Today)
Social and Economic Studies
Social Dynamics
Social Problems
Social Research
Social Science Information
Social Science Quarterly
Social Theory and Practice
Socialist Review

Society
Sociological Focus
Sociological Review
South African Law Journal
South Atlantic Quarterly
Southwestern University Law Review
Soviet Analyst
Soviet Law and Government
Soviet Military Review
Sports Illustrated
Stanford Journal of International Studies
Stanford Law Review
Strategic Review
Student Power
Survey
Survival
Swiss Review of World Affairs
Syracuse Journal of International Law and Commerce
Temple Law Quarterly
Terrorism
Thought
TIG Brief
Time
Today
Today's Health
Top Security
Towson State Journal of International Affairs
Trans-Action
TV Guide
TWA Ambassador
UN Chronicle
UNESCO Courier
United Service Institution Journal
University of Chicago Law Review
University of Florida Law Review
University of Pennsylvania Law Review
University of Toledo Law Review
US Naval Institute Proceedings
US News and World Report

Vanderbilt Journal of Transnational Law
Victimology
Villanova Law Review
Vista
Vogue
Washington Monthly
Washington Post Magazine
Weekly Compilation of Presidential Documents

Western Political Quarterly
Wiener Library Bulletin
William and Mary Law Review
World Affairs
World Federalist
World Marxist Review
World Politics
World Today
Worldview
Yale Studies in World Public Order

Author Index

The entries in this index are keyed to the entry numbers of references in the guide.

223